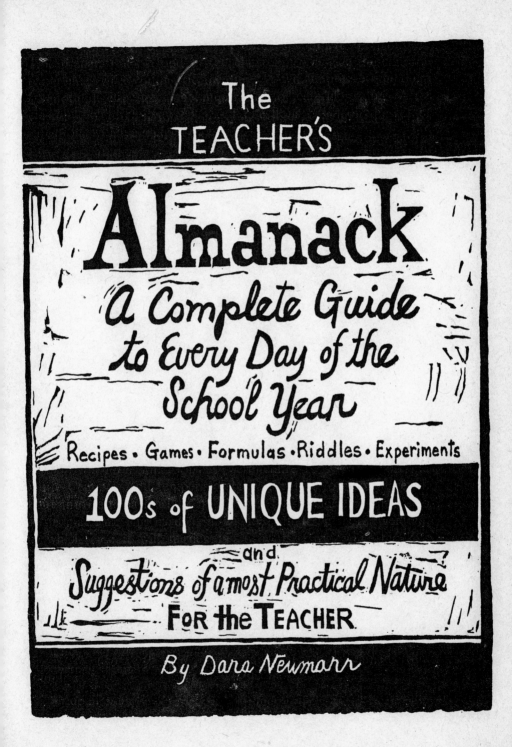

The TEACHER'S

Almanack

A Complete Guide to Every Day of the School Year

Recipes • Games • Formulas • Riddles • Experiments

100s of UNIQUE IDEAS

and

Suggestions of a most Practical Nature

FoR the TEACHER

By Dara Newman

THE TEACHER'S ALMANACK
Practical Ideas for Every Day
of the School Year

Dana Newmann

The Center for Applied Research in Education, Inc.

West Nyack, New York 10994

Printed in the United States of America
C-8720-9

About the Author

Dana Newmann has been involved in elementary education for more than ten years as a classroom teacher and reading specialist. Her experience includes teaching in the public schools of Monterey and Carmel, California, and with the U.S. Army Dependents Education Group in Hanau, Germany. A graduate of Mills College with a B.A. in Fine Arts, Mrs. Newmann lives in Santa Fe, New Mexico.

a word of introduction

I remember very clearly how my grandfather would consult his almanac as a guide to the planting & farmwork. I've often thought how handy such a book would be for the teacher.

It would be so helpful to have a ready source of teaching suggestions geared to the seasons of the school year — a book that would primarily be a statement of ideas & recipes. You could open it to a day of the month & find a stimulating entry appropriate to that day. It would offer intriguing science experiments not requiring hours of preparation & practice; it would have a collection of uncommon riddles; it would give historical anecdotes that make famous people come alive.

'The Teacher's Almanack' is such a book. You will find it a complete guide to the school year, containing unusual lesson suggestions for every subject & grade level. It covers such varied topics as: Rebus symbols, manipulative bulletin boards, Creative Writing self-starters, classroom cooking, formulas for art supplies & sources of free teaching materials. It gives the addresses, the formulas, the recipes so that you know _where_ to find them _when_ you need them.

A few of the teaching ideas included are standards that I use nearly every year, e.g. the directions for making an erupting volcano. I hope most of the suggestions will be fresh & novel to you as in many cases they are originals, e.g. games for helping & rewarding slow readers, an Interest Inventory to give you insight into the personality & interests of each child in your class.

I hope 'The Teacher's Almanack' helps this be the most rewarding year of teaching that you've ever had!

Dana Newmann

9

Table of Contents

11

Room environments, activities pertinent to October, e.g., original reading & math games; educational pumpkin projects; complete directions for a Halloween party that WORKS.

November 73

Calendar of important dates; etymology & quotations; historical background; activities related to:

Birth of R.L. Stevenson (76) . Birth of Robt. Fulton (79) . Assassination of John F. Kennedy (79) . Thanksgiving (79) . Birth of Jonathan Swift (89)

Room environments, activities pertinent to November, e.g., Indian finger puppets; suggestions to facilitate Parent-Teacher Conferences; crystal gardens; instructions for the organization of relay races.

December 94

Calendar of important dates; etymology & quotations; poetry; information & activities related to:

Birth of Eli Whitney (97) . Bill of Rights Day (97) . Birth of Beethoven (97) . Wright Brothers Day (97) . 1st Day of Winter (98) . Birth of Clara Barton (98) . Hanukkah (99) . Birth of Pasteur (126)

Art activities & helpful hints for the month of December, e.g., historical origins of Christmas traditions; suggestions for a meaningful holiday party; complete guide to a joyous & creative Christmas season.

January 127

Calendar of important dates; etymology & quotations; ideas & activities related to:

New Year's Day (130) . Birth of Betsy Ross (132) . Birth of Ben Franklin (132) . Birth of Edgar Allan Poe (134) . Birth of Watt (134) . Birth of Ampere (135) . Edison's Electric-Light Patent (135)

Games & ideas to spark-up the new year, e.g., 111 *uncommon* riddles; 28 plants from the kitchen; a complete guide to classroom printmaking; rainy-day games.

February 153

Ideas pertinent to the month of February, e.g., activities to help combat spring fever; directions for making new & novel valentines; a bulletin board that tells how we got our standards of length; sound exploration; haiku poetry.

March 176

Room environments, activities & games pertinent to the month of March, e.g., science experiments with the Irish potato; all kinds of number and scientific magic tricks; a *Rebus Dictionary;* how to make 17 different rhythm instruments.

April 199

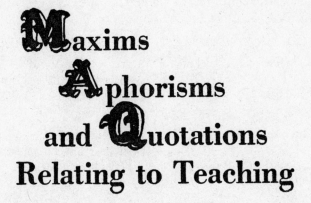

Maxims
Aphorisms
and Quotations
Relating to Teaching

Who teaches, learns. *Anonymous*

Those who educate children well are more to be honored than they who produce them; for these only gave them life, those the art of living well.—*Aristotle*

What we like determines who we are and is the sign of what we are, and to teach taste is inevitably to form character.—*John Ruskin*

Education is not to reform students or amuse them or to make expert technicians. It is to unsettle their minds, widen their horizons, inflame their intellects, teach them to think.—*Robert M. Hutchins*

A great teacher has always been measured by the number of his students who surpass him. *Anonymous*

Only the educated are free. *Greek*

There is just one way to bring up a child in the way he should go and that is to travel that way yourself.—*Abraham Lincoln*

Kids need a challenge and a sense of achievement. There is no pride and no satisfaction in having things handed to you.—*Ann Landers, 4/29/70*

Perhaps the most valuable result of all education is the ability to make yourself do the thing you have to do when it has to be done, whether you like it or not.—*Huxley*

The teacher who is attempting to teach without inspiring the pupil with desire to learn is hammering on cold steel.—*Horace Mann*

Human history becomes more and more a race between education and catastrophe.—*H.G. Wells*

"The wisdom of nations lies in her proverbs which are brief and pithy. Collect and learn them. You have much in little; they save time in speaking; and upon occasion may be the fullest and safest answers."

(Edifying quotations appear throughout The Teacher's Almanack. Any of these which are appropriate for your class can be clearly printed on large rectangles of paper or card stock & posted about the room. Frequent changes will be especially effective in keeping the children's attention & interest.)

Patience and the mulberry leaf become a silk robe. *Chinese*

Think; do not guess. *Greek*

Better lose the anchor than the whole ship. *Dutch*

To silence another, first be silent. *Latin*

A little too late is much too late. *German*

Fear less, hope more;
Eat less, chew more;
Whine less, breathe more;
Talk less, say more;
Hate less, love more;
And all good things will be yours. *Swedish*

Good manners and soft words have brought many a difficult thing to pass—*Aesop, c. 620-560 B.C.*

Gratitude is the memory of the heart. *Greek*

A candle loses nothing by lighting another candle. *English*

The man who removes the mountain began by carrying away small stones. *Chinese*

Sow a Thought, and you reap an Act;
Sow an Act, and you reap a Habit;
Sow a Habit, and you reap a Character;
Sow a Character, and you reap a Destiny.

A Very Short History of the Calendar

(including a description of the major Jewish holidays)

Thirty dayes hath November
April, June, and September,
February hath xxviii alone,
And all the rest have xxxi.
—Richard Grafton: 1562

Early man kept track of time by counting the suns &
darknesses, by tying knots in ropes, making notches on sticks &,
eventually, by noticing the changes in the positions of the sun,
moon & stars.

Most of the holidays are in some way related to divisions of
time—especially to the seasons. Primitive man celebrated the
beginning of each of the four seasons; those early holidays exist
today in differing forms throughout the world.

The Babylonians made the first calendar & based it on the
moon, counting twelve lunar months to a year. An extra month
was added about every four years to keep the seasons straight. The
Greek, Semitic & Egyptian peoples adopted the Babylonian
calendar. Later the Egyptians created a calendar that more nearly
matched the seasons. This lunar calendar is used today by the
Mohammedans & the Jews.

Therefore, the exact dates of the Jewish holidays vary from
year to year. The Jewish calendar reckons from the year 3761
B.C., which is traditionally given as the date of the Creation.
(Although most of the world now operates on a Gregorian
calendar, which is a solar one, the lunar calendar is still of some
contemporary significance. Your Jewish students celebrate holidays based on it.) The Jewish holidays include: Rosh Hashana,
Yom Kippur, Sukkoth, Hanukkah, Purim, Pesach & Shabuoth.
Each is noted in this book as it occurs during the school year.

In 46 B.C. Julius Caesar ordered a new calendar developed.
This Roman calendar made use of the Egyptian year & encom-
passed 365 1/4 days, every fourth year having 366 days. There

were twelve months in this calendar; Augustus & Julius Caesar each named one for himself, each taking a day from February, making August and July months having 31 days. (A complete historical description precedes each month as it is covered in the almanack.)

Pope Gregory XIII in 1582 requested that the error in the old calendar be corrected; the resulting Leap Year system is still in use today. The Gregorian calendar also made January first New Year's Day.

English-speaking countries began using the Gregorian calendar in 1752 & moved the calendar up eleven days. China adopted this calendar in 1912, as Russia did in 1914, & it is the standard in use throughout the world today.

Calendars for the Classroom

Lower grades. Stretch white oilcloth over a two-foot-square piece of lightweight wood. Screw 35 hooks into the board through the oilcloth as shown below. Each month, use rubber cement to affix cut-out paper letters in an appropriate color to the oilcloth at the top of the calendar. Keep 31 tagboard cards, each bearing a large, clear number, at the side of the calendar. Place the calendar upright in the chalk tray of the blackboard & each morning hang the card bearing that day's date on the appropriate hook.

Middle and upper grades. This calendar provides a striking bulletin board display & a fascinating class project that will motivate students to do extra research work. Each month, have every child research & illustrate one day's history of events. Allow pupils who have a birthday that month to illustrate their own date of birth. Illustrations may include drawings, photos, paper cutouts, objects & replicas. Use a large sheet of butcher's paper to provide a neutral background for the calendar.

Some First-of-the-School-Year Suggestions

On the first day of school have the children date a paper & write a few short sentences around a theme such as "What I Hope to Learn (or Want to Accomplish) in _____Grade." Put these finished papers in the bottom drawer of your desk & save them until Open House. At that time display each paper next to an up-to-date paper by the same child. The title of such a bulletin board might be "WOW! What a Difference a Year Makes!" or "See How Much My Penmanship Has *Improved*!" The children's morale will be given a boost by this concrete proof of their progress.

For the first few days of school, have several short periods in which the children practice the routines involved in passing out paper & handing in Spelling Tests, etc.

During the first week of school give the class a spelling "test" composed of words that the children have not been assigned to study. Such a list might include: "United States of America," the names of their city, state & school, the names of Presidents, an ocean, a nearby body of water, & any states that border theirs.

The results of this test will give you an indication as to the phonetic, capitalization & penmanship reviews needed. Save these papers until Public School Week & at that time have the children retake a test on the list of words. Perhaps the class will want to compare these two papers. Display some examples of extraordinary improvement.

Display a huge blowup of a correctly done homework paper, emphasizing heading, margins, paragraphs & placement of name.

Rather than presenting the children with an artificial confrontation of "Now we are going to write out rules for behavior at school," simply help the class to become familiar with the standing school policies ("No gum is allowed on playground," etc.). Then have the class set its own standards for conduct—as the particular problem arises.

A chart of the meanings of correction marks: ∧ ¶ sp. ⌣ inc. etc., could be permanently displayed in the room.

If there is a specific place for each working material (labeled drawers, boxes to fit and hold each size of paper used), classroom organization and cleanup will be facilitated.

Establish a general routine as to "cleanup." When planning allotment of time, include cleanup activities as a definite part of construction periods. Housekeeping jobs (watering the plants, closing the windows at dismissal, etc.) should be assigned to specific students each week. The last 10 or 15 minutes of each Friday* are set aside for cleaning out desks; try to keep *your* desk top uncluttered as a subliminal reminder if you wish to emphasize this type of organization.

Set aside time for a daily evaluation. A formal approach to discussion is helpful until the class is well organized. This daily evaluation will help alleviate the problem of students forgetting "what we did today" and should aid in getting the class to cooperate, function as a unit.

Always run through a science experiment yourself, at home the night before class, just to be certain that the experiment will be successful the next day. This saves time & patience. (And it's also a good procedure to follow if the class is to cook the next day; you'll find you have more confidence this way, too.)

---

*Why not try using a cooking timer which *audibly* clicks off these 10 or 15 minutes?

When presenting background information on each holiday, care should be taken to clearly distinguish between historic & legendary material. (Can the children?) It may be pointed out to the class that holidays are observed for specific reasons: to preserve a tradition, to mark a patriotic or religious event. (Can the children think of any other reasons?)

The use of holiday themes should not dominate a teaching program to the exclusion of other meaningful themes.

Be discriminating in your choice of the projects suggested here. Next year you can always try those projects which you were unable to fit into this year's schedule.

Allow the children to interpret these projects. In fact, different approaches to the same project should be encouraged whenever practical. Many times the children's variations will afford learning experiences that are especially fruitful.

September

Warm September brings the fruit,
Sportsmen then begin to shoot.

Note: The following dates, unless otherwise noted, refer to the birthdates of famous persons; dates within parentheses are the years of birth & death. This holds true throughout this book.

	First Monday of September is Labor Day.
1	World War II began, 1939.
2-6	Great Fire of London 1666 destroyed much of the city; c f. Sir Christopher Wren, Oct. 20, page 50.
3	Louis H. Sullivan (1850-1924), American architect. "Form follows function."
5	First Continental Congress met in Philadelphia, 1774.
	Jesse James (1847-1882), American outlaw.
6	Jane Addams (1860-1935), American pioneer social worker, winner of Nobel Peace Prize.
	The Mayflower set sail from Plymouth, England, for America, 1620.
7	Queen Elizabeth I of England (1533-1603).
8	Antonin Dvorak (1841-1904), Czech composer: *From the New World Symphony.*
	Richard the Lion-Hearted (1157-1199), King of England, Crusader.
	Peter Stuyvesant (1610-1672), last Dutch governor of New Amsterdam (New York).

9 Luigi Galvani (1737-1798), Italian scientist, discoverer of the metallic arc.
William the Conqueror (c.1027-1087), King of England.

10 Elias Howe patented the sewing machine, 1846.

11 O. Henry [William S. Porter] (1862-1910), American author.

12 Henry Hudson 1st saw the river that now bears his name, 1609.

13 Walter Reed (1851-1902), American bacteriologist, conqueror of yellow fever.

14 Friedrich von Humboldt (1769-1859), German naturalist.
Dante Alighieri died, 1321; 1st great poet to write in Italian: *Divine Comedy*.
Great Britain and its colonies (America) adopted the Gregorian Calendar, 1752.
"The Star Spangled Banner" was written by Francis Scott Key, 1814.

15 James Fenimore Cooper (1789-1851), American author.
William Howard Taft (1857-1930), 27th President.

16 Tintoretto [Jacopo Robusti] (1518-1594), Italian painter.

17 Citizenship Day (Constitution Day); U.S. Constitution signed: Constitutional Convention, 1787.

18 Samuel Johnson (1709-1784), English dictionary-maker.

19 Washington issued his farewell address to the American people, 1796.

20 Alexander the Great (356-323 B.C.) crossed Tigris River to battle Darius for Persian Empire, 331 B.C.

21 First daily newspaper published in the U.S., 1784.
H.G. Wells (1866-1946), English author.

22 Nathan Hale killed, 1776.
President Lincoln issued Emancipation Proclamation, 1862.

22-23 Autumnal Equinox—fall begins.
Euripides (484-406 B.C.), 3rd great tragedian of ancient Athens.
Augustus Caesar (63 B.C.-14 A.D.) 1st emperor of the Roman world.

25 Vasco Nunez de Balboa discovered the Pacific Ocean, 1513
First American newspaper, *Publick Occurrences*, began publishing in Boston, 1690.

Alfred Vail (1807-1859), American co-developer of Morse Code.

Dmitri Shostakovich (1906-   ), Russian composer.

26   Johnny Appleseed [John Chapman] (1775-1847), American nurseryman and folklore hero.

George Gershwin (1898-1937), American composer of musical comedy: *Rhapsody in Blue.*

American Indian Day.

27   William the Conqueror landed in England.

Samuel Adams (1722-1803), American patriot and leader of the Boston Tea Party.

28   Cabrillo Day: Juan Cabrillo discovered California, 1542.

These Jewish Holidays may occur in September :

Sukkoth: The date of the Feast of Tabernacles or Booths varies from year to year. For 7 days in the fall, many Jews eat in palm-branch-covered dwellings; this is in memory of the 40 years that their people hunted for the Promised Land. It was during these wanderings that the Hebrews lived in huts of palm branches.

Rosh Hashanah: The New Year (September or October) lasting 2 days. It is celebrated as a solemn occasion, ushering in 10 days of penitence which lead up to:

Yom Kippur: The Day of Atonement (September or October). It is a day of fasting and prayer, asking for the forgiveness of one's sins.

September

The early Roman calendar began with March, therefore September was its seventh month; *septem* = seven in Latin.

SEPTEMBER QUOTATIONS

(Unless otherwise noted, the quotations are from authors born on the date under which they are noted.)

6   Civilization is a method of living, an attitude of equal respect for all men (Speech, Honolulu, 1933)—Jane Addams

11   Love and business and family and religion and art and
      patriotism are nothing but shadows of words when a
      man's starving.— O. Henry

14   I despise mankind in all its strata.—Friedrich von Humbolt

      O, say can you see by the dawn's early light . . .
      'Tis the star spangled banner! O long may it wave
      O'er the land of the free and the home of the brave!
      ("The Star Spangled Banner")—Francis Scott Key

15   The cheerful loser is a sort of winner.—William Howard Taft

      Few men exhibit greater diversity . . . than the native
      warrior of North America. In war, he is daring, boastful,
      cunning, ruthless, self-denying, and self-devoted; in peace,
      just, generous, hospitable, revengeful, superstitious, mod-
      est and, commonly, chaste. *(The Last of the Mohicans)*—
      James Fenimore Cooper

18   The true art of memory is the art of attention.

      Few things are impossible to diligence and skill.

      Knowledge is of two kinds: we know a subject, ourselves, or
      we know where we can find information upon it.

      Dictionaries are like watches; the worst is better than none,
      and the best cannot be expected to go quite true.
                                              —Samuel Johnson

21   Were it left to me to decide whether we should have a
      government without newspapers or newspapers without
      government, I should not hesitate to prefer the latter.
      (Quotation of Thomas Jefferson)

      Human history is in essence a history of ideas.—H.G. Wells

22   I only regret that I have but one life to lose for my
      country.—Nathan Hale (before his execution: Sept. 22
      1776)

23   A bad beginning makes a bad ending.

      Waste not fresh tears over old griefs.

      Second thoughts are ever wiser.

      Who so neglects learning in his youth, loses the past and is
      dead for the future.
                                              —Euripides

26   The lands are ours. No one has a right to remove us, because
      we were the first owners. The Great Spirit above has

appointed this place for us, on which to light our fires, and here we will remain. (To the messenger from the President, 1810)—Tecumseh, Chief of the Shawnees, 1768-1815

A little while and I shall be gone from among you, whither, I cannot tell. From nowhere we come, into nowhere we go. What is life? It is a flash of a firefly in the night. It is a breath of a buffalo in the winter time. It is as the little shadow that runs across the grass and loses itself in the sunset. (Last words of Isapwo Muksika Crowfoot, Chief of Blackfoot Confederacy, ?-1890)

SEPTEMBER EVENTS

● **Labor Day**

The first Monday in September is observed as "Labor's holiday" in the United States. The word "labor" comes from the Latin *laborare,* which means "to be tired." This is the day on which the workers of America are honored.

● **Birth of Luigi Galvani, 1737-1798   [9]**

Galvani was an Italian physician & physiologist. One day he discovered, by accident, that an electrical current would pass through the legs of a dead frog when two different metals were connected to them. When the metals were joined to set up a circuit, the electrical current would cause the frog's legs to jump. This leg movement could then be used to indicate amounts of electrical current. Galvani thought that his observations might mean that electricity is generated by living organisms. Galvani's metallic arc actually led him quite close to the theory of the electric battery which Volta (see Feb.) later discovered.

"Galvanometer," "galvanism," "galvanic electricity" are some electrical terms that come from Dr. Galvani's name.

We get our word "electricity" from the Greeks. They knew that when amber was rubbed it became magnetic. Since friction causes amber to give off sparks, this phenomenom was named "elektron" from *elektor,* "the beaming sun." This word passed into Latin as *electrum* & was turned into the adjective *electricus,* from which we get our word "electric(ity)."

- **Adoption of the Gregorian Calendar   [14]**

In 1752 there was no September third—at least not in Great Britain or in any of her colonies. The calendar was changed from Old to New Style by a parliamentary ruling that the day after September 2nd would be September 14th. Many people felt that their lives had been shortened by 11 days & that everyone whose birthdays fell between September 2nd & 14th was legally dead. Crowds of angry Englishmen ran after Prime Minister Henry Pelham, shouting, "Give us back our 11 days!"

Language Arts

It is good for one's perspective to realize that something as widely used as our calendar has come into existence only through the knowledge & efforts of hundreds of people of various races & backgrounds.

- **Birth of Jacopo Robusti (Tintoretto) 1518-1594   [16]**

Tintoretto was among the last great Venetian painters of the Italian Renaissance. His work later influenced that of El Greco & Rubens. Named Jacopo Robusti, he was called "Il Tintoretto," the little dyer, because his father was a dyer. Tintoretto was apprenticed to the great painter, Titian, who soon dismissed him. Some legends say the older artist was jealous of the talents of the young boy. Other rumors allowed that Tintoretto was of an extremely impatient temperament.* He was to become a prolific painter, in any event. The largest "Old Master" painting in the world was painted by Tintoretto; entitled *Paradise,* it measures 72'2" x 22'11-1/2" & contains 500 figures!

- **Constitution Day   [17]**

Discuss with the children: "What *is* a constitution? How & why is it important?" Talk about the enforcement of the Constitution, the roles of the police, the Supreme Court, the Civil Liberties Union. Invite a police officer, lawyer, or representative of a

---

*The word "temperament" recalls a belief of olden times; medieval philosophers felt that the 4 qualities of hot, cold, dry & moist blended in varying quantities were what determined the nature of things. The Latin word for this mixture was *temperamentum.* When someone becomes temperamental, it means, figuratively, that there is an imbalance in the mixture.

legal-aid society to visit the class WHEN the children have sufficient background knowledge to appreciate (& participate in) the visitor's talk or discussion.

A bulletin board might display a parchment reproduction of the Constitution, an illustration of the signing, a list of men present at the signing, & short, interesting biographies of some of the men. An incidental aspect of this display might be the description of the step-by-step procedure involved in the making of a quill pen. Such a pen could be shown with the reproduction of the Constitution. If turkey quills are available, the making of quill pens could provide an enrichment project for one evening's homework. Complete instructions appear in Edward Johnston's standard work: *Writing and Illuminating and Lettering* (New York, Pitman Pub. Corp., 1958), p. 20.

- **First U.S. daily newspaper   [21]**

The 1st known "newspaper" was a clay representation of a scarab* containing carved lettering. It was made & circulated in Egypt in 1450 B.C.

The 1st historically dated newspaper was a series of clay tablets entitled "Acta Publica" which were begun by Julius Caesar in 58 B.C.

The oldest printed newspaper, *The Peking News,* which began publication 950 years before the invention of movable type, is 1400 years old.

The 1st newspaper of modern form was published in 1566 when the government of Venice, Italy, issued handwritten news-sheets & exhibited them in the streets. They could be read by anyone who paid a small coin called a "gazetta." These "gazettes," as they came to be called, were so popular that they began to be printed.

In the United States, Freedom of the Press was established in 1735 when John Peter Zenger published in his *New York Weekly Journal* a report of election frauds & an exposure of graft & crime by the Royal Governor William Cosby. Arrested for "seditious libel," Zenger found his bail set so high that he was unable to pay it. Andrew Hamilton, ablest of the colonial lawyers, defended Zenger. He admitted that Zenger printed the charges, but con-

---

*There are more than 20,000 species in the widespread Scarab family. Probably the most familiar in America is the June-Bug or May Beetle. The most famous is the sacred Scarab of the Nile, described by J. Henri Fabre as "rolling that pellet of dung in which ancient Egypt beheld an image of the world."

tended that they were true. Zenger was acquitted & the Fourth Estate was allowed its freedom.

Language Arts

At the end of each day the children dictate to the teacher a summarization of that day's happenings. The teacher writes this on the board & it is copied the next morning by a volunteer. These daily records combine to make a class broadsheet, *Our Daily News.* It is the best record of the year's activities for it is written *as* the children's interest is highest. It will be of special interest to guests during Public School Week.

A class newspaper could be published (mimeographed) for wider reader-consumption. It might boast of stories (fact and fiction), puzzles, riddles, poems, jokes, comic strips, sports news, science fiction, a serial, word games, science experiments, rebus (see March), arithmetic word games or problems, interviews with local people of interest, biographies of the school secretary, librarian, etc.

To stimulate a Creative Writing lesson the teacher passes out an actual newspaper want ad to each child. These ads should suggest a situation in an office, store, home, or in someone's personal life, i.e., an accident seen, a pet lost, an article found. The children use these ads as introductions or as endings to their stories.

• Fall begins [22] or [23] (Autumnal Equinox)

Discuss with the children the meaning of "equinox": equal night & day, twelve hours of night & twelve hours of day. The sun rises directly in the East & sets directly in the West; at the equator the sun is directly overhead at twelve o'clock noon. Discuss the cause of the ensuing longer days, the process & importance of hibernation, migration, & the possible reasons that this season is sometimes called "Indian Summer." Talk about deciduous & non-deciduous trees.

> *Riddle:* Why is autumn the best time for a lazy boy to read a book? (Because autumn can always be counted on to turn the leaves for him!)

FALL BULLETIN BOARDS

General suggestions. Remember that a bulletin board is a learning device to reward & encourage outstanding work; it is NOT a decoration. Try the incorporation of eye-catching titles, lead phrases, unusual textures, photographs & actual objects. Place (written) materials at children's eye-level. Ask yourself occasionally if the displays reflect the *current* interest of the children.

Lettering suggestions. Try the use of unusual materials, i.e., wallpaper (from outdated sample books, free, from hardware or interior decorating establishments); pipe cleaners (both the slender & the thick, fuzzy types); cut synthetic sponge (used for initial upper-case letters of bulletin board titles).

Sheets of dark pressed cork, pinned by four long "hatpins" to the bulletin board area, are good for breaking up the total layout, introducing a dark tonal quality to the display.

Theme ideas. The children paint on a large sheet of butcher paper a mural depicting woods, pond, leafless trees, cave, hills, dried fields, piles of leaves, grey skies. When the mural is dry, flaps are cut in it to reveal the sleeping places of insects, rodents & mammals & the migration of birds. A short story written in the first-person (as though dictated by the animal) appears on the inside of each corresponding flap. A few camouflaged animals & birds could also be included on the mural. VARIATION: Instead of cutting flaps in the mural, pin four signs at the appropriate places: "In the Air," "In the Trees," "In the Water," "Under the Ground." The children collect specimens that they find in each of these areas. Drawings, photos, parts of objects, feathers, can also be used. Each object should be labeled by the child & then pinned or taped to the correct area of the board. This bulletin board encourages children to LOOK, to become aware of details.

As the season changes, discuss with the children the adjustments needed to keep their display up-to-date: ice forms on pond, ground turns hard, tree loses last leaves. Take off each object, discussing, "Where will it (the tree toad, acorn, garden spider) go now that it's winter?"

"Beauty of Form" offers a more sophisticated title for an upper grade bulletin board. Beneath the title display objects (characteristic of autumn) whose forms are in some way repetitious of one another: a dried sunflower, a pine cone, the center of a daisy. A biographical brief similar to the following would be shown also:

> About 1170 a boy named Leonardo Fibonacci was born in Pisa. He became one of medieval Europe's greatest mathematicians and contributed to arithmetic, algebra and geometry. One

of his discoveries was a curious set of numbers that appears very often in nature, especially in the arrangement of individual seeds in a pattern.

Here is the Fibonacci Series: 1, 1, 2, 3, 5, 8, 13, 21, 34, 55, 89, 144. . . . . Can you tell how these numbers are related to one another? HINT: It has to do with addition. . . . Look below for the answer.* Another sign might ask: Can you discover the ratios involved in the seed patterns of the natural forms shown here? [Pine cones have 5 & 8 rows; daisies, 21 & 34; & the common sunflower has a 55-89 ratio.]

It may also be pointed out that the relationship of these numbers to each other approaches the golden mean, i.e., 1 to 1.618, & is found in the dimensions of the chambered nautilus (display a shell or a photo of it, if possible) as well as in hundreds of other designs in nature. Examples of man-made designs that correspond to forms in nature—the folded plate in architecture & a jade plant, a piece of mushroom coral, the spore plates of a toadstool—could also be incorporated into the display.

Paper sculpture, original interpretations in color & design, might be an outgrowth of such a bulletin board. An excellent book to introduce to the class at this time is *The Anatomy of Nature* by Andreas Feininger (published by Crown Pub., Inc., N.Y., 1956).

To make a bulletin board pheasant, have the children collect & press brilliantly colored fall leaves; those of the oak & elm trees work especially well. Pin a large sheet of neutral-colored paper to a bulletin board area. Dab spots of rubber cement to the paper & to the back of each leaf when attaching the leaf to the board; two twigs form the legs. By adhering the leaves in this way, the children help the classroom pheasant to grow a larger tail with each day.

---

*The Fibonacci Series is that sequence of numbers each of which is the sum of the two previous numbers.

Language Arts

Once each season, if it is possible, take the class for a walk to a nearby hill or area of greenery. There the children sit & write down a few lines, phrases about their feelings. (No importance should be placed on rhyming.) The teacher may also write down her impressions. Once back in the room, the children should be encouraged to prune their sentences, keeping only those that they consider the best. It can be pointed out how editing is of great importance to all professional writers. Something worthwhile can be found in each child's efforts. The class may share their writings aloud if they like.

> Down, down
> Leaves of red & gold & brown
> Come falling down, down, down.
> Now the wind says,
> "Come & play."
> Outside our window
> The gull is gone.
> All is quiet.
> Only the swallows are heard.
> The green trees dance
> To the song of the swallow.

During their autumn walk the children can also collect twigs for sensitive line drawings, leaves to use for the Skeletal Leaf Science experiment & clippings to press & save for valentines.

After the walk the children can make a collective list of words describing natural forms, patterns, colors & sounds which they noticed while on their walk. This list may be permanently displayed in the room & may be used as a departure point for a science collection, creative writing, or haiku.

Natural form	Pattern	Color	Sound
water	ripples, repeating pattern	transparent magnifies moss,	rippling
rocks, stones	ripples, striations	reflects sky stones	plunk hitting water
leaves	ribbed	rust, grey green	whirling
bark	smooth, rough variations		
		golden rust	rasp as it is rubbed
tall grass	tall lines moving	shining when wet	slithering
sky (trees on skyline)	moving, clouds vary it	deep to light	rushing wind
		green ranging from light to darkest blue	buzz of insects
			hum of cars

Fall Poetry

The melancholy days are come, the saddest of the year,
Of wailing winds, and naked woods and meadows brown and sere.

W.C. Bryant

The day is cold and dark and dreary;
It rains, and the wind is never weary;
The vine still clings to the mouldering wall
But at every gust the dead leaves fall.
And the day is dark and dreary.

H.W. Longfellow

AUTUMN FIRES

In the gardens
And all up the vale,
From the autumn bonfires
See the smoke trail!

Pleasant summer over
And all the summer flowers,
The red fire blazes,
The grey smoke towers.

Sing a song of seasons!
Something bright in all!
Flowers in the summer,
Fires in the fall.

R.L. Stevenson

Also appropriate: "Fog" by Carl Sandburg; "The Pasture" by Robert Frost; "September" by Edwina Fall.

Fall Science

Have the children observe & record seed travels. Have the class watch caterpillars spinning cocoons. The use of a magnifying glass or the less expensive reading-glass will be helpful. Place a cocoon in a box outdoors & wait for the emergence in the spring. (See May Science.)

Fall is the season to collect:

Seeds. Keep them in small labeled envelopes in a dry cool place until they are planted. Larger seeds & pods are excellent for printing borders, designs during an art class.

Buckeyes and acorns. Soak the buckeyes & acorns overnight. Put a few small stones in the bottom of each small flower pot, being careful not to block the draining holes in the bottom of the pots. Fill each pot with rich garden soil. Plant one (soaked) seed an inch below the soil in each pot. Put the pots in a dark place & water regularly until the shoots appear, then bring the pots into the light. Keep the plants dampened; try tapping the side of the pot, if it sounds hollow, add water. Also keep the surface soil loosened. Next spring the tiny trees will sprout leaves.

Buckeye

Any of the trees of N.A., resembling the horse chestnut, of the genus Aesculus. The large nut-like seed was used as medicine for horses. The tree itself was brought from Constantinople in the early 16th century.

Weeds & flowers.* Gather plants at noon of a hot clear day. Don't put them in water. Strip lower stalk of leaves. To trap their natural colors, hang them upside down by the stalks in a warm, dry, dark place for several weeks. These plants can be used in autumnal bouquets (November Art).

Lichens. These are a combination of a fungus & an algae living together. Their wide range of colors makes them a stimulating natural material for collages.

Leaves. To make *Leaf Skeletons* you will need: a canning jar, 1 quart of water, 2 T. lime, a small stick for stirring, a pan, a hot plate & a piece of soft cloth which is folded & tied over the end of a 2nd stick, a soft towel.

Put 2 T. lime in the jar & partly fill the jar with boiling water. Drop two or three leaves into the jar & allow them to remain there for up to 40 minutes. Slowly stir the water in the jar.

---

*An excellent chart of methods for "Preserving Flowers & Foliage" can be found in *Traditional American Crafts,* by Betsey B. Creekmore, Hearthside Press, Inc., 1968.

Take out one leaf; place it flat upon a table & gently rub it with the cloth-covered end of the stick. The green part of the leaf should be easily removed; if it doesn't come off completely, submerge the leaf a second time in the jar of boiling lime water. When one side of a leaf is clean, turn the leaf over & clean off the reverse side. Once the leaf is denuded, blanch it in 2 T. Clorox & 1 qt. water until leaf reaches desired whiteness. Rinse leaf; dry between paper towels & press beneath heavy books overnight.

Mount the leaf skeletons on black paper & use them in science study or art work.

Fall Art

During art periods, as often as possible, allow the class a freedom of choice: size, color, texture of papers, various colors of inks, paints. This encourages personal interpretation of each project & allows the child to explore, investigate, grow.

Seed mosaics. Children collect various seeds (pumpkin, apple, sunflower, corn, lentil, rice, peas, different kinds of beans) & sort them into (cottage cheese) containers.

Examples of mosaics, executed both by children & by adults, are shown to the class via filmstrips, art history books and art prints. The teacher elicits ideas as to the successful elements present in all of the examples: strong contrast of color, repetition of colors, balance of dark & light areas, definite composition.

Use corrugated cardboard pieces (10" x 12") for backings; cut the cardboard in varying proportions. The children draw a half-inch border all around the edge of the cardboard. The mosaics will be made within this delineation as the border facilitates display & protection of the finished piece. Children begin experimenting with the placement of various seeds on the cardboard. Usually the seeds themselves suggest an idea for a design. Squeeze-bottles of milk (casein) glue are used in the attachment of seeds to the cardboard backings. The seeds are pressed down firmly with the fingers & allowed to set for several minutes. Seeds can be scraped off if their placement is unsatisfactory. Large tweezers, toothpicks, or table knives are used to push small seeds into place. Patterned seeds should all face the same direction. The edge of a knife is used to make lines in the design clear & distinct.

After being allowed to dry for 36 hours, the seed mosaics can be sprayed with a clear (matte-finish) plastic coating.

Skeletal leaf collages. Abstract shapes of colored tissue paper are dipped into liquid starch. These shapes are overlapped, while still wet, on tagboard backings. Skeletal leaves (described in Fall Science) are gently pressed onto the wet tissue paper shapes. Compositions are allowed to dry completely before they are mounted on contrasting construction paper for display in the classroom.

Sand-casting. Each child removes one side from a half-gallon waxed milk carton. The cartons are filled three-fourths full of sand. Using a sprinkling or atomizer-spray bottle, the child dampens sand with water. Designs are then outlined in the sand with a small stick. Tablespoons are used to scoop out the sand within the confines of the design; a depth of two or three inches should be reached. Objects can be stamped firmly down into the dampened sand: (eucalyptus) seed pod or heavily veined leaf outlines are appropriate. After the impression is made, remove the object. If any decoration is to be added to the piece (small shells, colored glass, ceramic fragments, little stones, marbles, pieces of metal, etc.), these are pressed lightly FACE DOWN in the sand.

In a plastic waste basket the plaster of Paris is mixed (by the teacher) according to directions on the package. Using a plastic cup, each child pours the plaster carefully onto the moistened sand, making certain that each scooped-out area is filled with the plaster. A toothpick or broomstraw is inserted & withdrawn at random in the plaster's surface to aid in the escape of any trapped air bubbles. The plaster is allowed to dry undisturbed for several hours, if not overnight. Then the finished piece of sand sculpture is lifted out of the carton & any excess sand is removed from it by lightly brushing the sculpture's surface with a dry paint brush.

Veneer prints. Materials needed include: airplane glue; sheets of plywood of various dimensions (8" x 10"); different textures of paper, i.e. oatmeal, stencil, several grades of sandpaper; different textures of fabric, i.e. net, waffle-weave, embossed, Indianhead; yarn; string; toothpicks; masking & adhesive tapes; paper doilies & any textural materials that are flat & which the children find interesting. X-acto knives & linoleum block cutting tools are also helpful. Several brayers (a rubber roller with a handle), sheets of glass, linoleum block printing inks, turpentine & newsprint are needed for making the prints themselves.

A design is lightly drawn on the plywood with a pencil or is transferred to the plywood from a drawing. Flat textural materials (i.e. paper or fabric) are cut to fit the different areas of the design & are then glued firmly in place on the plywood. *All* edges of textural materials must adhere to the plywood. There should be some repetition of texture throughout the design. If the outline of any area is to be emphasized, glue yarn, toothpicks or string around the edge of that area. For negative lines & areas (which will appear white on final prints), an X-acto knife or similar tool can be used to cut away the surface of the plywood itself. Whenever possible the texture of the plywood should be utilized in the design, i.e. a sky, a background for a landscape, still-life or abstract. The textural areas of the plywood can be emphasized by repeatedly dampening the grain of the wood with a moistened sponge prior to application of the ink.

When the glue is dry, ink is applied to the veneered surface in the same way that it is applied to a linoleum block: ink is squeezed onto the glass pane from which the brayer picks it up & transfers it to the plywood sheet's veneered surface. The completely inked surface is covered with a piece of newsprint which is then rubbed gently but firmly with the heel of the hand, the fingers, & the bowl of a spoon. The corner of one edge of the newsprint is grasped & pulled diagonally toward the opposite corner, thus lifting off a copy of the finished veneer print.

The use of more than one color of ink can be attempted once the student is satisfied with his trial print.

Ink is removed from the plywood's surface, as well as from brayers and glass panes, by the frugal application of turpentine with soft cloths.

• Birth of Alfred Vail, 1807-1859 [25]

Alfred Vail was a friend of Samuel F.B. Morse & provided Morse with money for his experiments with the telegraph. Vail subsequently made numerous improvements on this invention & it was *he* who invented the dot & dash system for the telegraph.

Discuss briefly the invention of the Morse Code (see also Jan. 6, Marconi, & April 27, Morse). Distribute to the children mimeographed sheets bearing the code below.

A ·—	G——·	M ——	S ···	Y —·——
B —···	H ····	N —·	T —	Z ——··
C —·—·	I ··	O ———	U ··—	(.) ·—·—·—
D —··	J ·———	P ·——·	V ···—	(,) ——··——
E ·	K —·—	Q ——·—	W ·——	(?) ··——··
F ··—·	L ·—··	R ·—·	X —··—	

Then write the following message on the front board & see if they can decipher it:

/—/· · · ·/ ·/ /·—/·—/·—/··/—/· · · ·/——/·/ —/·· ·/—·—/

/· · · ·/———/——/·/·/·——/———/·—·/—·—/

/·——/··/·—··/·—··/ /—····/·/

Codes give the children practice in perceiving details.

Simple announcements can be written on the board with the vowels in each word omitted. This reminds the children that the vowels are "the mortar holding together the consonant-bricks of our words."

The children can experiment with creating their own codes.

• American Indian Day [26]

Discuss the following exerpt from "Remarks Concerning the Savages of North America": (*Poor Richard's Almanack*, 1757)

At a treaty of Lancaster in Pennsylvania in 1744 the government of Virginia offered the Six Nations (Iroquois) a fund for the education of six Indian youth. One of the rules governing Indian politeness is that a public proposition not be answered on the same day it is made, as an immediate answer might imply that the proposition was being treated as a light matter. So it was on the following day that the representative of the Six Nations expressed a deep sense of kindness on the part of the Virginia government in making the offer: " . . . for we know," says he, "that you highly esteem the kind of learning taught in those colleges, and that the maintenance of our young men while with you would be very expensive to you. We are convinced, therefore, that you mean to do us good by your proposal, and we thank you heartily. But you, who are wise, must know that different nations have different conceptions of things; and you will, therefore, not take it amiss if our ideas of this kind of education happen not to be the same with yours. We have had some experience of it. Several of our young people were formerly brought up at the colleges of northern provinces. They were instructed in your sciences, but when they came back to us they were bad runners, ignorant of every means of living in the woods, unable to bear either cold or hunger, knew neither how to build a cabin, take a deer, nor kill an enemy, spoke our language imperfectly, were, therefore, totally good for nothing. We are, however, not the less obliged by your kind offer, though we decline accepting it; and to show our grateful sense of it, if the gentlemen of Virginia will send us a dozen of their sons, we will take care of their education, instruct them in all we know, and make men of them."

Also discuss the quotations listed under September 26 Quotations.

Have the children listen to Buffy Saint-Marie singing "Now that the Buffalo's Gone," in the album: *It's My Way,* (Stereolab VSD79142, a Vanguard recording),* & then talk about feelings roused by the lyrics she has written.

If your class is interested in learning of a service project that they can undertake as a group to help Indian children living on a reservation, write, requesting information, to: American Friends Service Committee, 160 N. 15th St., Phila., Pa. 19102.**

Authentic American Indian recordings are published by the Folkways/Scholastic Records, 50 West 44th St., New York, N.Y. 10036 & may be obtained directly from them, or through record stores. ("Music of the American Indian, Southwest," 1420; &

---

*or "My Country, 'tis of Thy People You're Dying," in *Little Wheel Spin and Spin* (Vanguard: VSD 79211).
**Hereafter referred to as A.F.S.C.

"Music of the Sioux and Navajo," 1401.) Other long-playing records of tribal music may be obtained from the Music Division, Library of Congress, Washington, D.C. 20540. Write direct for price list.

Interpretive Art Forms

While listening to a record of American Indian music, the children can create interpretive art forms:

Leather collages (abstract or representational). Leather scraps can be obtained, usually at no charge, from any commercial tannery. Milk glue works well as an adhesive for the leather.

Sand pictures. Using a squeeze bottle, each child "draws" with milk glue on paper. A bit of sand is then blown onto the drawing. Parts of a design can be connected with solid lines of color & some areas may be filled in with tempera paint. VARIATION: (see November Art).

Soapstone sculpture. Soapstone (steatite) deposits are common in California, New York & North Carolina. This stone can easily be "mined" on a weekend & it is simple to work. A wood rasp, kitchen utensils & several grades of sandpaper are the only tools needed. A coat of wax is applied, after the finest sandpaper has been used, to bring out the subtle tonalities of the stone. When executing soapstone carvings, the children should allow the natural texture & veining of the stone to inspire the design of the sculpture.

If soapstone is not available, Girostone or Vermiculite (see Recipes for Art Supplies) also offer appropriate sculpture materials.

Educational materials & information pertaining to the American Indian are available through any of the following sources:

Publications Service
Haskell Institute
Lawrence, Kansas 66044

Bureau of Indian Affairs
Dept. of Interior
Washington, D.C. 20242

Superintendent of Documents
The Govt. Printing Office
Washington, D.C. 20402

Museum of the American Indian
Broadway at 155th St.
New York, N.Y. 10032

The Museum Shop: The American
Museum of Natural History
Central Park West and 79th St.
New York, N.Y. 10024

SEPTEMBER ACTIVITIES

Language Arts

Pen-pal projects. This is a good time to set pen-pal projects in motion. Bulletin board displays of pictures, coins, stamps (covered by sheets of clear acetate plastic to discourage the disappearance of valuables) can stimulate student interest in (international) correspondence.

Sources of pen pals can be found through:

World Pen Pals   35¢ apiece
World Affairs Center   ages 12-20
Univ. of Minnesota
Minneapolis, Minn. 55455

or contact your local Red Cross Chapter and inquire about their "School-to-School Program."

A permanent classroom chart might be made to display these pen-pal writing suggestions:

When writing letters abroad, REMEMBER:

Answer promptly. You'll be most enthusiastic about writing on the day you receive a letter from your pen-pal.

Write legibly. You have to keep in mind that your penmanship will be unfamiliar to your pen-pal.

Tell all about yourself. Tell about your family, friends, school, home, hobbies, pets, favorite books, sports. Be careful not to sound as if you're boasting; be sincere about what you write; be polite.

Don't use slang. Foreign pupils will often not be familiar with slang (& as a rule children from other countries write in a more formal manner than we do).

Avoid controversial subjects. Don't talk about things that might make your pen pal uncomfortable, e.g. comparisons of religions, political views.

Suggest exchanges: Think about things you'd like to exchange—photos, coins, stamps, slides, drawings, shells, tape recordings.

Learn your pen pal's birthday: Be sure to send him a card or small gift.

The teacher can distribute a mimeographed sheet of leading questions to assist the writer in eliciting information from his pen-pal.

Handmade stationery. This is another pen-pal spur. On bright colored strips of paper, the children stamp a border design by using seed pods or a simply cut potato cut away & dipped into rather thick poster paint. The strip of paper is then adhered (with rubber cement) to the top of a sheet of plain white paper. The design can be printed directly onto the writing paper & the corrected letter re-copied onto the sheet of handmade stationery. Initials, or a design incorporating them, make a pleasing decoration for stationery.

Personalized greeting cards: These can be made of felt or fabric scraps or yarn pictures which are adhered to the card with milk glue. Tissue paper* may be dipped in liquid starch & laid on the card to form a collage; this makes a vibrantly-colored card. The starch acts as an adhesive & gives a varnish-like effect to the tissue.

---

*Crystal Craft Tissue® mfg. by Crystal Tissue Co., Middletown, Ohio, is available in beautiful brilliant colors & costs about $1 for a package of multi-colored tissues.

Science

Easy microscope. With a pin, prick a hole in a piece of stiff paper. Hold your eye close to the hole & look at a strongly lit object which is about one inch from the hole; you will be unable to see the object clearly if it is closer than one inch to your eye as the eye cannot focus on an object which is that close. The pinhole in the paper acts as a diaphragm & greatly increases the depth of focus. This same principle applies to the camera: the smaller the opening of the lens, the greater the focus.

Waterdrop microscope. Make a small *round* hole in a piece of light-weight tinplate or heavy aluminum foil. Hold the piece of metal absolutely horizontal & let a drop of water from the tip of a watercolor brush fall directly onto the hole; the water will remain in the hole & act as a lens. Under a strong light, try observing different objects (grains of sand, salt, sugar, parts of insects or pieces of fabric). Place each object an eighth of an inch below the waterdrop.

Experiment with different sizes of holes; the size of the hole determines the curvature of the drop. And it is this curvature which determines the number of times the waterdrop microscope will be able to magnify the objects.

Waterdrop microscope* No. 2. Cut a 4-inch strip of metal from a tin can; round off the corners by using emery cloth or a fine sandpaper, so that no sharp edges remain. Using a hand drill & a 1/16"-inch bit, drill a hole in the metal strip a half-inch from the end. Score two lines down the width of the metal strip: one at 2-1/2 inches & the second at 2-3/4 inches. Bend the strip along these lines.

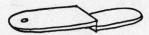

Use the hand drill with a quarter-inch bit to drill a hole toward the end of one side of a cigar box. Place a 15-watt bulb so

---

*From Ronald Roos, "Waterdrop Microscope," *Child Life Magazine* (June-July 1967). Copyright © by Review Publishing Company, Inc. Reprinted by permission of the publisher.

that it shines up through the hole. Mount a large sewing thread
spool over the hole in the box. The specimen on the slide (plain
glass one inch square) is placed over the hole in the spool. By
means of a small paint brush, make a drop of water fall onto the
hole in the metal strip. Line up the hole in the metal strip with the
one in the spool & observe the specimen, now magnified.

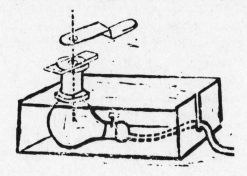

September Art

An excellent little magazine, *Everyday Art,* is free to (Art)
teachers, & may be received by writing to The American Crayon
Co., Eastern Office, P.O. Box 147, Jersey City, N.J. 07303.

Visual aids designed for classroom use are available from The
Extension Service, National Gallery of Art, Washington, D.C.
20565. Ask for their catalog of reproductions & publications.

September P.E.* (grades 1-3)

Squirrel in the Tree. Divide the class into groups of three:
two children hold hands to form a "tree trunk" & the third child
stands in the middle of the ring & represents "the squirrel." Any
extra players can be incorporated in the formation of "the trunk
of a giant redwood tree."

At a signal from the homeless squirrel, *all* squirrels, including
the homeless one, must change trees. The squirrel who finds
himself without a tree becomes "the homeless squirrel." Game
continues. Any player who has been "the homeless squirrel" twice

---

*The Fun Encyclopedia, by E.O. Harbin, published by Abingdon Press (201-8th
Ave. S., Nashville, Tenn. 37203), is a storehouse of games & would be especially useful
to teachers of P.E. & dramatics.

The Encyclopedia of Games by Doris Anderson is a Pyramid Book (444 Madison
Ave., New York N.Y. 10022) published by arrangement with Zonderian Pub. House.
This is the definitive collection of games & will be useful to all elementary school
teachers.

in a row automatically becomes a tree. Every child should have the opportunity to be "the homeless squirrel" at some time.

September Puppet (grades 1-4)

"Alexander" can become a regular feature of classroom activities; he may ask the class to please be quiet or to line up. He can enliven short review exercises, & he's always a dependable source of advice.

Stuff a three-year old's clothes with pieces of soft cloth; a straightened clothes hanger may be inserted through the middle of each appendage, as shown in the illustration. The hands are neutral-colored children's gloves & can be sewn in place to join the long-sleeved shirt. The head is papier-mâché modeled over a paper-filled sack. With poster paints apply a skin tone & facial features. When paint is dry, a clear mat plastic can be sprayed over the painted areas to protect them; adhere a large piece of (raccoon) fur to the top of the head. The finished puppet can wear glasses. Mainly, Alexander should express the personality of the teacher *& of her class.*

He may, when speaking, be made to sit on the teacher's lap. Lip movements need not be hidden while he is speaking; a change of voice, tonal quality, is sufficient. Because the children *want* him to speak—he can.

A hole may be made in the back of the torso so that by inserting a hand, movements of his head & torso will be achieved to further the illusion created.

Helpful Hints for Teachers

Fit 1 or 2 plastic containers for tableware into your top desk drawer. Use the little compartments for organization of, & easy access to, paper clips, pins, map tacks, tape, string, etc.

A picture file greatly simplifies the problems of bulletin board creation; collect large, clear, interesting pictures, photos. Make large tagboard folders to hold them & file them in alphabetical order (Animals, History, Holidays, Insects, Inventions, People, Sea, Weather, etc.). Obtain a large cardboard box, the top of which is cut on just 3 sides, forming a flap. The picture folders can be filed upright in the box & it can be kept in the classroom closet for easy reference.

There should be some stable month-to-month classroom activities, e.g. a nature walk, the recognition of students' birthdays, entries made in a Class Log or Diary.

For classroom book display: screw 2 metal coat hooks into a thick board.

From sturdy white cardboard, make 2 molar-shaped covers. Inside include at least as many pages as there are children in the room. Whenever a child loses a tooth, he has the honor of dictating "the whole story" to you: when, where, how. Type up the tale and include it in the book. Each story is signed by the child involved. This makes a Free Reading Time favorite, & visitors may enjoy it too.

One morning in the fall the children select a deciduous tree for year-round observation. They describe the tree in detail & record the date. Occasionally, throughout the year, they will visit the tree, illustrating & describing it & keeping a permanent record chart of it in the classroom. The height of the tree may be estimated (see March Science) on each visit.

It is always discouraging when a child arrives home & tells his parents that he has learned & done "nothing" in school that day. For lower-grade children, an aid-to-recall device can be set up beside the classroom door: a larger than life-sized paper scarecrow in September, witch in October, Indian in November—& each with outstretched arms. Every afternoon, as the class prepares for dismissal, it decides what the figure should hold in its arms, e.g. a penmanship paper, a science mimeo, a painting. As the work is attached to the figure by the teacher, she briefly discusses with the class their achievements of that day. This procedure need not take more than a few minutes & it has a calming effect on the group sending each child home with a clear image of what he did in school that day.

Set aside in a classroom cupboard the materials & equipment for 1 or 2 specific projects. On a day when you need a pick-me-up, 1 of these projects can be brought out, & the enthusiasm it evokes will be natural. An example of such a lesson might be the experiment below.

Volcano experiment. Purchase some crystals of ammonium dichromate at a chemical supply store. From 2 colors of modeling clay, make a realistic-looking crater on a large smooth rock. The crater should be about 6'' across at the base & 2-1/2'' across at the summit. Hollow out the crater so that it can easily hold 1-2 teaspoonfuls of the crystals. Following a discussion of volcanic action, during which such words as *lava, magma, pumice, igneous, vent, molten, dormant, extinct* are introduced, have a classroom display of volcanic power. Encourage the children to watch for different aspects of an eruption: what happens to the lava that is initially thrown upward? Where is lava most likely to flow? How is pumice formed? . . . etc. Strike a wooden match & insert it into the mouth of the crater, igniting the crystals. Viewers should stand clear of volcano until eruption has ceased.

Make a large bar graph on the blackboard by listing each student's name. Give every child the same 3 addition problems & 5 minutes in which to work them. Allow the class to correct these problems, & then you put the results on the graph. Repeat this procedure with subtraction, multiplication & division problems. This is an appropriate lesson to present when the children have become tired of the routine Math period.

Occasionally prepare a mimeo of incorrect grammar, spelling, punctuation examples which you have taken from *their* written work. The fun of recognizing a sentence, identifying its author, will help to enliven language review lessons for your class.

Younger children are delighted to receive a little special attention on their birthdays. Buy a box of trick birthday candles (the type that re-light whenever they are blown out) from a magic shop. Announce to the class that this is a special birthday candle

that cannot be blown out. Let the birthday child make a wish &
blow out the candle. Verbally encourage the candle to re-light (or
profess a lack of confidence in its powers). Once it has re-lit, the
candle may be "blown out" a 2nd time or permanently put out by
pinching its wick. Little children look forward to this "special
attraction" each birthday.

# October

Fresh October brings the pheasant,
Then to gather nuts is pleasant.

1　James Lawrence (1781-1813), American naval officer in War of 1812.
2　Mohandas Gandhi (1869-1948), Hindu Nationalist leader, pacifist.
3　Child Health Day.
4　Jean Francois Millet (1814-1875), French painter.
　　Rutherford B. Hayes (1822-1893), 19th President.
　　1st artificial satellite launched by U.S.S.R.: "Sputnik," 1957.
5　Chester A. Arthur (1830-1886), 21st President.
6　Le Corbusier (1887-1965), Swiss architect.
7　Hans Holbein died 1543 (born c. 1497), German painter.
　　Fire Prevention Week: always held during week of Oct. 9, anniversary of Great Chicago Fire, Oct. 9-11, 1871.
9　Camille Saint-Saens (1835-1921), French composer.
10　Guiseppe Verdi (1813-1901), Italian composer: *Aida, Falstaff, Il Trovatore.*
11　Eleanor Roosevelt (1884-1962), American diplomat, humanitarian.
　　Columbus Day: San Salvador was sighted by Columbus on Oct. 12, 1492. (This holiday is celebrated on the 2nd Mon. of Oct.)
13　Molly Pitcher (1754-1832), heroine of the Revolutionary War.
14　William Penn (1644-1718), founder of Pennsylvania.
　　e.e. cummings (1894-1962), American poet.
　　Dwight D. Eisenhower (1890-1969), 34th President.

15   Virgil (70 BC-19 BC), Roman poet.
      Poetry Day.
      1st public demonstration of ether as an anesthetic: Mass. Gen.
         Hospital, 1846.
16   Noah Webster (1758-1843), American lexicographer: com-
         piled *Webster's Dictionary.*
19   John Adams (1735-1826), 2nd President.
20   Sir Christopher Wren (1632-1723), English architect.
21   Ferdinand Magellan 1st sailed into strait that bears his
         name, 1520.
      Katsushuka Hokusai (1760-1849), Japanese artist.
      Alfred Nobel (1833-1896), Swedish inventor of dynamite;
         established Nobel prizes.
      Edison invented electric light, 1879.
22   Franz Liszt (1811-1886), Hungarian composer.
      Veterans Day (3rd Monday in October) was traditionally
         Nov. 11, changed by Monday Holiday Bill.
24   United Nations Day.
25   Geoffrey Chaucer, died 1400 (born 1340), English poet.
      Johann Strauss Jr. (1825-1899), Austrian composer.
      Georges Bizet (1831-1875), French composer: *Carmen.*
      Pablo Picasso (1881-   ), Spanish artist.
      Adm. Richard E. Byrd (1888-1957), American Polar
         explorer.
27   Theodore Roosevelt (1858-1919), 26th President.
      Dylan Thomas (1914-1953), Welsh poet.
      Navy Day.
      Captain James Cook (1728-1779), English explorer.
28   Statue of Liberty dedicated, 1886.
      Jonas Salk (1914-   ), American, developed polio vaccine.
29   Stock market crash, 1929.
      Edmund Halley (1656-1742), English astronomer.
      John Keats (1795-1821), English poet.
      National Children's Book Week: last week of October.
31   Jan Vermeer (1632-1675), Dutch painter.
      Halloween.

October

In the early Roman calendar, October was the 8th month: *octo=* eight in
Latin.

OCTOBER QUOTATIONS

1   Don't give up the ship! (His dying command, now watchword of U.S. Navy)—James Lawrence

2   If you think the world is all wrong, remember that it contains people like you.—Mohandas Gandhi

4   He serves his party best, who serves his country best.—Rutherford B. Hayes

14   Have a care where there is more sail than ballast. ("Advice to His Children")—William Penn

     Whatever America hopes to bring to pass in this world, must first come to pass in the heart of America. (Inaugural Address, 1953)—Dwight Eisenhower

     nobody, not even the rain, has small hands. ("Somewhere I Have Never Travelled")—e.e. cummings.

15   They are able because they think they are able. (*Aeneid*) —Virgil

19   I pray Heaven to bestow the best of blessings on this House and all that shall hereafter inhabit it. May none but honest and wise men ever rule under this roof.—John Adams: first tenant of the White House

25   A man doesn't begin to attain wisdom until he recognizes that he is no longer indispensable. *(Alone* "August: the Searchlight")—Richard Byrd

     Time! That's the thing. When it's gone, it's gone. No argument! Like a taxi meter ticking over. (*The Private World of Pablo Picasso*)

     When asked whom he considered the greatest painters of all time: "It depended upon the day."

                                  —Pablo Picasso

27   Speak softly and carry a big stick; you will go far. (Speech, 9/2/01)

     Free peoples can escape being mastered by others only by being able to master themselves.

     The things that will destroy America are prosperity at any price, peace at any price, safety first instead of duty first and love of soft living and the get-rich-quick theory of life.

                               —Theodore Roosevelt

28   Give me your tired, your poor,
Your huddled masses yearning to breathe free,
The wretched refuse of your teeming shore.
Send these, the homeless, tempest-tossed, to me;
I lift my lamp beside the golden door.
(Inscription on Statue of Liberty) — Emma Lazarus (1849-1887)

29   A thing of beauty is a joy forever:
Its loveliness increases; it will never
Pass into nothingness.
(*Endymion:* Book 1, Line 1)–John Keats

National Children's Book Week:

Something is learned every time a book is opened.—*Chinese proverb*

May blessings be upon the head of . . . whoever invented books.—*Thomas Carlyle.*

For a jollie goode booke whereon to looke is better to me than golde.—*John Wilson*

OCTOBER EVENTS:

- **Fire Prevention Week**

The 1st salaried fire department in America was that of Boston in 1679; it used a hand-operated engine which had been ordered from England & which required 13 men to operate it. The 1st volunteer fire department in the U.S. was founded by Benjamin Franklin in Philadelphia, 1736.

On October 8, 1871, at 9:00 P.M., Mrs. O'Leary's cow allegedly kicked over a lantern & started the Great Chicago Fire, causing $196,000,000 damage & leaving 98,860 homeless. Fire Prevention Week always occurs near Oct. 8 in memory of this disaster.

"Man the Bucket Brigade," a game that helps build coordination, may best be played outdoors. Each child, on the 2 or more equal teams, has a paper cup. Each team forms a line. A chair is placed at the head & at the end of each line. A water-filled milk carton stands on the chair at the head of the line. An empty milk carton is on the chair at the foot of the line.

At the starting signal, the 1st child on each team fills his cup from the milk carton at his side. He then pours this water into the cup of the child standing behind him, who pours the water into the cup of the child behind him, & so on. The last child pours the water into the empty carton. The game continues until the container at the head of the line is empty. The winning team is that with the most water in the carton at the foot of its line.

Riddle: What are the 3 main causes of forest fires? (Men, women & children!)

• **Columbus Day**

Social Studies

Columbus' voyages can be told in such a way as to include these 15 geographical references: Portugal, (Lisbon) Africa, Asia, China, Japan, India, Iceland, Europe, France, the Canary Islands, the West Indies, S. America, Central America, U.S.A., & Spain. Once each of these places is located by the class on the globe or wall map, Columbus' travels can be retraced.

Language Arts

Crossword puzzles. The letters in (Christopher) Columbus are used vertically as the backbone of the puzzle. Each child supplies definitions for each of the 8 words, e.g., Line 1 (7 letters): "the month in which Columbus sighted land." Line 2 (6 letters): "movement." Previously studied spelling words may be used. After the puzzles have been corrected, they might be recopied & exchanged between students.

Writing game. Each student is given a paper on which he is to write as many words as he can which have the word "ship" in them, e.g., friend*ship*, *ship*mate, craftsman*ship*. "At the sound of the bosun's whistle," writing begins. After 3-5 minutes, children stop & words are counted, results compared.

Dramatic play. This can be introduced at this time of year, using Columbus as the initial theme. Each month will afford opportunities for the use of this technique if you find it useful in working with your particular group.

" ... [D] ramatic play in the classroom is an educational technique under which the children explore an area of human experience (1) by reliving the activities & relationships involved in that experience in their own way, (2) by acquiring, under teacher-guidance, needed information & skills & (3) by increasing the satisfactions inherent in play that is meaningful & extensive. Dramatic play encompasses the following procedures:

1. The introductory situation is an arranged environment planned by the teacher.
2. Children explore the arranged environment & are permitted to respond in their own way, to manipulate tools and materials & discuss them.
3. A story may be read by the teacher to further the interest of the children in the selected area & to provide initial data for use.
4. Children are invited to play out any part of the story or set their own situation.
5. First play is spontaneous & unguided, but is carefully observed by the teacher.
6. Play is followed by a sharing period in which satisfactions are expressed or dissatisfactions are clarified, under teacher guidance, into statements of questions & expressed needs.
7. Planning for meeting the expressed needs includes the processes of problem-solving, making of rules, assignment of work to be done. [Steps 8, 9 & 10 are particularly suitable to culminating of Social Studies units.]
8. A period of extension of experiences through such activities as research, excursions, firsthand processes & utilization of multimedia ensues before, & beside, further play.
9. Play proceeds on higher levels (involving more accurate activities & more interrelationships & interpretations) as a result of enriched experience.
10. This is a continuous & expanding procedure, progressing on an ascending spiral that may, in the upper grades, eventuate, after weeks of growth, into a structured drama."*

Dramatic play may be facilitated by collecting, & then keeping in the classroom, a box of small simple props such as assorted hats, costume jewelry, eye glasses (or frames), shoe-boxes, a flashlight, wooden spoons, coffee cans, a baby blanket, a few pieces of fabric, etc. The use of such devices as signs, drawings, guide-lines, crepe-paper (to indicate a stream or the sea), and notation of important facts & dates on the chalkboard can also enliven these sessions.

Etymology. Ancient maps were marked with lines of longitude & latitude just as contemporary maps are, except that long

---

*From Fannie R. Shaftel and George Shaftel, *ROLE-PLAYING FOR SOCIAL VALUES: Decision-Making in the Social Studies* (Englewood Cliffs, N.J.: Prentice-Hall, Inc., 1967), pp. 134-35. Copyright by Prentice-Hall Inc. Reprinted by permission of the publisher.

ago these lines indicated the length & breadth of a flat world. The Latin words *latitude* and *longitude* were derived from *latus* (wide) & *longus* (long), as the world was then thought to be only wide & long.

The Greek prefix *ge* means "earth" & *graph* means "to write or describe," so then, *geography* is "a description of the earth."

Riddles: What BUS crossed the Atlantic? (Columbus.) As Columbus sighted America on his right hand, what did he see on his left hand? (5 fingers.)

Columbus Day Poetry

Introduce your class to Joaquin Miller's "Columbus" with its famed "Sail on! Sail on and on!"

Columbus Day Art

Ship in a Bottle. The children familiarize themselves with various ships either via book illustrations or a bulletin board display, e.g., "The Evolution of Ships." Differences in hull-shapes, number & size of sails, masts & riggings can be emphasized. The structure of Columbus' ships might be studied. This should help young children eliminate the stereotyped ship from their drawings.

Each child cuts a large bottle shape from tagboard. Hopefully, a wide variety of shapes will appear. By cutting masts, sails, & hull from colored paper & then pasting these on the center of tagboard, the child constructs his ship in a bottle. The riggings are pieces of string cut & glued in place. Varying shades of blue & green paper are torn, or cut, & overlapped along ship's hull to simulate waves. The entire bottle is tightly covered with plastic wrap, creating a glass bottle effect. The ends of plastic are taped to back of bottle. A slice of cork, or brown paper to represent a cork, is glued to "mouth" of bottle. VARIATION: Cap the waves with foam made of thick white poster paint. Allow this to dry before covering bottle with plastic. Fluffy cotton clouds, a seagull, or waving banners may also add variety.

• Poetry Day   [15]

The following is a list of poets whose birthdates occur within the school year. You may wish to have appropriate samples of their work available (on a bulletin board or at a reading area), or even provide mimeographed sheets of poems for the students to enjoy during free times.

Matthew Arnold, W.H. Auden, the Benets, Wm. Blake, Eliz. &
Robt. Browning, Lord Byron, Lewis Carroll, Eliz. Coatsworth, e.e.
cummings, Emily Dickinson, Ralph Emerson, Rachel Field, Robt.
Frost, John Keats, Kipling, Longfellow, J.R. Lowell, Pasternak,
Poe, Sandburg, Shakespeare, R.L. Stevenson, Edna St. Vincent
Millay, Whitman, Whittier, Wm. Wordsworth.

An order form describing Caedmon recordings of special
interest to teachers may be obtained by writing to the Houghton
Mifflin regional sales office serving your school. These recordings
include "Carl Sandburg Poems for Children," on which the poet
discusses poetry & reads some of his own works.

• Birth of Noah Webster   [16]

Webster's 1st dictionary was published in 1828 & is used
today in a bigger & better edition. Children are often intrigued by
the mere length of words. Contrary to the belief of many children,
the longest word in the dictionary is NOT "antidisestablish-
mentarianism." This word was merely created as an example of a
string of prefixes & suffixes & it isn't in Webster's Dictionary. The
longest word in "common usage" in the English language is
"pneumonoultramicroscopicsilicovolcanoconiosis," the name of a
lung ailment that afflicts coal miners as a result of inhaling fine
coal dust. The children might enjoy dissecting "the longest word"
& breaking it down into syllables to better understand its meaning.

• Birth of Theodore Roosevelt   [27]

Your class can listen to the voice of this great American
President; his voice (& those of 40 other famous persons, e.g.,
Tennyson, Robt. Browning, Admiral Perry) has been re-recorded,
filtered & amplified from the original wax cylinders & 1st flat
discs. (Two LP albums & a descriptive book: "Forty-two Great
Lives"; $6.98; "Voices of History," 2025 Greenland Bldg., Miami,
Fla. 33054.)

• Birth of Edmund Halley   [29]

Halley observed a comet in 1682 & decided that it was the
same comet that had been known to re-appear every 76 years. He
predicted that it would again be visible in 1758 or 1759. It was.

A comet is described as a star with a tail; the original Greek
word *kometes* meant "wearing long hair."

Halley's Comet last appeared in 1910. Its head was approximately 161,000 miles in diameter & its tail was 27,800,000 miles long. This comet travels some 100,000 m.p.h.

Information source: American Astronomers' Assoc., 223 West 79th St., N.Y., N.Y. 10024.

- **National Children's Book Week**

Bulletin board suggestions: (Title: Books help make a friendly world where people live in peace.) Ask the public librarian for the use of some book covers illustrative of the bulletin board title. Pin these beneath title. It's important to question the children as to why each of the books represented is an appropriate choice. Discuss book titles that might not be correct to include in this display. Ask the class to give examples of ways in which the written word *has* worked (& can work) for peace in the world today.

Through Books We Discover
How Other People Think   How Other People Feel   How Other People Live

The children are asked to think of ways in which they could fill the areas beneath each of these subtitles; e.g., pictures of famous people could be used with balloons in which their thoughts & feelings would be expressed; exact quotations (as noted in this book) are possibilities. Under the 3rd subtitle, various dwellings (e.g., those of Heidi, Mowgli, Clara Barton, Sir Lancelot) could be shown, or examples of various methods used in different places to solve the same problem (transportation, acquisition of food, clothing, art, music).

Language Arts

Creative writing topics include: "Seven Books & Why I Own Them," "A Book That Changed My Life"; or ask the class to write a complete new ending to a book they've read, or to tell about the funniest, meanest or most daring book character they've met; or have the children pretend that they are to be exiled to an uninhabited desert island: "What (10) books would you choose to take with you—& *why?*"

Prepare a set of tagboard playing cards. On half of these print the titles of well-known books; on the remaining cards print the corresponding names of authors or book characters. Children may match the cards by themselves or play "Authors" with 3 or more players. Whitman & Co. produces an inexpensive card game of "Authors" which could be introduced to your class at this time.

When children write their own books, variety should be encouraged. Unusual formats could be shown to the class: samples of a scroll book, a Japanese accordion fold-out book (e.g., Sesshus' *Long Scroll: A Zen Landscape Journey*, $2.95: 1969 Charles E. Tuttle Co., Rutland, Vermont 05701) or books of unusual design. Suggest that the children include any of the following in their handmade books: marbleized paper fly-leaves (see Dec.), a complete title page with copyright date & place of publication, the name of person to whom the book is dedicated.

Older children might enjoy making individual readers, using a controlled vocabulary such as the Dolch 220 Basic Words List; these books could be donated to the school library or used by a student-aide during a 1st or 2nd grade reading class.

If you have your students make book reports, here are some suggestions for varying the forms throughout the year:

> This is a book for boys___ girls___ both___. Why do you think so? Give the main idea of the story in one sentence. Did anyone in the book overcome a difficulty or solve a problem? If so, what do you think about the way he/she did it? Why do you feel this book would/would not make a good movie? Would you like to change the ending? Why? Do you feel the author wrote this book for the reader's entertainment or to give the reader information? What makes you think so? If the book was non-fiction, tell 4 things you learned while reading it. What information did it make you want to know?

Etymology. In Old English, *boc*, from which we get "book," meant "Beech" as that was the bark on which words were then scratched. "Author" comes from the Latin *auctor*, meaning "he who originates or makes things grow."

Social Studies

A two-generation book display can be organized by having the children bring to class books which their parents read or used as children. As a contrast, display modern editions of the same titles or exhibit recently published children's books. Discuss any differences, similarities which the children discover.

> Information source: The Children's Book Council, Inc., 175 Fifth Ave., New York, N.Y. 10010

- Halloween   [31]

The Romans honored the goddess of harvest, Pomona, during this time of year. Druids of ancient England celebrated the New Year on the 1st of November, believing that on the last day of the old year, Oct. 31, the souls of the dead were allowed to return to Earth. The American Indian held special dances at this season. Our Halloween is a mixture of these celebrations. Traditionally, Halloween is the ancient holy, or hallowed, eve'n (evening) of All Saints' Day.

In pre-Christian England, disguises were worn to confound any spirit that might have been out looking for you; today costumes are worn "for the fun of it."

During medieval times "Soulers" roamed the streets of England, praying, singing hymns & asking for alms. In return for the money, the Soulers were to pray for the donor's relatives who might be in Purgatory. "Trick-or-treating" is an outgrowth of these Soulers' parades.

Bulletin Board Suggestions

For attention-getting titles, burn the edges of letters you have cut from construction paper or burn the sides of a sheet of paper on which lettering appears.

A display for older students is shown here. Appropriate vocabulary enrichment words are printed on the ghost shape. On the 2nd day of this display, definitions are made to float at the side of the ghost. By this time the class should be familiar with the words & ready to matchthem with correct definitions.

Using the title "A Witch's Guide to Gardening,"* you can achieve an interesting science enrichment display. Illustrate the following information with drawings or photos; not all of these plants need be included on the board at one time. (Older students may enjoy & benefit by taking the responsibility for the entire execution of this display.)

> IMPORTANT: It should be noted that ingestion of most of these plants is dangerous & can be deadly. Any safety precautions deemed necessary should be taken.

Wild Angelica (the Holy Plant): Its name means "the angel-like herb." It is used as a flavoring & in medicines & perfumes. In olden days, it was hung over the front door of your house to ward off witches.

Mandrake: It was thought to feed on earth in which a murderer was buried. It is a deadly plant when eaten, & has a forked root which is said to resemble a man.

Wormwood: This plant was supposed to have grown in the track of the serpent as it slithered out of the Garden of Eden. It gives us absinthe, a drink that is harmful to health, but which was taken long ago "to counteract the bite of a shrew or of a seadragon." Its name has become a noun meaning "a bitter, mortifying experience."

Parsley: The most maligned of the plants. It was believed that it should only be planted on Good Friday in order to take off its curse & that it should *never* be transplanted. Plutarch wrote of a battle that was completely broken up as a parsley-laden mule crossed the path of a Greek army!

Belladonna: (Deadly Nightshade): A poisonous European plant (Atropa belladonna), it has purplish-red bell-shaped flowers. A tincture drawn from its leaves & roots is used to treat colic & asthma. Its name is Italian for "beautiful lady" & supposedly refers to its early use in cosmetics.

The Three Deadly H's: *Hemlock:* The Greeks administered capital punishment by giving a drink made of hemlock to criminals. Socrates died from drinking a cup of hemlock. *Hemp:* From its flowers & leaves, hashish, an intoxicating tobacco, is made.

---

*From Dorothy Jacob, *A Witch's Guide to Gardening* (Elek Books, London, 1964 and Taplinger Publishing Co., New York, 1965). Reprinted with permission of the publishers.

Henbane: A foul-smelling plant that is the bane (death) of hens—or any other bird that might eat it.

Information source: Write to Geigy Agricultural Chemicals, Ardsley, N.Y. 10502 for a free folder, "Plants That Poison."

The following is not specifically a Halloween bulletin board, but it might be used at any time during this month. With the exception of the definitions which are hidden under flaps, the body of the information is printed on a large sheet of butcher paper. The definitions are printed on bright colored paper to contrast with the predominant tan of the board. Students raise flaps to verify or discover correct word meanings.

OCTOBER was the eighth month of the early Roman calendar. *Octo,* or *Octa* (before a vowel) is a combining-form meaning "eight." Knowing this, can you figure out the meanings of these words?

Octagon (*gonos* is Greek for "corners")
Octopod (*pod* = "foot")
Octopus (*oktopus* is Greek for "8-footed")
Octogenarian (*octogeni* is Greek for "80")
Octillion (*octo* + *mille,* the French word for "million")
Octennial (*octo* + *annus,* the Latin word for "year")
Octave (*octavus* is Latin for "eighth")
Octet (*octo* + duet)

Classroom Door. Have the children make a large scary witch & attach her to the outside of the classroom door. In her hand place a sign that states: "Welcome to Room 7. Come in—if you dare!"

Language Arts

Halloween Surprise. 5-line compositions are written by the children in answer to the questions below (final stories need not be completely logical):

Sentence 1: Who? Where? When?
Sentence 2: What is the problem in this story?
Sentence 3: Why does this problem *have* to be solved?
Sentence 4: How do they try to solve it?
Sentence 5: What is the surprising outcome?

The variety shown in the finished compositions is a pleasant surprise in itself.

Ask the class to write the "Life History of a Monster," including such details as where he lives, what he does in his free time, how he gets friends or his food or clothing.

Have each child invent the imaginary origin of some superstition held today; e.g., the practice of saying, "God bless you" when someone sneezes, the belief that Friday the 13th is a day of ill-luck, etc. Encourage the children to include as many details as possible in these stories.

You can prepare for the following creative writing lesson the evening before presenting it. Cut as many pieces of 6" x 8" white (typing) paper as you have students. Fold each sheet in half—either crosswise or lengthwise. Using India ink (magenta is effective), apply several drops from the stopper along each side of the fold. Crease the sheet along the original fold & press firmly, rubbing with the palm of the hand. When paper is unfolded, a Rorschach-like pattern appears. Allow ink to dry completely. The next day, pass out writing paper to each child. Place the ink blot sheets, face down, on their desks. Advise students to listen to instructions before turning over ink-blot sheets. Direct them to look at the ink blot from any angle they like & let it give them an idea for a descriptive paragraph. Older students may be interested in hearing how Dr. Rorschach originated a method of analysis that utilized ink blots: his patients made up stories about what was seen in the blot & Rorschach interpreted these stories in much the way that Dr. Freud analyzed dreams.

When the paragraphs are corrected & recopied, they can be pinned up with their accompanying ink blots to make a quick display & fascinating reading.

A review spelling mimeo might direct the children to "supply the missing letters in these SKELETON words." Previously studied spelling words or words that your class frequently misspell might be included: The princip_l helped the ch_ldr_n find th_r ball.

A classroom cave for dramatic play. Overturn a table, with its top to the wall; use butcher paper (painted gray) for the sides of the cave. The top is made by attaching the 4 corners of a sheet to the 2 uppermost table legs. Sew a long string to the middle of the sheet. By pulling up on this string (& tacking it to the ceiling) a tent-like structure is achieved. Drape it over with crepe paper vines & leaves.

Etymology. During the Middle Ages in England so many people died from the Black Plague that the bodies had to be burned every day in huge fires. These fires were called "fires of bones" or "bonefires." Later, when burning of heretics at the stake became common, these were also called "bonefires." Gradually, it came to be that any large fire was referred to by this name, but with a shortened spelling: bonfire. A costume is something that is the custom (from Italian *costuma*) to wear. The Latin *skello* means "to dry up," so a skeleton is a dried up body! Loot is a corruption of the Hindustani *lut,* meaning "something plundered."

> *Riddles:* How does a witch tell time? (With a witch-watch.) How can you get into a locked cemetery late at night? (Use a skeleton key!) Why is a haunted house a good place to play baseball? (There's always an extra bat handy.) What's the difference between a match & a black cat? (The cat lights on its feet & the match lights on its head.) Which burns longer: a black candle or an orange candle? (Neither—they both burn *shorter!*)

Halloween Poetry: This is a fine time to introduce your class to the image-eliciting "Windy Nights" by Robt. L. Stevenson.

Halloween Reading. An eerie introduction of new words can be achieved in this way: The night before the lesson, using a fine brush & evaporated milk, print each new word on a separate slip of paper. Each child in the reading group will have the chance to hold his "blank" slip of paper over a candle's flame & watch the "new word" appear. Once he can say the word, he shares it with the group, or the group may try to guess the word as it appears, letter by letter. The word will appear most quickly if the paper is held milk-side to the flame. This might best be used several days prior to Halloween, as the children will probably need little additional stimulation on the 31st!

Here is a reading game that gives the children the incentive to sound out unknown words: Make up tagboard cards, one for each child in the reading group. The instructions printed on the cards should utilize, & emphasize, whatever phonics the group is presently studying. Each child gets a card, reads it silently & prepares to perform. The other children watch until the performer is finished & then the group tries to guess the identity of the creature, & action portrayed, e.g.: "You are a little black bat. It is still daytime and so you are hanging upside down, sleeping. There goes the bell! Can that be seven o'clock already? It is seven o'clock and that means it's time for you to wake up! Stretch your wings. Now fly outside & swoop by the trees. Fly upward. Fly down again. Fly a———way."

Séance. This game can be played at any time during the year. It is basically a phonics-review device that affords the teacher a quick check on an individual student's progress. It also gives the teacher an opportunity to be *very* dramatic. A tagboard turban may be worn. An elaborate rhinestone earring can be attached to the front of the turban; the clip of the earring goes through the tagboard & is secured by tape to the backside of the turban. Fasten the ends of the turban with a rubber band so that the turban will fit any size head.

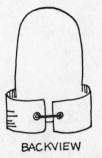

BACKVIEW

FRONTVIEW

Explain to the class that you are going to act as "a medium" & that they must be very quiet & concentrate as it demands a great deal of energy for you to make contact with the spirits. Stretch out your arms, & with just your fingers touching the table top (around which the reading group is seated) close your eyes & speak: "I'm thinking of a word that has the sound of 'oi' in it. This word means 'earth' or 'ground'; do any of you know the word? *Soil!* That's correct, Bob. Do you know how 'soil' is spelled? Absolutely right. . . . The next message I'm receiving is in the form of a word with a long 'A' sound. This word is a verb that means 'to lose consciousness' or 'to pass out,' " etc.

Sometimes the children themselves may be capable of conducting the séance. A new medium should be chosen only when he already has "a message" in mind.

These sessions, like all review-exercises, should be kept short: after a while simply note that the vibrations are growing weak & that you are very tired from the strain of transmitting these messages & so "now today's séance must end." By stopping a bit before the group grows restless, you will insure their being enthusiastic about having a séance at some future time.

Halloween Math:

Watch the Ghost Disappear (a flannelboard drill). On each piece of the ghost, which is made of felt, a problem is written in felt-point pen. Each child touches that part of the ghost which he wishes "to make disappear." If he gives the correct answer, he may keep the piece of felt; answers may be written on the back of each piece of the ghost. When the entire ghost has been taken from the board, children may work "to help make the ghost re-appear." VARIATION: "My Favorite Ghost." Children have the choice of 3 ghostly felt figures, each is devoted to a different multiplication table or math process.

Plus Cat (or Minus Cat)—a mimeo review sheet. Children fill in the differences at the bottom of the sheet, e.g.: left eye: 9 minus 5, 9 minus 8, 9 minus 2 etc. Following completion of the left eye, students do the right eye (11), nose (10), & mouth (12), each in succession.

Science Experiments

Bendable Bones. Soak a large clean uncracked chicken bone

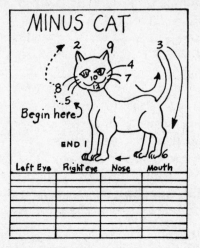

Left Eye	Right eye	Nose	Mouth

in a glass of vinegar for 12 hours. The acid in the vinegar dissolves the bone's calcium which gave it its initial stiffness. The resultant bone can be tied in a knot.

Halloween Art:

Discourage the stereotyping of Halloween motifs. Ghosts and devils can be presented as exciting, historically interesting phenomena. Nature can be personified, e.g., mountains that are watching you. It would be helpful if the children could observe from life in order to avoid generalizations, e.g., how a person, astride a broom, grasps the broom handle; how the leg of a cat comes out of the haunch; what happens to the back of a cat when he sits down.

Lesson suggestions. Let the children paint in accompaniment to Saint-Saens' "Danse Macabre," or "Night on Bald Mountain" by Mussorgsky.

Watercolor witchery. A red & orange watercolor wash gives a glow-like effect when applied over drawings of ghosts, goblins, witches done with white crayon on white paper.

Wet chalk drawings. Prior to the lesson, chalk may be soaked

in a solution of ⌒⌒⌒ sugar & ⌒⌒⌒ water; this mixture helps prevent chalk from rubbing off drawings. A water container (1/2 pint milk carton with top removed) may be placed on each desk; children can then repeatedly moisten their chalk while drawing.

During recess you prepare for this lesson by dampening large sheets of newsprint: hold each sheet under running water & loosely fold paper in halves or fourths; or submerge loosely folded sheets in basin of water. Pile dampened papers in large square plastic dishpan in order to transport them to the desks. Pass between the rows of desks, handing out dampened papers to children on either side of you. This procedure cuts down on confusion & wet floors. Designate an area at the back of the room where the children may lay their finished drawings to dry.

Witches. This lesson helps strengthen listening skills. The teacher may describe, in geometric terms, the pieces to be cut. In this way the identity of the witch is concealed as long as possible; e.g.: "Choose a long piece of the cotton yarn in any color you like (choices may include red, purple, green) and two partitions (egg holders) of an egg carton. Then return to your seat. Take out a black crayon and blacken the bottom (inside) of each of the egg holders; tear the holders apart from one another if they are not already separated. Now cut from black paper a medium-sized triangle (hat). Cut out a thin rectangle that is longer than the base of your triangle (brim of hat). Cut a very large triangle that's about 2 times as big as your 1st triangle (dress)," etc.

Arms, legs, fingers, high-heeled shoes could also be described in geometric terms for older children. Oral instructions continue until black shapes, egg carton eyes, yarn hair, are pasted in place on bright orange paper. Young children will add appendages with black crayon. A paper broom is optional.

Sculpted masks. Sheets of 12" x 18" construction paper or tagboard are used. Cut along dotted lines & fold in (or overlap) one piece, stapling it in place. Variations are countless.

Goblin mask. Children fold a sheet of 9" x 12" red orange

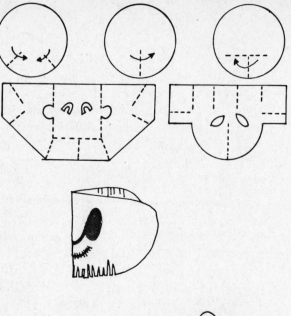

construction paper in half. Using scissors, they make the cuts shown.

Then they open the mask out flat & spread the teeth & whiskers with their fingers. A second piece of 9″ x 12″ construction paper is cut lengthwise & long slits are then made from these long strips. Using pencils, the children curl each strand separately, making some curl forward & some backward. This hairpiece is then glued to the goblin's forehead. Holes can be punched & backed with hole-reinforcers (this eliminates tearing of mask), & elastic or string ties attached.

OCTOBER ACTIVITIES

Plant Projects for October

Your name on a pumpkin. Cut letters from aluminum foil & attach them with petroleum jelly or waterproof glue to an unripe pumpkin. Put the letters on the side of the pumpkin which faces the sun. Since chemical reactions caused by the sun turn the pumpkin from green to orange, when the foil is finally removed bright green letters will stand out against the orange pumpkin skin.

Class pumpkins. If you are able to contact a farm-produce market, you can often purchase, or even order in advance, a tiny pumpkin for each child in your class. Then, armed with a spoon, each child can carve out his own jack-o'-lantern. You may walk around the room & slice off the tops of pumpkins with a knife, but usually the handle of the spoon can be used by the child himself to cut off the top. Newspapers are spread on each desk so that the seeds may be saved (recipe follows) & as an aid to clean-up.

As the pumpkins are scooped out, discuss the layers of the shell, the way in which the pumpkin grew from a blossom & the importance of water to the growth of the pumpkin.

The basic geometric shapes may be listed on the front board so that the children may use them as a guide to cutting features in their pumpkin. Also remind the children to bore a small hole with a pencil in the lid of the jack-o'-lantern in order to allow candle's smoke to escape.

Toasted pumpkin seeds. Thoroughly wash & clean the seeds. Drain them well on paper toweling. Sprinkle the bottom of a cookie sheet with a solid layer of salt. Arrange the seeds in a single layer on the salt. Place the cookie sheet in a moderately slow oven (300°) for 40-45 minutes or until the seeds are lightly browned. Allow to cool in the pan.

Flower bulbs. Now is the time to plant bulbs indoors. Hyacinths should bloom by Christmas; daffodils, tulips & mauve crocus are also usually successful. (Yellow crocus will not bloom indoors.) Plant bulbs in special fiber purchased at a nursery, or in a bulb jar (which need not be set in a dark place until roots appear, & therefore allows class to watch growth.)

October Puppets

Easy Witch Finger Puppets. Cut a circle from matboard. Tape a paper loop (the size of your finger) onto the back of the circle; on the front paste a witch's face. Black crepe paper taped beneath this head becomes the witch's cloak.

Matchbox Owl—October finger puppet. Attach an owl's head made of paper to the front of a small matchbox cover. Tape construction paper wings to the back of the box cover. Insert finger through opening to make owl move.

Halloween Party

Children, in committees, are encouraged to do the majority of the planning. A time schedule is set up as a guide for these committees, e.g.: 2:15, recess: children may be dressing in their costumes in the restroom or cloakroom. Supervision may be needed. 2:30, everyone is in his seat. 2:35, short games, a story. 2:55, ON THE DOT—refreshments (soft "spooky" music may be played as a calming device). 3:10, napkins discarded, everyone seated. 3:15, dismissal; clean-up committee remains in classroom (to wash paint off windows).

Decorations. The classroom windows have been painted with Halloween motifs, (a combination of kitchen cleanser mixed with poster paint). The cleanser facilitates window-washing on Friday afternoon. Torn tissue paper ghosts may have been lightly glued atop these paintings. Small scraggly tree branches have been suspended from light fixtures; brightly colored shapes (bats, owls, witches, moon) twirl on threads tied to these branches. The children can draw a large graveyard scene on the chalkboard, using only yellow & white chalks. This drawing might be done during free time on the day of the party.

Entertainment. Games should be kept fast-paced, quickly rewarding & controlled. This helps prevent younger children from becoming overly excited.

Each child is given an 8'' x 8'' square of yellow, gold, or orange construction paper. The children are asked to stand beside their desks. "Put the paper behind your back. Using no scissors & *without* looking, tear out an entire jack-o'-lantern. Now, remember, no looking!" When they bring out their finished pumpkins, the class will enjoy comparing results & choosing, perhaps, "the funniest," "the most realistic," "the most cleverly executed," etc. (These pumpkins can be quickly stapled, after school, to a vacant bulletin board for a cheery new 1-2 day display.

Pass out paper & see who can make the most words from the letters in (HAPPY) HALLOWEEN. Any word—proper noun, verb—counts, with the exception, if you wish, of abbreviations. It seems wise to state beforehand if searching in books for word suggestions will be permitted. Perhaps this might be allowed during the last five minutes. All writing of words begins at the same minute, e.g., at the next click of the classroom clock. The teacher may pass between rows giving spelling assistance, when needed. At the end of the game a winner is announced & the papers are collected. (A composite list of words cited by the class as a whole can be printed in large lettering after school & posted for the children to read the following morning.)

Finally, the teacher may read a short spooky story as the refreshment committee passes out napkins & treats.

Other entertainment possibilities include the "Halloween Science Experiments" or "Magic Experiments & Tricks" (see April & May).

Refreshments. Children can vote on the choice of food prior to their party. It need not be elaborate as, of course, an abundance of sweets will be consumed that evening. Treat suggestions include: hot or cold cider or orange Kool-Aid; cupcakes in which foil-wrapped fortunes & tiny prizes have been baked; or caramel apples; doughnuts with icing faces.

Two Notes to the Teacher. (1) Try to keep the day of the party as calming in mood, & as organized in method, as you can. (2) Bring an extra mask or two (or a sheet) for "that one kid who couldn't have a costume this year."

November

Dull November brings the blast;
Then the leaves are whirling fast.

1   All Saints Day.
2   Father Junipero Serra (1713-1784), Spanish explorer, founder of many Calif. missions.
Daniel Boone (1734-1820), American frontiersman.
Gaspar de Portola (1734-1784), discoverer of San Francisco Bay.
James Polk (1795-1849), 11th President.
Warren G. Harding (1865-1923), 29th President.
Auguste Rodin (1840-1917), French sculptor.
Election Day is the 1st Tuesday after the 1st Monday in November.
4   Will Rogers (1879-1935), American humorist.
5   1st black woman (Shirley Chisholm) is elected to the House of Representatives, 1968.
6   John Philip Sousa (1859-1932), American bandmaster.
7   Lewis and Clark sighted the Pacific Ocean 1805.
Marie Sklodowska Curie (1867-1934), Polish-French physicist, co-discoverer of radium, received 2 Nobel Prizes: 1903 & 1911.
8   1st circulating library in USA established in Phila., 1731.
9   Sadie Hawkins Day.
10   Martin Luther (1483-1546), German theologian, leader of the German Reformation.
William Hogarth (1697-1764), English painter.

US Marine Corps created by Continental Congress, 1775.
Stanley found Livingston, 1871.

11   Abigail Smith Adams (1774-1818), wrote persuasive, warm letters urging women's rights to her husband, U.S. Pres. John Adams.
Traditional date of Veterans' Day (now in Oct.).

12   Aleksandr Borodin (1834-1887), Russian composer.

13   Robert Louis Stevenson (1850-1894), British author.

14   Robert Fulton (1765-1815), American inventor.
Claude Monet (1840-1926), French impressionist painter.
Aaron Copland (1900-   ), American composer.

15   Articles of Confederation adopted by Continental Congress, 1777.
Pike's Peak was discovered by Zebulon Pike, 1806.

17   1st meeting of Congress in Wash. D.C., 1800.

18   Louis Daguerre (1789-1851), French inventor of 1st practical photography.

19   George Rogers Clark (1752-1808), American explorer— "conqueror of the N.W. Territory."
James Garfield (1831-1881), 20th President.
Lincoln delivered his Gettysburg Address, 1863.

20   Atahualpa, Inca of Peru, agreed to fill a room with gold for Pizarro, 1532.

21   Mayflower Compact signed, 1620.

22   John F. Kennedy assassinated, 1963.

23   Henry Purcell died 1695 (born c. 1658), English composer.
Franklin Pierce (1804-1869), 14th President.
Thanksgiving is the fourth Thursday of November.

24   Zachary Taylor (1784-1850), 12th President.
Carlo Lorenzini [Collodi] (1826-1890), Italian author of *Pinocchio.*
Henri Toulouse-Lautrec (1864-1901), French painter.

25   Andrew Carnegie (1835-1919), American capitalist, philanthropist.

26   1st national Thanksgiving proclaimed by Geo. Washington, 1789.
Sojourner Truth died 1883 (birthdate unknown); illiterate freed slave who became civil rights advocate, eloquent black feminist.

28   William Blake (1757-1828), English poet, engraver.

29   Louisa May Alcott (1832-1888), American author.

30   Jonathan Swift (1667-1745), English author, satirist.

Samuel Clemens [Mark Twain] (1835-1910), American author.

Winston Churchill (1874-1957), English statesman.

Children's Book Week varies from year to year (see Oct.).

Hanukkah: The Festival of Lights or The Feast of Dedication (November or December).When the Maccabees recaptured the temple in Jerusalem only one vial of sacramental oil (enough for one day's use) was found. However, this oil lit a light which lasted for seven days and allowed sufficient time for additional oil to be prepared. Each evening of this seven-day celebration a new arm of the menorah is lit in honor of the freeing of the Maccabees.

November

For the Romans, November was the 9th month: *novem* = 9 in latin. ("November; n. The eleventh twelfth of a weariness": Ambrose Bierce, *Devil's Dictionary*).

NOVEMBER QUOTATIONS

4   A man only learns in two ways, one by reading and the other by associating with smarter people.

Don't let yesterday use up too much of today.

Everybody is ignorant, only on different subjects. *The Illiterate Digest*

I never met a man I didn't like. (Address, Boston: 6/30)

Will Rogers

5   I have been discriminated against far more because I am a female than because I am black.—Shirley Chisholm

13   Everyone lives by selling something. *Across the Plains*

To be what we are and to become what we are capable of becoming, is the only end of life. *Famous Studies of Men and Books*

The world is so full of a number of things, I'm sure we should all be as happy as kings.

—Robert Louis Stevenson

19   A pound of pluck is worth a ton of luck.

—James A. Garfield

25   Surplus wealth is a sacred trust which the possessor is bound
      to administer in his lifetime for the good of the com-
      munity.

                                                —Andrew Carnegie

26   The man over there says women need to be helped into
      carriages and lifted over ditches, and to have the best
      place everywhere. Nobody ever helps me into carriages
      or over puddles or gives me the best place . . . ain't I a
      woman? Look at my arm! I have ploughed and planted
      and gathered into barns and no man could head me—ain't
      I a woman? I could work as much and eat as much as a
      man—when I could get it—and bear the lash as well! And
      ain't I a woman? I have born 13 children and seen most
      of 'em sold into slavery, and when I cried out with my
      mother's grief, none but Jesus heard me. . . . and ain't I a
      woman?

                                                —Sojourner Truth, 1851

30   We shall defend our island, whatever the cost may be, we
      shall fight on the beaches, we shall fight on the landing
      grounds, we shall fight in the fields and in the streets, we
      shall fight in the hills; we shall never surrender. (Speech
      in House of Commons, 5/4/40)

      Never give in! Never give in! Never, never, never, never—in
      nothing great or small, large or petty—never give in
      except to a conviction of honor and good sense.

                                                —Winston Churchill

      Supposing is good, but finding out is better.

      It is differences of opinions that make horse races.

      Don't, like the cat, try to get more out of an experience
      than there is in it. The cat, having sat on a hot stove lid, will
      not sit upon a hot stove lid again. Nor upon a cold stove lid.

                                                —Mark Twain

      May you live all the days of your life.

                                                —Jonathan Swift

      ┌─────────────────────┐
      │ **NOVEMBER EVENTS:** │
      └─────────────────────┘

• **Birth of Robt. L. Stevenson   [13]**

      Have children design their own Treasure Island maps, incor-
porating vocabulary words, e.g.: reef, cove, stockade, paces, grove,

westerly, marker, beneath, strides, doubloon, curse or Evil Eye. A story or journal may then be written to "explain" the map.

"Search for Treasure" reading game (2 teams): Distribute mimeos of sentences taken from the latest reading story; each sentence is missing a key word. Teams search for answers in their readers. First team to find all the answers "reaches the treasure."

Reading group Treasure Hunt, a culminating activity, e.g., a special reward for having mastered all of Dolch sight words & phonics, word-analysis skills. Schedule the hunt at the end of the day, the last 30-45 minutes on Friday. Eight participants, or less, work well. Advise them to come back to the room if they find they are having problems with any of the clues. Encourage them not to run as running causes accidents, & to keep their voices low because other children are still in class. Appoint one child to collect all the clue-papers & bring them back to the classroom wastebasket. (You will have taped clues in place during a recent coffee-break.)

Children wait outside classroom door initially. You tack up the map (brown paper bag wrinkled, dampened & ironed flat; then burnt around the edges) by piercing it through with a bloody-handled paring knife (red poster paint is applied to your hand before you grip knife's handle). When you are ready, call in the children. They find map & the hunt begins!

Sample clues (wording emphasizes phonics that have been studied by class): The 1st clue is taped to underside of the reading table: "This hunt is for fun, but still don't be loud & shout! No audible voices, please! To find Clue #2 go outside & look high up where Old Glory is raised."

Clue #2, taped to flag pole: "Clue #3 is at a place outlying from here, attached to a red & yellow fire-hydrant."

Clue #3, taped to the fire hydrant: "Look for a message tied to the handle of a broom at the top of the stairs. The broom is near a drain pipe."

Clue #4, tied to broom handle: "On the younger children's playground is a bench made of concrete. Look beneath it for your next clue."

Clue #5, taped to underside of bench: "The tether ball holds clue #6."

Clue #6, attached to tether ball chain or written on ball with felt pen: "Look on the ground for a number 3 and clue #7."

Clue #7, taped to number 3 which is permanently painted on playground black top: "Clue #8 is on a fountain. You must stoop to be able to see it, though!"

Clue #8, taped beneath water fountain: "Attached to a stick that is divided into 36 sections is your next clue. You're almost at the TREA-SURE!"

Clue #9, taped to yardstick which leans against nearby wall: "Go back to the classroom! Look in the book written by Webster. Look up 'oyster.' You're almost there!"

In an unconcealed dictionary at page on which "oyster" appears is this note: "Your treasure awaits you beneath a large table-like object. Look for the skull & cross bones . . . hee, hee, hee." (Signed with a skull & crossbones.)

You gauge, by watching their progress, when to bring ice cream bars from Faculty Room refrigerator & place them in "treasure chest" hidden beneath your desk. The chest is made from a large cardboard box & may be saved for future hunts.

Trunk is a corrugated cardboard box; lid is a piece of cardboard, curved & taped to inside back of box. The entire trunk is painted with a coat of tan opaque poster paint. When paint is dry, details (wood grain, metal hinges, lock) are added. A skull cut from white card stock is attached to lid. Stuff bottom of trunk with crushed butcher paper.

- **Birth of Robert Fulton   [14]**

Fulton did *not* invent the steamboat; he was, initially, a painter & the inventor of machines for making ropes & for sawing marble! The steamboat was largely the invention of John Fitch in 1785. When Fitch died in 1798, he was poverty-stricken. Fulton studied all of Fitch's plans & all of the patents relating to it. With financial backing, Robt. Fulton built the Clermont in 1807 & consequently grew rich & famous.

- **Assassination of President John F. Kennedy   [22]**

In World War II, Kennedy distinguished himself in the Navy, most notably when his torpedo boat was rammed by a Japanese destroyer. Rallying his crew on a few pieces of wreckage, Jack Kennedy got his men to safety & then towed a badly wounded sailor for 3 miles through shark-infested water with the man's life-belt strap in his teeth.

There had never been a Roman Catholic President of the United States before John F. Kennedy.

He worked hard for the Civil Rights Bill which would guarantee equal status for the American Negro. By doing this, he alienated the South, which usually voted Democratic, & partly to help alleviate this situation he set off on a tour of the Southern states. It was during this tour, & just after he had been in office 34 months, that on Nov. 22, 1963, in Dallas, Texas, the shots were fired that killed the youngest elected President our country has ever had.

Etymology. 800 years ago Christian Crusaders were ambushed & killed by members of a secret band of Moslems who had worked themselves into frenzies by smoking hashish. Such fanatics were called "hashish eaters" or "hashashin." This East Indian word entered medieval Latin as *assassinus,* becoming the English "assassin" & so retaining its murderous history in its meaning.

- **Thanksgiving**

"Harvest season is a time to be aware of the generosity and riches of nature and the effect of the productiveness of man. For thousands of years people in many lands, worshipping in different ways, have expressed joy and gratitude when their crops were harvested."* The Romans' Thanksgiving holiday was called "Cerelia"**& was dedicated to Ceres, goddess of harvest.

---

*From Days of Discovery, an A.F.S.C. publication.
**This is where we get our word "cereal."

The Pilgrims of Plymouth probably patterned their celebration after the Hebrew "Feast of Ingathering" described in the Bible (Exodus 23:16, Leviticus 23:33-44, Deuteronomy 16:13-15). The first Thanksgiving in America was proclaimed by Governor Bradford 3 years after the Pilgrims had settled at Plymouth. Here is a copy of that first Thanksgiving Proclamation.

To all ye Pilgrims:

Inasmuch as the great Father has given us this year an abundant harvest of Indian corn, wheat, peas, beans, squashes and garden vegetables and has made the forests to abound with game and the sea with fish and clams, and inasmuch as He has protected us from the ravages of the savages, has spared us from pestilence and disease, has granted us freedom to worship God according to the dictates of our conscience; now I, your magistrate, do proclaim that all ye Pilgrims, with ye wives and ye little ones, do gather at ye meeting, on ye hill, between the hours of 9 and 12 in the daytime on Thursday, November ye 29th of the year of our Lord one thousand six hundred and twenty-three, and the third year since ye Pilgrims landed on ye Pilgrim Rock, there to listen to ye pastor and render Thanksgiving to ye Almighty God for all His blessings.

(signed) Wm. Bradford, Ye Governor of Ye Colony

President George Washington proclaimed November 26, 1789, to be the first officially observed Thanksgiving in the U.S.A.

It wasn't until 1941 that Congress fixed a national date for Thanksgiving: the fourth Thursday of November.

Bulletin Board Suggestions

Try cutting out title letters from construction paper; texture these by gently tapping with a sponge lightly dipped in poster paint. Glue seed (pods) to letter shapes cut from tagboard. Or soak Indian corn, beans, fruit seeds, cloves in water; then when they can be easily perforated by needle (& before they begin to split), seeds are strung on heavy thread. Simply wind a long string of seeds around a straight pin outline of the first letters of the title of bulletin board display.

Where will your Thanksgiving dinner come from? Discuss typical menus. Explain the importance of including vegetables, fruits, grain, milk, meat on every menu. Talk about the sources of these foods (orchards, milk delivery, bakery, fields of pineapple, wheat, dairy farms, pumpkins from roadside stands, refrigerator R.R. cars & trucks, gelatine processing plants).

Illustrations may be made individually, or as a class mural, that emphasize how many people are involved in providing us with Sunday dinner. A short neatly written description can accompany each illustration. Arrows of red or orange may serve as connecting devices.

In a lower economic area—or in any school—the class might discuss "the story of the child (or family, town) that couldn't have a Thanksgiving turkey," talk about the meaning of the turkey as a symbol, the relative importance of the bird & of feasting. Stress the deeper meaning of the holiday.

Use "As Americans We Are Thankful For . . . " as a topic. Children each choose an appropriate subject & write about it, illustrating their papers with photographs, actual objects or cut-outs. Written papers are backed with a square of red or blue & pinned against an all-white background.

Classroom Co-op Turkey. This activity for young children will facilitate small muscle control. Before introducing project, cut strips of tan construction paper (1" x 4" long). Pin a large tan turkey body to the bulletin board. Each tail feather, backed in orange, is a different color: tan, purple, green, grey, brown, blue. Eye is 3 circles: tan, purple, & the smallest is white. Red wattles, yellow feet & beak complete basic bird. Children curl & attach paper strips to bird's body. Curling is done by wrapping strips around a pencil, or by pulling them across the blade of a pair of dull scissors. This curling might occupy the 15 minutes prior to dismissal. Once bird is finished, children suggest a message for their turkey to convey. Individual birds can be made.

Language Arts

Prominently display a "November Remember Words" chart as a vocabulary & spelling aide. Such a chart could include: cornucopia, banquet, forefathers, endure, arduous, bountiful, Puritans, Plymouth. Words can be added to the chart as they come up during class discussions.

Have the children write down the first word they think of after they hear you read each of these stimulus words: life, freedom, school, food, America, our world, church, home, God, thanks. Their papers will indicate spelling needs & the phonetic weaknesses of the class. A bulletin board entitled "What Thanksgiving Means to Me" could be developed from such lists.

The class can practice their penmanship while writing thank-you notes to people who have been especially thoughtful or helpful, e.g., the school's secretary, nurse or librarian.

Classroom Game. "Why-When-Where?" facilitates spelling & noun study. One child leaves the room & a secret word, related to Thanksgiving, is chosen by the class. The children spend a few minutes getting sample answers in mind & then the player returns & asks each child in turn: "Why was it used? When was it used? Where was it used?" Each student must give a different answer to each question. The game continues until questioner guesses the secret word. If he can then spell it correctly on the chalkboard, he is allowed to choose the next questioner. If, however, he misspells the word, the teacher, after writing the word correctly, chooses the next questioner; the child who had especially thoughtful answers may be rewarded in this way. (Secret word suggestions: musket, prayer, feather, Bible.)

Dramatic play will be facilitated by having the children familiarize themselves with the historical details, background information of the 1st Thanksgiving. Children collect props & make simple identifying head-gear. Wigs for both Pilgrim men & Indians are made from crepe paper.

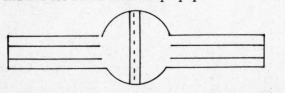

For Indian wigs, machine stitch a center reinforcing strip of tagboard. Children braid ends of crepe paper. Pilgrims wigs have bangs attached to cover forehead. Plays should incorporate historical facts & appropriate vocabulary.

Etymology. The word "pilgrim" is nearly 800 years old. As "pelegrim" & later in French as "pelerin," it dealt with traveling & wandering. The Latin *peregrinus* was a combination of *per* (through) & *ager* (field); a pilgrim was, originally, one who wandered through the fields on his way to the Holy Land. A banquet has come to mean a large feast, but in French it meant "the little bench" (on which you sat when you were seated for dinner). When the colonists arrived in America they sighted a large bird that reminded them of the guinea fowl of Turkey, so they named the strange new bird "Turkey-cock."

> *Riddles:* Exactly where did the Pilgrim Fathers stand when they landed on Plymouth Rock? (On their feet.) Who is never hungry on Thanksgiving? (The turkey: he's already stuffed.) What does everybody want on Thanksgiving, but they try to get rid of it as soon as they have it? (A good appetite.) What 3 letters spell the name of the first house built in America? (A T-P, the house of the Plains Indians.) Two Indians were standing on a bridge. One was the father of the other one's son. What relation were they? (Husband & wife.)

Thanksgiving Poetry

The classic "Over the River and Through the Woods" by Lydia Maria Child evokes the holidays of turn-of-the-century America.

> "So once in every year we throng
> Upon a day apart
> To praise the Lord with feast and song
> In thankfulness of heart."
>
> Arthur Guiterman

Thanksgiving Reading

The following was adapted from a choral reading suggestion published by the A.F.S.C. in their Fall Guideposts series. As a group, the class compiles 3 appropriate responses wherever asterisks appear. Then the reading is practiced by the group, as a body, & ultimately taped (with appropriate music).

Leader: Thanksgiving is a time to thank. It is also a time to think.
At this season of the year we think more than usual about our
many blessings. We remember the gifts that we don't often
notice just because they are all around us. They cost nothing.
They can be enjoyed by everyone. Such gifts are 3 very
precious ones: sound, color, & taste. They put gladness in our
hearts.

Girls: We are thankful for sounds we hear:*(e.g., birds singing in
the early morning.)

Boys: We are thankful for colors we see:*(e.g., orange pumpkins
against black earth.)

Everyone:*(response.)

Boys: We are thankful for colors we see:*(e.g., scarlet maple
trees.)

Repeat response.

Silence.

All: We are thankful for foods we taste:*(e.g., juicy grapes.)

Response.

All: We are thankful for foods we taste:*(e.g., spicy cookies.)

Response.

Silence.

Phonetic Drill

Farmer Jones' Turkey Ranch. Cut 8 or 10 medium-sized (6"
wide) turkey bodies from tan paper. Details & color are added
with crayon. A word-ending is printed on each turkey body.

Six or 8 bright colored paper feathers, with a blend printed on
each of them, are tucked behind turkey body to form a fan-like
tail. Turkeys are laid flat on the table & children in the reading
group try "to pluck all the turkeys on Farmer Jones' Ranch. Each
turkey (phonetic structure) is tackled in turn by each student; a

child may have more than 1 try at a turkey, if necessary. Children withdraw each tail feather as it & word-endings are successfully pronounced. In this way turkey is "plucked." When a child has plucked 8-9 turkeys, he gets the chance to try his hand with "the toughest Tom," a difficult, tricky phonetic structure, e.g., "_ough," Once the toughest Tom is conquered, child earns the title "King of the Turkey Pluckers"!

Thanksgiving History Activities

Compare on a classroom map the different routes taken to the New World: that taken by Columbus & that by the Pilgrims.

Discuss with the children: Which people, according to skills, trades, professions, would have been chosen to come on the Mayflower? (There were 102 passengers on the Mayflower.) What food, tools, objects would the Pilgrims have chosen to bring with them? How might people have occupied themselves on the trip? (The trip required over 2 months: 10 times longer than it takes today.) In what ways did the advantages outweigh the hardships the Pilgrims were forced to face in the New World?

A classroom chart entitled "Now and Then" can be compiled by class: Pass out mimeographed sheets that list modern inventions, equipment or have class as a group compile such a list. Each child then fills in the Early American equivalent of each modern aid or appliance. There are innumerable "correct answers": if child can give a logical reason for giving a response, it's correct; e.g., hair dryer: wind & sun; clock radio: hour-glass, rooster or song bird singing at dawn; tape-recorder: handing down stories father to son. . . . A large class chart could then be made, displayed & added to throughout the year.

Thanksgiving Math Enrichment

Here are 2 recipes for classroom cooking experiences:

Young children can make Cranberry-Orange Relish (20 jars):

8 large cans whole cranberry sauce	4 pkgs. orange gelatin
8 fresh seedless oranges	2 cups hot water
(plastic wrap, ribbon)	20 small clean jars

Peel oranges & remove all the pith you can. Cut oranges into little pieces.

Add hot water to gelatin & stir until dissolved; add cranberry sauce to gelatin.

Add oranges to gelatin mixture. Ladle into jars. Cover jar

openings with pieces of plastic wrap. Refrigerate until children take relish home.

Tie ribbon around each jar top securing plastic wrap in place.

Secure a note (via a gummed sticker) to each jar stating how well this relish goes with turkey.

Older students may enjoy contributing a pint of homemade mincemeat to their holiday dinners. Here is a recipe (with modern equivalents) used by my Great Grandma Alden:

Simmer 2 lbs. beef neck (or chuck) covered, in water to cover, until tender (about 3 hours). Cool. (This step might be taken the evening before; the prepared meat could be brought to school and the children could continue from here on.) Put meat through a food chopper, using the coarse blade. Mix 1/2 lb. ground suet with ground meat. Put these into a large kettle & add 3 lbs. (or more) red tart apples which have been pared & diced. Add the following:

1½ c. sugar	1 pint pineapple-apricot jam
1 pkg. currants	1 pint plum jelly
1 pkg. white raisins	2½ tsp. salt
1 pkg. dark raisins	3 tsp. cinnamon
1 pint strawberry preserves	2 tsp. allspice
1 #2½ can apricots (& their juice)	1 tsp. cloves
1 #303 can pineapple tidbits & juice	
1 #2½ can pickled peaches; remove seeds, dice (& add juice).	
1 #303 can red tart cherries: drain & discard juice.	

Cover & simmer for 1 hour. When cool, mincemeat may be put into pint containers & frozen or into glass jars & sealed while it is still hot. *(Thank you, Mother.)*

Thanksgiving Art

Many children have never seen a live turkey. These children cannot be expected to draw or paint a personal impression of the bird; their work will, at best, be an interpretation of a photograph or drawing they've seen at some time. If a live turkey cannot be brought to class ("borrowed" from a poultry farm for an afternoon), perhaps a film featuring turkeys could be shown.

Turkey drawings. Ask the children how an emotion makes itself visually evident through posture, gestures, etc. Then have the children depict a turkey in an appropriate setting & have the bird express an emotion: fear, happiness, surprise, suspicion.

Collage turkeys. Have the class collect & sort magazine pictures into different colors, tonal groups: this helps children learn to recognize shades, tones. Feathers, neck, wattle, legs & feet are torn from appropriate shades of illustrations, regardless of subject matter. Background details are kept simple. Collage is glued to a piece of tan or light yellow paper. This type of lesson helps loosen up those children who always seem to need the security of using a ruler.

Giant Pilgrims & Indians. Have on display many reference illustrations showing differing dress, tools, footwear of colonists & Indians. This lesson necessitates use of newsprint, large sheets of colored paper, tape, glue, scissors & plenty of floor space. Children initially draw & color (on small sheets of newsprint) their interpretation of an Indian or Pilgrim man or woman. Next discuss briefly the sections of the body (head, neck, torso, legs & feet) & how the children should try to use as much of each sheet of paper as they can. (E.g., 1st a very big torso is cut out; then 2 legs to fit this torso; then feet to fit the legs, etc.) No pencils or crayons are used, if possible. Children try to cut shapes directly from the pieces of paper & refer back to their drawings as they cut out the sections of their figures. Rather than "dressing" the figures, clothes are cut out directly from colored paper & glued together (taped on underside). Once general form of figure is achieved, the addition of details, e.g., buckles, feathers, aprons, muskets, etc. (also cut from paper) should be encouraged. Finished Pilgrim & Indian figures may be from 40"-55" in height. Figures can be stored flat on top of a cupboard if more than one art period is required to finish this project. Staple the finished figures above the chalkboard; overlap their arms so that the Indians & Pilgrims will appear to be holding hands. Then they will look down on your class, watching over your November activities.

Quick paper-bag puppets. Draw facial features (of Pilgrim) rather high up on sack, using felt-tip pens. Fill sack with crushed newspapers. Insert a sturdy stick (dowel or ruler) into mouth of sack. Secure the sack to stick with rubber band &/or masking tape. Stovepipe hat or collar, made of construction paper, can be taped or stapled to bag. Children manipulate puppet with stick. Show puppets in a doorway, across the lower half of which a blanket is suspended, or turn a table on its side with its surface toward the audience; puppets pop up from behind the table top.

Thanksgiving P.E.

"Pilgrim Father" requires no equipment & emphasizes running, tagging. "It" (the Pilgrim Father) says to the Pilgrims standing on the goal line, "Come with me to hunt turkey." All the children fall in line behind him & march around in any direction he chooses. When he has led the pilgrims all away from the goal line he calls "BANG!" The children run back to the goal line; the Pilgrim Father catches as many as he can. These players become "turkeys" & are put in "a cage" & the game continues. Each Pilgrim Father has 3 turns & then he picks a successor from among the remaining Pilgrims. Turkeys leave cage & join game again; play continues.

Information sources:

Boys' Clubs of America
381 — 4th Ave., New York,
N.Y. 10003
"Crafts from Mayflower Times"
(35¢)

John Hancock Mutual Life
Insurance Co.

"Story of the Pilgrims"
(free)

Thanksgiving Culmination

Discuss a class gift project with your principal before introducing it to the class. Suggested outlets for classmade gifts include: hospitals & schools for children with special needs,* settlement houses, homes for the aged (all listed in the classified section of the phone book), or contact the local chapter of the Cerebral Palsy Assoc. or Council of Social Agencies; a staff worker can tell you of any special needs to be filled, e.g., the names, birthdates of children who would appreciate mail.

Discuss with your class: "Ways we can share with others who may not be as lucky as we are."

Two class gift projects. Have the children collect brightly colored, perfectly shaped autumn leaves. Press these between sheets of newspaper topped by heavy books. When the leaves are dry, spread them on newspaper & shellac them. Allow leaves to dry; then shellac reverse sides. A shut-in or hospital patient will be cheered by the sight of a bright autumnal leaf lying on his tray or pinned to the curtain. A.F.S.C.

---

*Write Mr. Kenn Kroska, Director, Volunteer Services, Faribault State Hosp., Faribault, Minn. 55021 to learn how your class may lend a helping hand.

Autumn bouquets. Using a bulletin board display of dried plants as a guide (& as a warning against poisonous plants), children collect wheat, Chinese lantern, bittersweet, cockscomb, milkweed, money plant & other appropriate weeds. Hang these plants upside down & allow to dry. Artistically grouped, these plants become decorative pieces & make kind, lasting gifts to shut-ins.

Bittersweet. A North American ornamental vine (*Celastrus scandens*); its small green flowers develop into yellowish tan capsules that burst, when ripe, to reveal brilliant orange seed coverings (the antils). Sometimes it is called "false bittersweet." Container suggestions: A small jar is dipped in Spackle, twirled, removed & allowed to dry (at which time it may be painted if you wish).

Using a funnel, children pour plaster of Paris into an attractively shaped soft drink bottle. Weeds are inserted into soft plaster. When plaster is hardened (& weeds secure), the bottle is placed in a heavy paper bag & held tightly at the neck. The bottle is smashed, leaving broken glass inside bag; the remaining plaster impression becomes "the vase."

• **Birth of Jonathan Swift [30]**

Ask children to choose one of the following to write about: "The adventures of Vegetable Man, " of " ... a Flying Ghoul," " ... an Imp Caught in a Bottle," " ... a Spider Man," " ... a Snake Woman," or of " ... a Creature That Invades One's Sleep." Illustrations of these stories may be confined to 1 color, e.g., Veg.

Man: orange; Spider Man: brown, etc. If students are older, discuss with them the nature of satire, the lampoon.

NOVEMBER ACTIVITIES

Parent-Teacher Conferences are often scheduled during November. If the sample form given here is mimeographed & a separate sheet is dedicated to each student, you should find this a real aid to organization & a valuable post-conference guide.

Parent-Teacher Conference

Name: Date:

Teacher's Opinion   Parent's Opinion

Strengths:

Needs:

Follow-up

November Poetry:

> ... No warmth, no cheerfulness, no healthful ease,
> No comfortable feel in any member—
> No shade, no shine, no butterflies, no bees,
> No fruits, no flowers, no leaves, no birds,
>   November!
>   Thomas Hood (19th c.)

Science

"The Study of Crystals" (a mimeo-sheet suggestion). "Do you know how grains of sand, salt, sugar, & a snowflake are all alike? (No, this isn't a riddle, but just a way of introducing you to the subject of crystals, for that is what sand, salt, sugar & snowflakes have in common: Each is a crystal.)

Crystals have flat faces & regular (geometric) shapes. This is because their atoms are arranged in an orderly & repeated pattern.

Each snowflake is actually made of many tiny crystals of ice. Snowflakes are always 6-sided & yet no 2 snowflakes are ever exactly alike!

Grains of sand are crystals of quartz, but the wind & water have battered them so long that their edges have been worn smooth.

Let's plant a Crystal Garden & then you can watch some crystals "grow" right before your eyes! You'll need small pieces of brick (the size of walnuts), small pieces of briquette, a fairly deep glass bowl (plastic cottage cheese containers work well)*, & 3 T. bluing, 3 T. water, 3 T. *uni*odized salt, 1 tsp. ammonia, tiny twigs (toothpicks), & food coloring.

A few PRECAUTIONS : Ammonia is poison-ous if swallowed (so wash your hands after using it). Ammonia also has a strong smell (it's a good idea to do your gardening in a room with the window open). Bluing can stain clothing, so push up your sleeves. And now on to the planting!

Place the brick & coal pieces in bowl. Prop the twigs, toothpicks between the brick & briquette. Add a little water to the bowl. Combine salt, bluing, ammonia, water in a cup. Mix well. *Slowly* pour this mixture over the broken coal & brick. To give color to your garden, sprinkle a few drops of food coloring over the mixture in the bowl. Place your garden in a warm place where it will not be disturbed.

In a short time tiny crystals will begin growing & in a few hours your crystal garden will have odd & interesting shapes. To keep your garden growing, just add 1 T. of ammonia to it once a week.

More fun with crystals (crystal candy). Each child will need a drinking glass, a pencil or ice cream stick, a piece of clean string 6" long, 1/2 cup of water, a paper clip & granulated sugar. Tie the string to the middle of pencil or stick. Tie the paper clip to the other end of the string. Put water in a pan & boil (on classroom hot plate). Add sugar, teaspoon by teaspoonful, until no more will dissolve in the water. Pour this liquid into each glass. Place the pencil across mouth of glass, with paper clip on bottom of glass. The glasses are then set in a warm spot where they won't be disturbed.

---

*Do not use aluminum containers, e.g., TV trays, frozen pie pans. The solution reacts with aluminum & causes tiny holes to develop in container.

In 1 or 2 days crystals begin to form along the string. After a week or 2 each child will have a large crystal candy suspended in his glass.

A very interesting Science publication:

Nature and Science $1.15 per child per semester or
$1.95 per school year (16 issues)
Natural History Press
American Museum of Natural History
Central Park West at 79th St.
New York, N.Y. 10024.

Art

Classroom frescoes. A mixture of sand, thick white tempera & a small amount of flour is applied to pieces of cardboard. Don't apply mixture too thickly. When dry, the cardboard is painted with tempera (water color), achieving a fresco-like effect.

Punched metal plaques. Display pictures of work by early tinsmiths, & point out how their designs served a purpose (radiation of light, air or heat) as well as beautified the object. Have the children collect a variety of lightweight aluminum containers. T.V. dinner trays, various sizes of frozen pie pans. With the aid of pencil, compass & ruler, a design is drawn onto the metal's surface. Then using hammer, different sizes of nails, a small chisel & adequate newspaper padding, the children perforate the aluminum along the pencil lines or in a designated area. Display the punched metal plaques in such a way that light is allowed to come through the holes (against a window) or against a dark-colored bulletin board.

November P.E.

Some suggestions for the organization of Relay Races: Relays are usually not introduced before the second grade. Never use relays before the skills involved have been practiced or learned. Initially, the children might want to walk through the procedure once before the race begins. Since the purpose of relays is the practice of skills & improvement of teamwork, competition is not overemphasized. Teams are of equal numbers of players. If necessary, the teacher can play, or 1 child could run twice, or extra children might be rotated into the teams. The starting line is specifically marked. Infractions are penalized by the subtraction of a point from that team's score or by sending the player back to the starting line (an infraction never disqualifies an entire team). Every team may receive points: 5 for 1st team, 4 for 2nd team, etc. The winning team is declared, in a classroom situation, when the whole team is seated, the last person over the line having also seated himself. (See June for additional relay races.)

Cranberry relay race. Divide children into 3-4 equal teams which line up at 1 side of the room. At the opposite side of the room are 3-4 empty bowls. The 1st child in each team has a sack containing 4 cranberries. He places these berries on the back of his hand & when the teacher calls "Go," he gives sack to 2nd player, runs to bowl, drops in berries, & runs back, tagging 2nd player. If any berries roll off a player's hand, they must be replaced BEFORE he may continue on his way to the bowl. The 2nd player gives sack to 3rd player, runs to bowl, puts berries on back of his hand & returns to the team putting berries into sack. This procedure is repeated until 1 team finishes first.

November Puppet

These are teacher-made finger puppets that can be re-used each year; they are introduced to enliven a drill period or as an aid to Language Arts work. The face, body, feathers are of colorful felt scraps. Hand-stitch the body down back. Glue ends of feathers about head shape. Glue black bias tape to encircle head shape; this adds rigidity & forms hair of puppet. Feather tips are also glued down to cover back of head. Facial features are glued to face.

December

Chill December brings the sleet,
Blazing fire and Christmas treat.

1 1st atomic nuclear reaction demonstrated 1942, Chicago.

4 Kandinsky (1866-1944), Russian painter: one of the origi-
nators of non-objective painting.

5 Martin Van Buren (1782-1862), 8th President.

6 St. Nicholas Day celebrated in Europe.

8 Eli Whitney (1765-1825), American inventor of the cotton
gin.

10 John Smith began trip on which his life was saved by
Pocahontas, 1607.
Emily Dickinson (1830-1886), American poet.
1st state, Wyoming, grants women the right to vote, 1869.
Human Rights Day.

11 Hector Berlioz (1803-1869), French composer.

12 Marconi sent 1st radio signal across Atlantic from Newfdld.
to England, 1901.

13 Sir Francis Drake started voyage around the world, 1577.

14 South Pole discovered, 1911.

15 Bill of Rights Day: 1st Amendments to Constitution rati-
fied, 1791.

16 Boston Tea Party, 1773.
Ludwig von Beethoven (1770-1827), German composer.
1st rendezvous in space (U.S. Gemini VI & VII), 1965.

17 John Greenleaf Whittier (1807-1892), American poet.
Wright Bros. Day: 1st successful aeroplane flight at Kitty
Hawk, N.C., 1903.

18   1st colonial Thanksgiving celebrated, 1777.
      Slavery abolished, 1865.
20   U.S. took possession of La. Territory, 1803.
21   Forefathers' Day: landing of Pilgrims at Plymouth Rock,
         1620.
      Winter begins.
      Giacomo Puccini (1858-1924), Italian operatic composer.
24   Kit Carson (1809-1868), American frontiersman.
      Matthew Arnold (1822-1888), English poet.
25   Isaac Newton (1642-1727), English mathematician, 1st per-
         son to identify the "law of gravity."
      Washington crossed the Delaware, 1776.
      Clara Barton (1821-1912), founder of American Red Cross.
      CHRISTMAS DAY.
27   Louis Pasteur (1822-1895), French chemist, developer of
         the Pasteurization process.
28   Woodrow Wilson (1856-1924), 28th President.
29   Andrew Johnson (1808-1875), 17th President.
      Charles Goodyear (1800-1860), American inventor of vul-
         canization process.
30   Rudyard Kipling (1865-1936), English author: *The Jungle
         Book.*
31   Henri Matisse (1869-1954), French painter.
      Hanukkah (Feast of lights) may occur in December or
         November: 8 days. This holy day has been observed for
         2000 years by Jews in many lands. (See page 75.)

December

This was the tenth month in the calendar of ancient Rome; in Latin
decem is ten.

DECEMBER QUOTATIONS

5   The second sober thought of the people is seldom wrong
         and always efficient.—Martin Van Buren
10   There is no frigate like a book
      To take us lands away,
      Nor any courser like a page
      Of prancing poetry.
      ("There Is No Frigate Like a Book")—Emily Dickinson

17   "Shoot, if you must, this old grey head,
      But spare your country's flag," she said.
         ("Barbara Frietchie": line 35)—John G. Whittier

      Success four flights Thursday morning all against 21-mile
         wind started from level with engine power alone average
         speed through air 31-miles longest 59 seconds inform
         press home Christmas. (Telegram to their father, Kitty
         Hawk, N.C., Dec. 17, 1903)—Orville Wright, Wilbur
         Wright

24   Where the great whales come sailing by,
      Sail and sail, with unshut eye.
         ("The Forsaken Merman")—Matthew Arnold

25   And the angel said unto them, "Fear not for, behold, I bring
         you good tidings of great joy which shall be to all people.
         For unto you is born this day in the city of David a
         Saviour, which is Christ the Lord." (Luke 2, v. 10-11)

      People say Christmas Day is too commercial. But I have
         never found it that way. If you spend money to give
         people joy, you aren't being commercial. It is only when
         you feel obliged to do something about Christmas that
         the spirit is spoiled.—Eleanor Roosevelt

28   The world must be made safe for democracy. (Address to
         Congress: Feb. 2, 1917)

      Liberty has never come from the government. . . . The
         history of liberty is the history of the limitations of
         governmental power, not the increase of it.
                                                    —Woodrow Wilson

A General Word about December Events

      Think through your ideas in response to the following
questions:

      Can you state concisely what Christmas means to you? What
      does it mean in our culture today?

      What aspects of Christmas can be meaningful to your students
      who are non-Christians?

      How much of this can be part of your December teaching
      plans? During this season outside activities accelerate & multiply.
      How can you use the activities presented here to lessen or to

channel pre-Christmas excitement in young children? And which might be used to prevent older students from wasting December in a mounting spiral of over-activity?

DECEMBER EVENTS:

• Birth of Eli Whitney [8]

It is said that while struggling to find an easier way than manually removing the seeds from cotton bolls, Eli Whitney happened to glance out the window & see a fox trying to snatch a hen from its coop. The fox clawed at the chicken wire pen & although he didn't get the chicken, he got plenty of feathers! This chance encounter gave Whitney the idea for the basis of his cotton gin—a metal claw that would pull cotton fibers through a strong wire mesh, leaving the seeds behind.

• Bill of Rights Day [15]

Receive a free chart showing the Bill of Rights by writing to:

Standard Oil Co. of California
225 Bush St.
San Francisco, Calif. 94120

A free illustrated booklet is available from:

Boys Life
New Brunswick, N.J. 08903

• Birth of Beethoven [16]

Beethoven was a lonely child who spent hours each day practicing the piano. He wrote great music for the piano, the violin & the entire orchestra. However, at an early age his hearing began to fail. By the time he was 34, he could no longer hear. Yet Beethoven lived to write his most wonderful symphonies AFTER he was deaf!

As December often needs a soothing classroom atmosphere, from time to time try playing excerpts from Beethoven's work (e.g., Moonlight Sonata). Children may draw while the music is playing, or simply listen for "pictures."

• Wright Brothers' Day [17]

Read to the class from John Dos Passos' "Big Money" (published in 1936), an excellent short description of what led up to that famous flight.

Free packets of aviation materials:

Smithsonian Institution Press
Wash. D.C. 20560

United Air Lines   Air Transport Assoc. of America
P.O. Box 66141   1000 Conn. Ave., N.W.
O'Hare International Airport   Washington, D.C. 20036
Chicago, Ill. 60666

- **Winter begins   [21] or [22]**

This is the day of winter solstice when the sun is farthest
from the equator & its apparent northward motion along the
horizon ends. In Latin *sol*=sun & *sisto*=to stand still.

Discuss non-deciduous trees; make a collection of cone &
needle samples: from these the children can learn to identify
the 7 most common genera (Arborvitae, Pine, Yew, Hemlock, Fir, Spruce, Juniper). Emphasize the difference between
the shapes of the trees. Use pictures from a seed or nursery catalog
(see Jan. Science) to illustrate a mix-match quiz or a bulletin
board display. Remind the children that the shape of the needles
begins with the same letter as the name of the tree: the fir (&
balsam) has flat needles; the spruce has square needles.

Talk about "cold" & its relativity. Discuss how snow, sleet,
hail & rain are each formed.

Review the subject of crystals (see Nov.). Discussing how
coarse salt is used during winter to melt the ice on northern roads
can lead up to this simple set of experiments: Dissolve salt in hot
water. Allow water to evaporate, revealing salt crystals. Repeat
procedure, using sugar. Compare the 2 crystal formations under a
microscope. Repeat procedure using borax. Next look at a piece of
sandpaper (which is usually covered with quartz crystals) under a
microscope. For further crystal investigation, obtain samples of
alum, sulphur, & camphor crystals from a druggist. Let the
children see if they can eventually identify the crystals by their
formations.

"If winter comes, can Spring be far behind?"
P.B. Shelly: 18 c. English poet.

- **Birth of Clara Barton   [25]**

Clara was so shy as a child that her parents became worried
that she would never be able to successfully relate to the outside
world. They consulted a phrenologist who, after feeling Clara's

head, assured the Bartons that the shape of Clara's skull meant that she would spend her life working for others. A lucky guess? Perhaps. Clara Barton grew up to teach school, tend the wounded of the Civil War & finally to persuade our government to sign the Red Cross Convention, organizing the American Red Cross—which is dedicated to helping humanity.

• Hanukkah

Hanukkah is a movable feast. Here is a cooky recipe that you might use as a math enrichment activity.

Hanukkah Cookies

Cream butter & sugar in a big bowl. In a second bowl beat egg & add milk & vanilla. Now combine these 2 mixtures in the big bowl. Sift together flour, salt, baking powder. Add these to the mixture in the big bowl. Refrigerate dough for 1 hour. Dust rolling pin & board with flour. Roll out dough to 1/4" thick. Cut into fancy shapes using cardboard patterns like those shown here. Place cookies on an oiled cooky sheet & bake for 12 min. in a 350° oven. (A.F.S.C.)

• Christmas   [25]

There have always been midwinter celebrations following winter solstice, when the days begin to lengthen & grow lighter. In ancient Egypt this time of year was celebrated with a Feast of Light; in Scandinavia they call it "The end of the Frost King's rule."

The American celebration of Christmas, as centered around the tree, its lights & presents, is a comparatively recent tradition. It arrived in our country via England, from Germany, after 1840. Until then Christmas in America was strictly a religious holiday.

Germany is generally credited as being the country of the Christmas tree's origin. Some feel St. Winifred created the first tree; others say Martin Luther, one Christmas Eve, envisioned a candle-lit tree as he gazed at the starry heavens. The 1st authenticated mention of decorated trees occurs in an Alsatian manuscript (1604). It is also recorded that the German soldiers in the British army decorated evergreens to celebrate Christmas in 1776 at Trenton, N.J. But it wasn't until 1841 that decorated trees became popular here & abroad. In that year Queen Victoria had a tree decorated for her children at Windsor Castle, at the suggestion of Albert, her German Prince Consort.

In pagan times bonfires were built to keep the waning sun alive during winter solstice. Christmas tree lights, fires & candles may be descendants of those primitive blazes.

In the 12th century, St. Francis of Assisi, Italy, wanted to make the Christmas story come alive for the people of his church. So he constructed the 1st creche scene. It was a doll in a simple manger set upon the grass near the church; live farm animals grazed by it. St. Francis also popularized carol-singing as he relied on the use of carols in the services held around the creche.

The word "holly" comes not from "holy," but from "holm oak," the leaves of which holly resembles. The Christmas wreath commemorates Christ's crown of thorns. Pre-Christian legends held that witches despised holly & that they would stay away from any house where it was hung (as a wreath on the door).

A pre-Christian custom dictated that Roman enemies were to reconcile with one another if ever they met under mistletoe!

Why do we have turkey at this time of year? Because James I hated boar's head. His taste for turkey at Yuletide became popularized when he became, in 1603, the King of England.

Legend says that one Christmas another English king found himself snowbound. His cook had no idea of what to prepare for a holiday meal. Then he had an inspiration; he collected all the supplies in the camp: stag meat & dried apples & plums. He threw in some flour, eggs & sugar & salt & wet these down with brandy & ale. Finally he took the resulting lump of dough, tied it in a cloth & boiled it. The outcome? The very 1st Christmas Plum Pudding!

Christmas Bulletin Boards

Lettering suggestions. Cut letters from holiday materials, e.g., gift-wrap, felt, ribbon.

Recipe for Fireproof Non-melting Snow: beat 2 cups deter-

gent & 1/2 cup water, adding more soap or water until snow
stands in peaks. Apply snow to cardboard letters or to fir
branches, which may then be used as a bulletin board border.

Theme ideas. Cover a bulletin board with white butcher
paper. Wind fluffy green nylon yarn around pins forming a large
geometric outline of a Christmas tree. Below each branch, in felt
tip pen print "Merry Christmas" in different languages. Include
greetings from those countries which reflect the heritages of your
students: Froeliche Weihnachten (Austria & Germany); Joyeux
Noel (France, Switzerland & Belgium); Stretan Bozic (Yugoslavia);
Buon Natale (Italy & Switzerland); Boldog Karacsony Unnep
(Hungary); Glaedelig Jul (Norway & Denmark); Felices Navidades
(Spain, Mexico); God Jul (Sweden); Wesolych Swiat (Poland);
Kung ho shen tan (Chinese); Merry Christenmass (Scotland);
Vrolyk Kerstmis (Holland); Um Feiz Natal (Portugal); S Rozh-
destvom Christovom (Russia); Kala Hrystoughena (Greece); Glae-
delig Jul (Norway); Nodlaig Mhaith Dhuit (Ireland).

Older students may enjoy studying lay-outs of the cities of
Bethlehem or Jerusalem & topographical photographs of Israel.
Resultant discussion topics might include how cities grow &
change, & how nature imposes itself on the growth of cities.

Angel-inspired bulletin boards. Have the children collect &

bring to class any angel pictures they can find. Supplement these, if at all possible, with reproductions of Giotto's crying angels, Byzantine & Romanesque angels, &/or those of Signorelli, Memling, Fra Angelico. (The Christmas card catalog which can be purchased for 25¢ from the Metropolitan Museum of Art, New York, N.Y., is illustrated with small good pictures, many of which are of angels.) These may all be combined in a large class-made collage; pieces of colored foil can be used to highlight eyes, wings, halos.

After acquainting themselves with various illustrations of angels, the children are prepared to make their own artistic interpretations. Have them bring different types of musical instruments to class. Display pictures of instruments. Then let your class color & cut out pictures of angels playing different musical instruments. What easier way to learn the mechanics of drawing a flute, violin or trumpet? An angelic orchestra can then be assembled to herald the coming of the Yuletide.

A decorative bulletin board, a pyramid of angels: Each child receives a piece of white paper (6"x 8") & is asked to cut out an angel, using as much of the paper as possible. The finished cut-out is turned over to hide any pencil outlines that may have been made. Assemble these, with wings almost touching, in the following manner: base of pyramid is 6 equally tall angels pinned one next to the other. 5 angels are pinned above base, each cut-out supported by the wings of the 2 beneath it. Continue building pyramid, always using angels of equal height for each tier, arriving finally at the zenith with a gold star atop the shortest angel.

Just for fun & in a hard-to-fill area, display the following Mystery Xmas Trees: children lift up large printed tagboard labels in order to find answers. "The Oldest Xmas Tree" (a fossilized fern imprinted in clay); "The Newest Xmas Tree" (tree shape cut from Mylar or other newly developed substance); "The Youngest Xmas Tree" (a pine nut taped to tagboard).

Room Environment

Walls. A time-line based on Christmas carols, e.g., early 1500; "God Rest Ye Merry Gentlemen"; 1692, "O Come All Ye Faithful"; 1703, "While Shepherds Watched Their Flocks by Night"; 1709, "Joy to the World"; 1739, "Hark the Herald Angels Sing"; 1751, "Adestes Fideles"; 1833, "The First Noel"; 1849, "It Came Upon a Midnight Clear"; 1867, "O Little Town of Bethlehem." (Also see "Xmas Music" for additional carols). Let children choose the carols THEY want to include; this may lead to vocabulary & spelling word enrichment Bring time-line up to date by including "Frosty" & "Rudolph" if children wish.

"The 12 Days of Christmas" mural. Divide class into groups. Staple a long sheet of butcher paper to cover one entire wall. Divide this paper into 13 equal parts, if title is to be in 1st space. (Title can be placed above mural, if you prefer.) Before beginning to draw, the class briefly discusses each of the 12 subjects: "What is a colly bird?* And a turtle dove?** How do the leaves of a pear tree look? How does a drummer keep his drum in place? What is a partridge, & a lord? And a French hen? How DOES a piper pipe?" (Later, you might explain how each came to be included in the song.) Children who enjoy being graphic technicians should be given the 1st, 2nd & 4th areas Section 5 requires only 1 or 2 students while areas 8-12 require most of class. Have each group draw up their ideas on scratch paper. This plan may then be drawn on the butcher paper in LIGHT pencil. Children select colored papers from numerous piles of construction paper, including dull metallic gold & silver wrapping paper. These papers are cut out & glued in place on the butcher paper. Discuss with the group handling of the title: effective use of color; how title should tie up with, & NOT distract *from,* mural; different lettering possibilities. Those whose areas are 1st completed may begin careful cutting & pasting of lords or ladies.

Windows. Stained glass window effect can be obtained in several ways:

1. Draw a design on tracing paper; divide large areas into sections (mosaic-like effect). Lay newspapers beneath windows to catch any drips. Tape tracing paper to outside of clean windows. For each color required, pour 6 T. clear mucilage into a small container & add 2 T. food coloring. Test on window for intensity of color. Children paint all areas calling for one color before mixing (or using) a 2nd. A 1/3" strip is left between all areas to prevent running & to simulate leading of stained glass. A damp Q-Tip will help correct mistakes.

2. Cut shapes from lightweight colored tissue paper. Cut a

---

*The word "colly" used in England means "soot"; collybird is a blackbird.

**A slender European dove having a white-edged tail; some sources say that the 5 golden rings = 5 golden ring-necked pheasants.

piece of plastic film slightly larger than completed design will be. Heavy duty kitchen wrap may be used, or 12 gauge vinyl, $1.50 a yard at awning, auto seat-cover shops. A 9 x 12 plastic drop cloth is most economical, but is rather opaque & must be cellophane-taped to window. Brush shellac on plastic; smooth on 1st shape. Apply shellac between each successive tissue shape & on top. Allow to dry. Trim plastic around finished design. *Clean* window. Smooth on finished design. It will remain in place. If corners should at some time begin to peel away, remove design, wash it & window with water & then re-press design to glass.

3. Buy some clear plastic storm window covering; it is sold in 36" & 42" widths & easily cut with scissors. Felt-point pens work beautifully on it. (Vivid hues are obtained by squirting ink from felt point refill-can directly onto plastic.) Crayons give a rough texture; water colors mixed with Knox Gelatin give tints, pastels. To remove ink from an area, dip Q-Tip in shellac thinner & gently rub plastic. Finished compositions are adhered to classroom windows with double stick cellophane tape. You might mat small compositions & stand them along a window ledge.

Door. A cheerful Santa can greet visitors to your class. Tagboard or light tan (pink) construction paper is used for face. Score along & beneath eyebrows. Cut out eyeholes & make a slit along either side of nose. Pink cheeks are gently curved outward & then glued in place. Beard & hair are curled by gently pulling each paper strip along blade of scissors. Shaggy eyebrows, hair, & beard are glued to face. Eyes are glued behind holes. Red mouth is glued on the beard & a bushy mustache completes face. Bright pink,

orange or red paper is used for Santa's hat. White trim completes your paper sculpture. (Another paper Santa idea appears in "Let's

Have Fun," a free booklet copyrighted in 1966 by The Borden Co.)

Language Arts

Note: Check with your principal before presenting the following creative writing lesson as it could be considered too religious by some standards.

Have the children write stories based on the following:

"Each of the Animals Brought the Baby Jesus a Gift on His Birthday" (i.e., "Friendly Beasts"). Choose any animal, bird, fish, reptile, & tell about his gift & the travels he made to deliver it to the stable on Christmas Eve. VARIATION: Each child chooses & writes his impressions of an object that was present on the 1st Xmas, e.g., the star, the road, the straw, the inn, the barn, the night, a camel's saddle, frankincense, myrrh, gold, a piece of clothing worn by a Wise Man.

"Why We Use (or Have)_____at Christmas." Each child chooses an object & invents an imaginary historical background, developing this into a creative writing story. A list such as the following (in mimeo form, or written on the front board, may facilitate getting started): angel-hair, bells, holly, candles, wreaths, candy canes, fruit cake. Later you might briefly describe to the class actual historical data, comparing it with the stories they have written; an interesting tape-recording could be developed from the combined materials.

One day, as a change-of-pace activity, bring in a huge gift-wrapped cardboard box. Have young children suggest by pantomime (older students might write a descriptive paragraph) just what they think is in the box. (Contents? Tiny candy-canes for the class.)

Very young children may write about, or dictate to you, a story based on "The Time I Rode in Santa's Sleigh!"

An unusual spelling lesson can develop from asking the children to make up individual gift lists. These are handed in, & while you are correcting any misspelled words you can also be noting the specific phonetic review needed by each student. Any misspelled words become personal (extra credit) Spelling Words for the week.

The most frequently misspelled Holiday words: wreath, sleigh, icicles, poinsettia, reindeer, mistletoe, Bethlehem, creche, nativity, myrrh, frankincense, Jerusalem.

Etymology. "Angel" is from the Greek *angellos,* a messenger or herald.

"Carol" stems from the Greek *choraules* (*choros* dance & *aulos* flute), which meant a flute player who accompanied the Greek choral dances.

"Christmas" is the celebration *maesse,* the Anglo-Saxon word for rite or celebration of Christ's birth.

"Creche" is a French word meaning crib.

"Noel" is also French, coming from the Latin *natalis* which means birthday.

"Poinsettia": This bright Christmas flower (which is actually tiny yellow flowers surrounded by brilliant red leaves) is a native of Mexico. It is named for Joel Poinsett who, when he was a special minister to Mexico, found it & brought it back to America.

"Xmas": the Greek letter *X* or *Chi* stands for "Christ" & so "Xmas" is an abbreviated spelling of "Christmas."

Yule is *Jol,* the Norse word for the Xmas feast, originally a pagan festival held at winter solstice. "Yule" was also influenced by the Latin *jocus* which means "a time of happy talking"!

Riddles: What Xmas tree keeps you warm? (A fir tree.) What do we have in December that we have in no other month? (The letter *D.*) Which one of your toes can you never stub? (Your mistleTOE.) What do you fill every morning & empty every night except once a year, when it is filled at night & emptied in the morning? (A stocking.) What are some girls' names that you'll always find in a Xmas song book? (Carol, Merry, Angel, Holly, Joy, Noel, Chris, Bell[e], Beth [lehem].) What parts of the North Pole are in the United States? (The *N, T,* & *E.*) When does the postman bring you 29 letters in ONE envelope? (When he brings you a M-E-R-R-Y C-H-R-I-S-T-M-A-S A-N-D H-A-P-P-Y N-E-W Y-E-A-R card!)

Christmas Poetry

> Let's dance and sing and make good cheer,
> For Christmas comes but once a year.
>
> G. McFarren (prior to 1580)
>
> I heard the bells on Christmas Day
> Their old familiar carols play,
> And wild and sweet

The words repeat
Of peace on earth, good-will to men!

H.W. Longfellow

Also appropriate: "Carol of the Brown King" by Langston Hughes.

Christmas Reading

Try reading "The Christmas Mouse" (E. Wenning, Holt Publishing Co., 1959, $3.50) aloud to your middle-graders. It's entertaining & also explains the history of the carol "Silent Night." Older students may enjoy "A Child's Christmas in Wales," (as read) by Dylan Thomas. Some background & vocabulary build-up (i.e., jelly babies, etc.) will be most helpful.

Social studies topic suggestions. The manufacture of candles, the difference between mass-produced & individually created products, the production of stained-glass windows, Church Arts, a study of toys (their history & present-day counterparts; children each design a toy, e.g., jack-in-the-box), Xmas Tree Farms.

Christmas Math

Many children travel during the holidays. On the front board list the distances each child expects to travel. Let the children compute total mileage, (then you add your proposed mileage to list), average distance, greatest distance, shortest distance, 2nd greatest & shortest distances.

Let older students design & make tree decorations using ONLY pencil, compass, ruler, French curve, scissors & paper. Let children INVENT.

Help your class learn about postal rates for cards, packages, air-mail & parcel-post, & the meanings of 1st, 2nd & 3rd class mails. Have the children figure out various postage costs & then compare these in order to learn the most efficient way to dispatch their mail.

One day, for variety, let your class practice estimating by playing "Competent Consumers F.O.R.N." (Friends of Ralph Nader). To prepare for this game, cut out large pictures (from mail-order catalogs or magazines) of toys, food, tools, cars, books, furniture, appliances, sporting goods, musical instruments & pictures that illustrate a service, e.g., movies, gas, electricity, telephone, shoe-repair, water. Paste each picture to a piece of 9" x 12" tagboard. Beneath each picture indicate price of item (average monthly cost for a service). Mask-out price from view. Now children form "families" of 5-6 students (or "companies" of 10-12 students). You advise each group of its monthly income and the amount it may spend. A "salesman" holds up 1 of the tagboard cards & calls for estimates. Each family (or company) 1st discusses if they can AFFORD item & then each of group who wishes to is allowed 1 written guess at the cost. Price is then unmasked & item is awarded to the group whose bid was most nearly correct. At end of game children total up amount they "have spent that month." A "Competent Consumer" badge is awarded each member of the group with the most products or services (within their given budget). By playing this game, children become aware of how a toy may cost as much as a pair of shoes, a refrigerator costs less than a color T.V., & how a monthly income will go just so far.

Gingerbread for 45

15 cups flour	1²/₃ cups salad oil	3 tsp. cloves
1¼ cups sugar	5 tsp. ginger	5 tsp. salt
4 cups molasses	5 tsp. cinnamon	raisins or red hots
5 eggs	5 Tbsp. baking powder	for decoration

Children measure, sift & mix ingredients.
Chill dough well (15-25 min.).

Each child writes his name on a slip of paper & then receives a piece of wax paper for his desk top & a bit of flour. Using a large knife, cut dough into appropriate number of pieces. Once his hands are washed & his sleeves pushed up, each child gets a lump of chilled dough. Advise children to make men rather thin as fat men do not bake evenly. As each gingerbread man is completed, it is decorated with raisins or red hots & is transferred to an oiled baking sheet & the name tag is slipped under an edge of the man. Bake at 325° to 350° for 8-15 minutes depending on thickness of men. (Recipe may be halved.)

Christmas Science

The theory of electric currents can be demonstrated if you bring 2 strings of tree lights to class—a single strand (all bulbs go out when bulb burns out) & a double wire type. Electricity must make a complete circuit, a round-trip. The double set of wires gives electricity a round-trip to each bulb, while the complete circuit of the single-strand is interrupted whenever a single bulb burns out.

Christmas botany. American *holly* grows naturally from Massachusetts to Florida. In some places it reaches a height of 50'. At nurseries holly berries are sown & covered with mulch, & in the spring of the 2nd year the seeds germinate. Holly is evergreen, shedding its leaves every 3rd year.

Mistletoe. This is a parasitic air-plant growing on a host tree & manufacturing its own food. The roots of an air plant anchor it to the host tree; specialized rootlets of mistletoe delve into tissues of the host, drawing a water (& mineral) supply from it.

Christmas trees. *Balsam fir* has a symmetrical shape & its needles remain green even when dry. Its needles stay firmly attached, as they are arranged spirally on twigs & have no joints, brackets, at their bases. Its cones stand erect on the boughs, giving a candle-like effect. *White spruce,* while living, retains its bluish-green needles for 7 to 10 years! Once cut, it begins to shed. *Cedar* has short, scale-like needles. Long-needled pines are sometimes also used at Xmas.

This is a fine time for the children to work together on a class project such as "a gift for the birds." Such a lesson can induce quiet, thoughtful working conditions that may initiate meaningful ecological discussions. Consider for what type of birds you are making your tree & which of the following suggestions are appropriate fare for your birds:

Pine cones dipped in melted suet & rolled in seeds.
Strings of popcorn.
Balls of peanut butter, fat & seeds.
Stale bread dipped in honey.

These are tied to the branches of a living or dried tree or bush. Incidentally, this is a traditional Christmas activity in Norway.

A Few Thoughts on Christmas Art

Year after year in their school experience, children have a Christmas Art curriculum; try to develop plans which will alleviate boring repetitions. What symbolic material comes with Christmas? Choose a symbol & explore its meanings & possibilities for use in the curriculum. What visual elements are especially a part of Christmas? How can these be used in developing sensitivity?

When choosing gift or decoration projects for your class, be critical of the possibilities afforded for individuality of expression. Ask yourself if the project will give deeper meaning or understanding of old symbols—or is it more likely to perpetuate the cliché? Finally, what is the value of a "clever" idea when it is the teacher who initiated it?

Christmas Tree Ornaments. These ornaments may also be hung from light fixtures or along window casing or used to form a bulletin board display. Of course, in all cases, they should not be distracting to your class.

Stars. Easy star: accordion fold a 10" strip of paper (or a paper soda straw) into 9 equal folds. Glue ends together, forming star. Insert thread through a small hole in topmost point of star.

Five-pointed star.

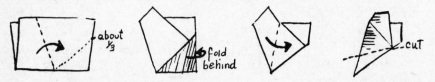

Six-pointed star. Fold a circle in half, fold this in half again. Fold this quarter of a circle into thirds. Cut on a slant as shown.

Any star at this point may have tiny holes & lacy edges cut, making snowflakes instead of stars.

Foam rubber snowflakes. Pattern is transferred to sheet of thin foam rubber (available at surplus stores). Cut out design.

Fold lengthwise & cut out centers of designs. Using 4" lengths of wire or thread, bind 3 or 4 foam strips together at their centers.

Glitter may be adhered to finished snowflake with white glue.
Starbursts. Cut several circles, 2" in diameter, from foil. Pinch foil
at 1 side & crease to center of circle. Bring opposite side of circle
over & lay atop crease, forming 2 small cone shapes. Join several
of these shapes together by passing thread through points &
pulling to form starburst cluster. VARIATION: Cut 3" diameter
circles of foil or metallic paper. Fold in 1/2 vertically & horizontally & slantwise. Open circle out flat again. Cut along each crease
to within 1/2" of the center of circle. Use pencil to make points
of stars as shown. Thread through centers forming a cluster or
starburst. VARIATION: Use 3" squares instead of circles. Fold in
1/2 vertically & horizontally ONLY. Continue as with circle
starburst, making 1" slits from center top, bottom & left & right
sides.

Hanging strands. From white paper cut small circles, bells, trees, or
diamonds. Cut 2 identical shapes of each form. Fold each shape
down the center. Apply paste to 1/2 of each shape & press 2
identical shapes together, forming a 3-sided figure. When dry,
shapes are strung together using a long needle & thread. Hang
strands so that they may gently twirl.

Beeswax ornaments from Mexico. Cut a basic shape from thin
cardboard (star, bell, moon). Lay a sheet of beeswax atop
cardboard, shape, & using your thumbnail (or a tableknife) gently
trim wax to follow outline of cardboard. Soften wax slightly by
placing it in the sun or near a heater & then press firmly onto
cardboard shape. Using various colors of thin yarn & beginning at
the outer edge of ornament, press yarn onto wax, eventually filling
entire area. Wax may be re-warmed occasionally to facilitate
adherence of yarn. Pattern should be uniform & variations in color
of yarn used will create an intricate design.

Fish. Trace fish onto sheet of soft aluminum (sold at hardware,
lumber stores). Cut 2 slits behind eyes. Fold in 1/2 lengthwise &
bend each little strip down & forward. Also bend each 1/2 of tail a
bit forward.

Danish string of bells. Trace pattern onto foil. Cut slits & curl paper around, forming bell-shapes. Glue paper in place. String of bells can be any length you wish. Size of bells may be varied also.

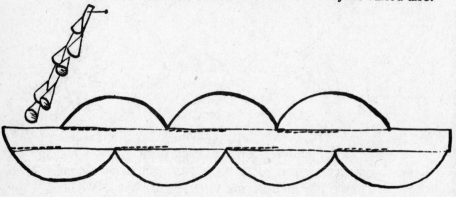

Dove. Insert body into wings. Let children design their own dove shapes.

VARIATION: Wings of 1-piece dove may be slightly bent in opposite directions. Again, let children come up with their own personal bird shapes; variety will be pleasant.

Swedish angel. Cut shape out of white paper. Curve & tape dress back, forming skirt. Gently bend arms forward so that hands

appear to hold trees upright. Adhere wings to center of angel's back. Bend wings slightly forward. Unless enlarged, this angel had best be presented to older children with good small-muscle control.

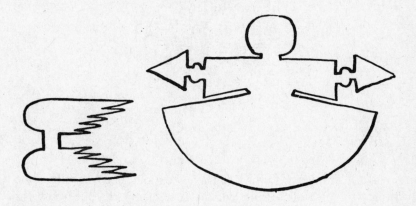

Snowy ornaments. Cut shapes from cardboard. Coat each with plastic starch. Shake in paper bag filled with soap flakes. Allow shapes to dry thoroughly before hanging.

Lasting Creations. For *a lasting ornament* which will be used each Xmas: Each child designs a basic shape (approx. 3" x 5"), e.g., snowman, toy, farm animal, bell, angel, etc. You cut these shapes from plywood, faithfully reproducing their original design. A jigsaw is used to cut plywood; each child sands his cut-out shape & then carefully paints it. Glitter may be sparingly used. If poster paints are used, the ornaments, when dry, may be sprayed with a protective coating of clear plastic.

Teacher's dowel-tree can be used each year in the classroom. May display ornaments made by children or God's Eyes interspersed with bright year tassels or bells—or Peppar Kakor, the thin crisp ginger cookies which the Swedes traditionally hang on just such a tree each Xmas. They also tie the trunk with a large bright bow, spear an apple on the end of each branch & festoon the top with a cluster of golden wheat stalks.

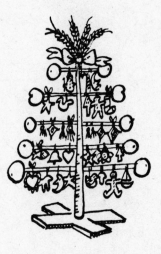

Gifts. *Teacher's gift to class.* Take your class caroling one evening (visit a local nursing home), & wind up at your house for hot chocolate & doughnuts.

Give the children a handmade piñata (as described in Christmas party suggestions later in this chapter).

Present your class with a set of holiday puzzles to be used during free time. Rubber cement a Xmas picture to tagboard. Press beneath books until dry. Paint the back of each puzzle with a different primary color to facilitate identification of pieces. Cut tagboard into pieces; each puzzle is kept in a hosiery box with a lid painted to match identifying color of puzzle it holds.

Class gift to school's principal &/or secretary. Candy or cooky-making can incorporate lessons in measurements, heat, & the action of leavening. Classroom cookery suggestions at the back of this book may be of help in preparing for this project. You might choose one of the recipes there or use the following gift recipe:

Toasted Coconut Chips

Pierce the eyes of fresh coconuts & drain off juice. Heat nuts in 300° oven for 1 hour. When cool, tap nuts with hammer until they crack into large pieces. Pry out meat, leaving brown skin on meat, & thinly slice with carrot peeler, the slicing side of a grater, or a slicing machine. Lay chips on cooky sheets & bake in a 200° oven for 2 hours or until chips are tan & crisp. Stir occasionally during baking. Sometimes an additional 1-1 1/2 hours baking time is required. Pack chips in airtight jars & wrap festively.

Children's gifts to parents. It seems wise to ask yourself if the gifts to be made by your class are appropriate, if they are likely to be used. Each child should have the joy of seeing that his gift is appreciated by his parents. Therefore, it helps to inquire as to how many children *have* fireplaces before making a gift for the hearth; avoid making ash trays in view of good health training & non-smoking parents. Personalize the gift: make it something that can be used each Christmas, something that will become a family tradition, e.g., an ornament, paper sculpture (see Bakers Clay recipe & suggestions at back of book), or a card that contains a Polaroid photo of the child. Have an easy-to-make substitute for the exceptional child who loses or breaks (or "hates") his gift at the last moment.

Classroom recipe books. Each child brings 1 of his mother's favorite recipes to class; variety should be encouraged. According to the abilities of the class, the teacher may (1) fold mimeograph master sheets in half & copy a recipe at the top of each side, leaving space at the bottom of each half for the contributing child's own signature & an appropriate drawing if he likes; or (2) have each child copy his recipe onto a paper which is checked for accuracy & spacing. If it is correct, it is transferred by the child to half of a mimeo master sheet. A second student will copy his recipe on the remaining half. Each signs his name at the bottom of his recipe & draws a picture of his mother, the reader, or of himself preparing the recipe in the kitchen, etc. A master-sheet bearing title page information is also designed & written up: "Our Christmas Recipe Book—Written by Miss Arter's Third Grade Class of River School, Christmas, 1973." Mimeos of the recipes & title page are run off for each student (& a few extras for your school librarian, the wife of your principal, etc.). Simple tagboard covers, secured by 2 brads, are added to the folded pages, completing your gift recipe books. In their free time, children may add color to illustrations.

Hot-dish trivet (a quick gift). Each child needs 15 ice cream bar sticks & a thick piece of cardboard. Eight of the sticks are painted with poster paints. When dry, the sticks are laid, alternating painted & unpainted, across the cardboard, forming a rectangle. Cardboard is cut to the size of this rectangle. Sticks are glued in place with milk glue. Weight is applied to trivet until it is completely dry. A light coat of clear plastic may be sprayed onto finished trivets.

Soap dish (for an easy gift). Neatly cut off the bottom sections of rectangular plastic detergent bottles. An awl is heated & used to make 5 holes for drainage in the bottom of each soap dish. Enamel paints may be used to add stars or polka dots around the edge of each dish. A bar of handmade soap might be a nice accompaniment.

Lemon soap. Mix 2 cups white soap flakes & 1/4 cup water. Add yellow food coloring & several drops of oil of lemon essence. Knead until well blended. Mold into lemon shape, packing tightly. Set aside to harden. A.F.S.C.

Key chain (another quickie)—for older children. Each child brings a smooth, interesting stone or shell to class. A light coat of shellac or clear nail polish may be applied to bring out deeper colors. Each stone or shell is snugly wrapped about with copper wire. On top is left a loose end, from which an inexpensive little key chain is securely attached.

Cryst-L Craze* bud vase. The children collect & bring to class

――――――――――
*Cryst-L Craze® spray is manufactured by Fry Plastic International Inc., Los Angeles 3, Calif.

a variety of interesting glass bottles. "Cryst-L Craze" is a relatively inexpensive solution sold in hobby shops. Following the directions on the bottle, the children can transform throw-away bottles into quite lovely vases. Re-cycling begins at school!

Tree ornament (for very young children). Teacher cuts out basic angel shapes from felt. Children choose fabric scraps, gold braid, buttons & yarn & decorate their angels. Glue the decorations firmly in place with milk glue. Weight is applied until angels are completely dry. Each child writes his name & the date in pencil along the bottom of his angel. Teacher machine stitches embroidery along name & date using bright colored thread—or you might use a fine pointed felt-tip pen.

Rose sachet. Have children gather & bring to class rose petals, geranium leaves, lavender. Spread these out to dry in a warm place. Using a dietetic scale, each child (if possible) weighs out the following: 4 oz. dried rose petals; 1 oz. dried lavender; 1 oz. geranium leaves; 2 oz. (granular) orrisroot; 1/2 oz. ground cloves; 1 oz. (granular) patchouli; 1 oz. benzoin (broken up). Mix these ingredients well by shaking them in a small paper bag, then spoon mixture into tiny silk squares. Gather up 4 corners & secure firmly with a pretty ribbon. Each sachet should be compact & NOT loose. (Makes 6 sachets.)

A gift for the hearth. Pine-cones tossed into a log-burning fire produce colorful flames. Have children collect & bring to class dried pine cones & small dry pine branches. Cones are dipped into a solution made by dissolving 1 T. of solid glue in 1 gallon of hot water. Skim out the cones & while they're still moist & hot, sprinkle generously with powdered chemicals:

> For red flames: strontium nitrate
> For bright green: borax
> For orange: calcium chloride
> For apple green: barium nitrate
> For blue: copper sulphate
> For emerald: copper nitrate
> For yellow: common table salt
> For purple: lithium chloride

Dry cones on newspapers for several days.

Easy gift wrap for cones, wood. The dried cones are put in new medium-sized brown paper bags. Neatly fold over opening & staple shut. Features of deer or bird are drawn directly on sack with felt tip pens. Cardboard appendages are painted, taped in place (brown paper tape works well). Deer's antlers are 2 appropriately shaped twigs.

Gift Wrapping Ideas. Other gift wrapping ideas include *marbleized paper.* Fill shallow (cooky sheet) pan with water. Mix left-over oil paints, enamels or lacquers with their thinners. Keep a bit of thinner in reserve for cleaning of pan. By snapping wrist or tapping brush, drop or spatter oils onto surface of water. If color immediately spreads out, you have added too much thinner. Stir water gently with a toothpick, causing a slight swirling of paint. Place sheet of paper lightly atop water, remove paper, "peeling" it off the water. Allow paper to dry face up on a flat newspaper-covered surface. Should globs of paint stick to paper, refusing to dry, you need to add more thinner to oil mixture. Two or more colors of paint may be used or a little bronzing can be sprinkled on the water (with a small salt shaker). The resulting papers are similar to those used as the end papers of books in the 19th century.

Hand holding gift. Each child wraps a tiny gift (i.e., key chain) in plain white or colored tissue. Child then traces around his hand on pink construction paper or tagboard. Hand is cut out & made to "grasp" gift. Double-stick tape or rubber cement holds hand in position.

Double-edged greeting. Wrap gift in a box covered with a solid color paper. Child writes "Greetings" in large letters along folded edge of a rectangular piece of paper. Bottoms of letters will touch fold. Letters are then cut around, always leaving some of the fold intact. The centers of the letters *G, E, & S* are cut out. Open out piece of paper. Adhere double-edged greeting to top of package. This idea can also be used on a card. A few sequins can be glued around edges of "Greetings."Older students will have the control of their scissors that is essential for this project.

Snowflake doily. Fold a round paper doily (according to the directions given for cutting a 6-pointed star, page 110). Starting at curved edge, cut INTO doily. Open out snowflake & glue atop gift package.

Cards or program covers (see "Jan. Printmaking" for other ideas). A handmade card is a thoughtful gesture to extend to your Room Mother & any other persons whom the children wish to remember at this time.

Standard greetings include: Joy; Peace; Noel; Rejoice; Season's Cheer; Happy Holiday; Glad Tidings; Yuletide Greetings. Children can be counted on to come up with personalized expressions of good cheer.

Card shape variations:

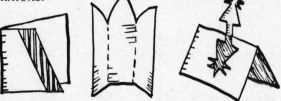

Gesso clay: Apply with a brush atop fine line pencil drawing. Gesso is diluted plaster of Paris & as such may be tinted appropriate colors. It may also be trailed from a squeeze bottle in intricate arabesque designs directly onto folded card. Rough textured paper (oatmeal paper) works well. Allow design to dry completely. Children may experiment with bronzing powder, blowing it on wet gesso. Dry designs may be lightly spray-shellacked for added protection.

Pine Print. Paint a small short-needled piece of pine with thick white poster paint. Press the pine carefully & firmly against a piece of dark green or blue paper folded into card form. Sprinkle print with mica.

Face in the window. Take snapshots of your students. Cut each photo to approx. 2" x 2" (including the head & torso of child). Hand out 7" x 8" sheets of tan tagboard. Pictures of varying house facades may be displayed. Have each child fill tagboard with a large detailed drawing of a house at Xmas time, including windows, one of which is 2" x 2". Houses are painted & carefully cut out. Photo of child is rubber cemented atop 2" x 2" window so that child appears to be looking out in greeting. Written date, message, signature may be added on back of card.

Inkblot Santa. Each child dips a big soft-haired brush into a rather weak solution of white poster paint. Tiny (2" x 2") pink construction paper cards are used. By touching brush to card, applying gentle pressure, dragging brush down, to left & up, a fat shape is produced with one sweep of the brush. Details are added with black felt-point pens. A wide variety of expressions should be the result.

Angels. Each child designs a simple angel (one that is flying) & cuts it out of a piece of inner tube which is then adhered to a hand-sized wooden block. Printing ink is applied to angel (using brayer) & angel is firmly pressed against folded card. Let children experiment with their prints; e.g., a slit is made above & below angel's hand and something is inserted. VARIATION: Each child stamps his angel somewhere on a bulletin board that is covered with light blue paper. A few soft cloud shapes are added. Each child, in his own way, designs & prepares a message of glad tidings for his angel to hold. This completed board becomes a classroom greeting. VARIATION (for older students): Each child folds in half, lengthwise, a piece of 3 1/2" x 5" gold foil-backed Japanese paper. Using sharp pointed scissors, the child makes cuts similar to those shown in the paper. Top corners are rounded off, paper is unfolded & glued atop a neutral colored card, e.g., oatmeal paper.

Xmas Music

In France they call Christmas songs "noels." In England & America they are called Christmas carols. The word "carol" comes from the Greek word meaning "to dance"; a true carol has a religious theme that is treated in a familiar, happy manner. Some of our Xmas songs are hymns rather than carols, e.g., "O, Little Town of Bethlehem," "It Came Upon a Midnight Clear." Carols date back to the 13th century (see Christmas Walls, page 102).

Historical backgrounds of 12 Xmas songs. What are some ways that your class might (re)-interpret this information?

Adestes Fideles: Origin unclear; scholars have spent years investigating 2 different claims—that it is Portugese & that it is English.

Away in a Manger: The German, Martin Luther, is said to have written this for his child.

Deck the Halls: Welsh; a very old melody which Mozart used for a piano-violin duet.

God Rest Ye Merry Gentlemen: English, traditional old song.

Good King Wenceslaus: Monarch of Bohemia, 928-935, this kind man was generous to the poor, especially on Dec. 26, the feast of St. Stephen. Carol, thought to be of Swedish origin, was 1st published in 1582.

I Heard the Bells on Christmas Day: This was written by Henry Wadsworth Longfellow at the time when America was involved in the tragic Civil War; peace on earth had, therefore, a special significance to Longfellow when he was composing this carol.

I Saw 3 Ships: English, traditional. Probably written in the 2nd half of the 15th century.

Joy to the World: Isaac Watts wrote this in 1719 when religion was at a low ebb in England. He paraphrased verses from the 98th Psalm & used music from Handel's *Messiah.*

O Little Town of Bethlehem: Phillips Brooks, a famous minister of Boston, promised his pupils a new Christmas song for the holiday. By Saturday he still had no song written. During the night he awoke. Suddenly a melody had come to him. He jotted it down & returned to bed. The next day he taught this new song to his children.

The Wassail Song: One of the oldest of carols. "Wassail" comes from the Anglo-Saxon "we shel" ("to be healthy"), & was used long ago as a toast ("To your health!").

The First Noel: French or English, it is the tune of medieval shepherds.

We Three Kings (1857); & It Came Upon A Midnight Clear: American.

Tell your class the story of *The Nutcracker Suite.* Let them hear excerpts from it while they paint.

Play Gian-Carlo Menotti's *Amahl & the Night Visitors.* Let the children follow the words being sung on the record by reading along with it a mimeo of the script of this opera. Discuss with the class how they might use this record as the basis of a puppet show to be presented to other classes or the sick ward of a local hospital—an appropriate gesture of thoughtfulness at this time of year. Take photos of the children involved in this activity & display these during Open House.

December P.E.

Your Left & My Right. Children are divided into pairs, all of which comprise 2 teams. Each pair of teammates is given a box, some wrapping paper (or newspaper) & ribbon or yarn, with instructions "to wrap the present." The only catch is that 1 child may use only his left hand & his partner may use only his right while cooperating in wrapping their package. Discuss, prior to playing, how class might insure that each player will use just 1 hand. The first team to successfully wrap all of its presents is the winner.

December Puppet

Quick Santa finger puppets. Each child designs his own Santa using a 3 1/2" Styrofoam ball for head, felt for hat & features, & yarn for hair & beard. Red corduroy is cut on the bias for his suit. White glue (or 2 straight pins) is used to adhere hat to head, facial features & head to suit, & edges of corduroy together. A little jingle bell may be sewn to the front of his suit, & a yarn tassel completes his cap.

Holiday Parties

Avoid chaos by being especially well-organized this month.

Entertainment. Hand out to each child a paper on which the same sprig of holly has been mimeographed. Children make up original pictures incorporating the holly outline in any way they like; paper may be used in any direction. The class might enjoy sharing & comparing the variety of results.

Present relay. Children stand in 2 (or more) lines. Each child must run to a chair or table on which there is a "gift." He must un-tie, unwrap, re-wrap, & re-tie the gift. Then he runs back to his line, tagging 2nd player who repeats above activity.

A Mexican-inspired piñata. A piñata made from a heavy duty, double-thickness brown paper bag works well & it is quick to make. Its only drawback is that it usually rips when struck, rather than bursting apart.

Older children especially like the feeling of striking a more solid pinata. A corrugated cardboard box can be made into an animal piñata which offers a bit more resistance to the "swinger." Put a trap door in the bottom of a cardboard box. After filling the cavity with small inexpensive wrapped gifts, candy & gum, tape trap door shut. This door should fall open after a couple of direct hits by the blindfolded child. Box can be decorated to resemble a bird or animal. Rolled newspaper serves as a base for neck, legs, wings, or arms; use staple or masking-tape to fasten these in place. Fold crepe or tissue paper (10-12 layers) & cut long strips. Along edge of each strip cut many short vertical snips. Pull strips apart; glue them 2 at a time about body of pinata, overlapping cut edge atop uncut edge to achieve a feathered effect.

Spread blanket on the playground under a basketball hoop.

Piñata, firmly tied to a rope, is strung over the basketball hoop. Class stands behind edge of blanket out of range of blindfolded child who attempts to break the dangling pinata which you lower & raise by slackening & pulling on rope. When, after several tries, he is not successful, a new child is blindfolded & given the bat (or broomstick) with which he strikes at the piñata. Once smashed, the piñata spills its contents & the children rush forward to collect them.

Party place mats. These also make an interesting border design (for above chalkboard) in January when you return & the room is bare. So have the children make 2: one for the party & one for the border.

Each child folds 1 segment of "Tree-Saver" (recycled paper) or paper toweling in half & thoroughly moistens it with water. Excess water is carefully squeezed out. Towel is opened out flat. It is folded in half crosswise & then in half lengthwise. Then it is folded into a triangle as shown: Design is begun at pointed end.

With water colors children paint different types of lines across folded paper. Dots, stars, hearts, crosses may be added. Undo 1 fold & check to see if paint is sinking through. If the lines are too faint, they are carefully re-traced afresh. Undo a second fold & repeat process of re-painting, if necessary. Towel is opened out flat & allowed to dry.

Refreshments. The children would probably enjoy preparing their own refreshments (see Classroom Cookery, e.g., Nut Log) & this activity could take the place of exchanging purchased gifts. The money that would have been spent in that way could be collected & used for a charitable cause. (Save the Children Federation: Boston, Post Rd., Norwalk, Conn. 06852.) This is in keeping with the meaning of Christmas.

• Birth of Louis Pasteur   [27]

Pasteur discovered in the 19th century that fermentation could be prevented if a liquid were exposed to extremely high temperatures. Milk that has been treated this way is called PASTEURized!

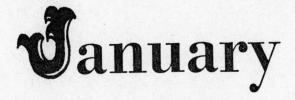anuary

January brings the snow,
Makes your feet and fingers glow.

1 New Year's Day.
   Bartolome Murillo (1617-1682), Spanish painter.
   Paul Revere (1735-1818), American patriot.
   Betsy Ross (1752-1836), maker of 1st U.S. flag.
   Lincoln issued Emancipation Proclamation, 1863.
3 Lucretia Mott (1793-1880), antislavery & women's suffrage
   leader.
4 Jakob Grimm (1785-1863), German author & collector of
   fairy tales.
5 George Washington Carver probably born on this date
   (1864-1943), American botanist.
6 Joan of Arc (1412-1431), French heroine.
   Carl Sandburg (1878-1967), American poet.
7 1st U.S. Presidential election, 1789.
   Millard Fillmore (1780-1874), 13th President.
9 Carrie Chapman Catt (1859-1947), American suffragist.
10 1st United Nations General Assembly, London 1946.
11 Alexander Hamilton (1755-1804), American statesman.
   William James (1842-1910), American psychologist, philosopher.
12 Charles Perrault (1628-1703), French author *(Cinderella,*
   Sleeping Beauty).

   John Hancock (1737-1793), 1st signer of the Declaration of
   Independence.

Jack London (1876-1916), American author *(Call of the Wild).*

John Singer Sargent (1856-1925), American painter.

14 Benedict Arnold (1741-1801), U.S. Revolutionary War traitor.

Albert Schweitzer (1875-1965), French doctor, philosopher.

15 Moliere (1622-1673), French writer of comedies.

Martin Luther King (1929-1968), American civil rights leader, winner of Nobel Peace Prize.

17 Benjamin Franklin (1706-1790), American inventor, statesman.

18 Daniel Webster (1782-1852), American statesman.

A.A. Milne (1882-1956), English author *(Winnie the Pooh).*

19 James Watt (1736-1819), Scottish inventor.

Robert E. Lee (1807-1870), Commander in Chief of Confederate Army, Civil War.

Edgar Allen Poe (1809-1849), American author *(The Telltale Heart).*

Paul Cezanne (1839-1906), French post-impressionist painter.

20 Inauguration Day: every 4 years U.S. President takes oath of office.

Andre Ampere (1775-1836), French physicist (developed science of electrodynamics).

American Revolution ended, 1783, after lasting 8 years.

Josef Hofmann (1876-1957), Polish-American composer.

21 Stonewall Jackson (1824-1863), Confederate general: Civil War.

1st Atomic submarine, "Nautilus," launched by U.S.A., 1954.

22 Lord George Byron (1788-1824), English poet.

Edouard Manet (1832-1883), French impressionist painter.

24 Gold discovered in California, 1848.

25 Dr. Mary Walker received the Congressional Medal of Honor 1866. She is the only woman to have received this honor.

26 Douglas MacArthur (1880-1964), Commander in Chief of Allied Forces in S.W. Pacific, W.W. II.

27   Wolfgang Mozart (1756-1791), Austrian composer.
      Lewis Carroll [Chas. Dodgson] (1832-1898), English author
      (Alice in Wonderland).
      Thomas Edison granted patent on incandescent light: 1880.
28   Jackson Pollock (1912-1956), American abstract-expres-
      sionist painter.
29   Thomas Paine (1737-1809), American Revolution patriot,
      writer.
      William McKinley (1843-1901), 25th President (assassinated
      in his 2nd term).
30   Franklin Delano Roosevelt (1882-1945), 32nd President.
31   Franz Schubert (1797-1828), Austrian composer.
      Explorer I launched 1958; 1st U.S. Earth satellite.

January

The name comes from Latin *Januarius,* after Janus the 2-faced Roman
god who was able to look back into the past &, at the same time, into
the future. Janus also busied himself with the beginnings of all
undertakings. The Romans dedicated this month to Janus by offerings
of meal, wine, salt & frankincense, each of which was new. The
Anglo-Saxons called January "Wulfmonath" because this was the
month in which hunger drove the wolves down into the villages.

JANUARY QUOTATIONS

1   No one ever regards the first of January with indifference.–
      (Charles Lamb)

      The American system of rugged individualism. (Campaign
      speech in New York 10/22/28)–Herbert Hoover

6   Shakespeare, Leonardo da Vinci, Benjamin Franklin &
      Lincoln never saw a movie, heard a radio or looked at
      T.V. They had "loneliness" and knew what to do with it.
      They were not afraid of being lonely because they knew
      that was when the creative mood in them would work.–
      Carl Sandburg

12   Every time I paint a portrait I lose a friend.–*John Singer
      Sargent

      *Quoted in *The Treasury of Humorous Quotations* by Herbert V. Prochnow,
Harper & Row Pub. Co., 1969.

15   I have a dream. I have a dream that one day this nation will rise up & live out the true meaning of its creed: "We hold these truths to be self-evident: that all men are created equal". . . . I have a dream that one day in the red hills of Georgia, sons of former slaves and sons of former slave owners will be able to sit down together at the table of brotherhood.—Martin Luther King, Jr. 1929-1968

17   He that can have patience can have what he will.

       Early to bed and early to rise makes a man healthy, wealthy and wise.

       A little neglect may breed mischief: for want of a nail the shoe was lost; for want of a shoe the horse was lost; and for want of a horse the rider was lost.
       ("Maxims"—preface to *Poor Richard's Almanack:* 1732)

A few words about January. When the children return, you may discuss their vacations by asking them to stop & consider: "What did you *learn* over the holidays?" Thoughtful answers to this question could be enlightening & would avoid extensive gift discussion, the comparison of presents.

Talk about what your class would like to do, accomplish this year. Do the students suggest any changes in rulings?

During this new year, try to help the children learn to savor the moment—not always be preparing for "when I grow up." A similar philosophy is not bad advice for a teacher either!

JANUARY EVENTS

• New Year's Day

This marks the beginning of the civil year. The date is inherited from the Romans; Julius Caesar designated Jan. 1st as the 1st day of the year, changing it from the traditional date in early March (near the spring equinox). When the Romans, under Constantine, accepted Christianity, New Year's Day changed from a day of feasting to a time of meditation & fasting. Now—and for the last 300 years—New Year's is, again, a time of feasting & rejoicing.

Social Studies

On the 1st day back in class, older students are given paper on which they list every major news event they remember as having occurred during the previous year. These lists may be compiled, discussed, used as the basis for a graph giving an overview of historic events of the last months.

Discuss different methods of measuring time (see Page 0). Let each child make a (9" x 12") poster "publicizing" one of the days in January. The date should be shown in large numbers (in the upper left-hand corner); a pertinent quotation, birthdate of famous person, anecdote should be added; & an illustrative collage or drawing will finish this piece of personal propaganda. If research uncovers nothing historically important about a date, the child then supplies an original theme, i.e., a scientific fact, a meteorological comment. These posters are collected & put in chronological order. Each day the new one is posted, adding to that month's hall display.

Language Arts

Discuss "resolutions," their meaning & possible values. Talk about symbols: old Father time & the baby New Year, their clothing, the scythe & hourglass. Consider how in life it is necessary to have opposites, to have the *old* in order to have the *new*.

Talk about the almanac. Is it important today? How? Compare a current (i.e., Farmers') almanac with Poor Richard's. Perhaps the children will want to keep a classroom almanac of room information, anecdotes for Open House visitors.

Vocabulary enrichment words: resolutions, hindsight, fortuitous, predictions, serendipity, valedictory, prophetic, auld lang syne.

Etymology. The Italian word for candy is "confetti." Long ago during the fun-filled carnival days, Italians used to pelt one another with tiny pieces of candy. Then as time passed, little pieces of cardboard were substituted for the candies. Now, centuries later, we throw tiny pieces of paper "confetti" at one another—usually at 12:00 midnight, New Year's Eve!

Riddles: Why is a New Year's Resolution like a mirror? (Because it's so easily broken.) What is it that you can't see on Jan. 1st although it's right in front of you? (The whole new year.) Which travels faster in January: heat or cold? (Heat. It's real easy to catch cold in January!)

New Year's Poetry

> Ring out the old, ring in the new
> Ring happy bells across the snow;
> The year is going, let him go;
> Ring out the false, ring in the true.
>
> —Alfred Lord Tennyson

While the earth remains, seedtime and harvest, cold and heat, summer and winter, day and night, shall not cease. (Genesis 8:22)

New Year's Art

The ancient Romans thought Janus to be so alert & watchful that they kept images of him above their doors to guard their homes. Let the children create their own interpretations of the 2-faced Janus, some of which may become appropriate decorations for your classroom door.

- **Birth of Betsy Ross   [1]**

Mrs. John (Betsy) Ross was an expert seamstress who had an upholstery shop at 329 Arch St., Phila., Pa. George Washington, Robt. Morris & Col. Ross, all members of a committee appointed by Congress, went to Mrs. Ross & gave her a sketch of a proposed design for the American flag. It was Betsy who thought of making the stars 5-pointed. She demonstrated how it could be done with one snip of her scissors! (See Page 110 for directions for re-creating Betsy's demonstration.)

- **1st public demonstration of the telegraph   [6]**

On this day in 1838 Samuel F.B. Morse & Arthur Vail demonstrated the telegraph at the Speedwell Ironworks in Morristown, N.J. The word "telegraph" comes from the Greek *tele* (far away) & *graph* (writing), so it is literally "long distance writing"!

- **Birth of Benjamin Franklin   [17]**

Benjamin Franklin's prospective mother-in-law was hesitant to consent to her daughter's marrying a printer. There already were two printers in the United States & she was not at all certain that the country could support a 3rd. As it turned out, Benjamin Franklin lived to become a prominent statesman, scientist, philosopher, inventor, & writer!

Bulletin board suggestions. Under the title "What Do All

These Things Have in Common?" display pictures of a fire engine, metal rimmed eyeglasses, a copy of *Poor Richard's Almanack*, a library bldg., a Franklin stone, a lightning rod.

Across your room string a clothesline high enough up so as not to be distracting. From it hang sayings by Franklin (i.e.: Man is a tool-making animal; Time is money; God helps them that help themselves; Don't leave for tomorrow what you can do today; A penny saved is a penny earned; In this world nothing is certain but death and taxes). Such a display may lead to a discussion of cliches (their cause` & significance & possible correction) that upper graders might enjoy.

Etymology. The Greeks knew that when amber was rubbed it became magnetic. Because friction could make amber give off tiny sparks, the Greeks named amber *electron* from *elector*: the beaming sun. *Electron* became the Latin *electrum* from which we have our word "electricity"!

> *Riddles:* What did Benjamin Franklin say when he discovered electricity in lightning? (Nothing, he was too *shocked* for words.)

Fun with electricity. Ask the electric power company if your class may see a lightning arrester & be given an explanation of how it works. Explain how to read the electric light meter. Have the children read theirs on the 1st & last days of 2 months & then estimate the family light bills for these months. Explain why fuses blow, how to change a blown fuse (why NOT to use a penny in place of a fuse), & what measures help prevent blown fuses.

Your class might enjoy reading Franklin's self-written epitaph:

The Body
of
Benjamin Franklin, Printer
(Like the cover of an old book,
Its contents torn out,
And stript of its lettering and gilding,)
Lies here, food for worms
Yet the work itself shall not be lost,
For it will, as he believed, appear once more
In a new
And more beautiful edition
Corrected and Amended
By its Author!

- **Birth of Edgar Allen Poe   [19]**

Write & read to your class an original mystery story. Then show them a list of clues which you have previously written on tagboard or have hidden beneath the pull-down map at the chalkboard. Older children make deductions & write possible solutions to the mystery story.

Bulletin board ideas. Lettering might be in the form of a ransom note, with individual letters cut from magazines & pasted together to form a "warning" or notice.

MYSTERY THEATRE

Fold bright colored pieces (6" x 8") of paper in half length-wise; on the outside print an appropriate vocabulary word (i.e., somber, hypnotic, cataclysmic) or paste a picture to illustrate such a word (i.e., horrific, catatonic, foreboding). On the inside print the definition of the word & its syllabication. These folders are stapled on a bright background beneath title. Children try to guess contents before raising the curtain on each little mystery.

"Can you solve this week's mystery with Detective Don?" Post a short intriguing list of questions on which the children will try their sleuthing techniques. Emphasize the importance of the search (through use of reference books) to solve a mystery. Have 4-5 books (i.e., Guiness Book of World Records, the World Almanac, a science encyclopedia set, etc.) right near (beneath) bulletin board for immediate use in tracking down the answers. Children may also write to Detective Don & ask HIM questions.

- **Birth of James Watt   [19]**

James Watt did not invent the steam engine while watching his mother's tea kettle. He actually conceived the idea while on a Sunday walk shortly after having rebuilt a Newcomen steam engine for the lab at the Univ. of Glasgow. Over a period of 15 years Watt developed an engine that launched a new age.

"History of Horsepower" bulletin board. Power is the rate at which work is being done or the rate at which energy is being spent. Horsepower has no real relationship to an animal's strength or work. What we call "horsepower" is the outcome of experiments that James Watt did with big draft horses over a century ago. He wanted to find the rate at which a horse under average conditions will do his work. He decided on the round number 550 foot pounds of work a second or 33,000 foot pounds a minute. So 1 horse power is the energy it takes to raise weight of 550 lbs. one foot in 1 second. Watt realized that this was a high rate of work for the average horse to maintain over a full day's time. Watt set up the horsepower measuring unit as a means of promoting his engines.

Etymology. The "watt" is a unit of electric power named after James Watt.

A simple steam turbine. Take a syrup can with a tight-fitting lever lid & with a sharp nail bore 2 small (1/10") holes, one on either side of the can & at *an angle to the can.* This may be done by twisting the nail as far as possible to one side after you've driven it through the can. Put 1" of *hot* water in the can & tightly secure lid in place. By strong elastic thread, suspend the can from a button on a cord, as shown. Hang as shown over a candle's flame. Steam escaping from holes sets up a force of reaction which makes can move in opposing directions (e.g., as in a jet plane, the hot gases escaping backwards push the plane forward).

- **Birth of Andre Ampere** [20]

The Paris Electrical Congress of 1881 paid tribute to Ampere who had made great contributions to the science of electro magnetism. They named in his honor the current that 1 volt sends through 1 ohm: the "ampere."

- **1st patent by Edison on incandescent light** [27]

(Also see Feb. 11.)

> *Riddles:* What is the best & cheapest light? (Daylight.) Who was the most clever inventor of all times? (Thomas Edison. He invented the radio & the phonograph so people would stay up all night burning his light bulbs!)

JANUARY ACTIVITIES

Now is the time of year to take stock of your relations with your students. You know each student quite well, but it's very enlightening sometimes to listen to a child talk about himself. Give the following Interest Inventory to each of your students either by "interviewing" personally or by having each older student fill out the mimeo-sheet himself. Not all of these questions need be included. You can edit this Inventory to suit your needs.

Name_____ Age_____ Birth-date_____ (good as quick reference for classroom celebrations.)

—What do you want to do (be) when you grow up? Why?
—What is your favorite T.V. program?
—Do you have anything that you feel superstitious about?
—If you could be Teacher, what would we study in Science this month? (I.e., outer space, the physical body, insects, sea life, animals, flowers, science experiments.)
—What's the scariest (most frightening) thing you can imagine? (Or: Tell me something that you think is really scary.)
—If you had $10 to spend in a book store, what kinds of books would you buy—what would they be about?
—If you could be any animal or bird or fish or snake in the whole world, what would you be? Tell me WHY.

  (Note: the answer to this question often affords real insight into the child's self-image.)

—What do you think is the best part about school?
—If you could be Teacher what would you change?
—Is there anything in particular that YOU would like to learn more about this year?

Things to Make for Absentees

During the 1st months of the year, there is often frequent absenteeism. When one of the students in your class is ill, have the children make him something *other* than the perennial raft of get-well cards. Here are some ideas:

Sewing cards. Firmly glue a colorful picture or greeting (Xmas) card onto tagboard. Use a picture that is not too detailed. Outline the main figure with dots about 1" apart. Punch through dots with small-holed paper punch or carefully use a darning needle to do so. With the group of sewing cards include several pieces of bright heavy yarn. Dip the tips of the ends of yarn in shellac & allow to dry hard; this will facilitate the threading of each sewing card.

A flannel board. Tightly stretch a bright piece of solid-colored flannel (less expensive than felt) over a 15" x 20" piece of corrugated cardboard. Firmly adhere flannel's edges to back of cardboard. Now children cut a series of figures or objects from bright felt scraps. These may be the cast & props of a specific fairy tale or they might be various people, things around which the child may build his own stories. The class dictates a letter (which will be enclosed with the flannel board set), explaining how the board is like the child's own personal stage & he can now make up plays using the felt figures.

A yucca-day tree. Each leaf is made by a different child; he colors one side a shade of green & on the other side he writes a riddle, joke or cartoon. To facilitate things, a mimeographed sheet of riddles (see page 139) may be prepared. Cut this sheet apart, giving each child a different riddle to copy. Once the yucca-tree is finished, each child may share his riddle with the rest of the class. Following this, you may give each child a complete mimeo to enjoy on his own.

A classmade surprise-ball. This can be appropriate for any age child depending on the surprises you include. Wrap a special little treat (Mexican jumping beans, a tiny clay whistle, jacks & ball) in a piece of cotton. Wind this round with a long thin strip of crepe paper. Continue winding crepe paper around this core. Occasionally wrap a small prize (balloons, coin, gum, tiny plastic toy, a magnet) into the ball. This is a good opportunity to use up any

faded crepe paper you may have. When surprise ball contains
10-12 prizes (& little get-well messages written on strips of paper)
the end of the last crepe streamer is fastened with a colorful
sticker, or finished ball may be made to resemble a funny face.

A Wonder Box. This can be of great comfort to a child with a
prolonged illness. Use a good sturdy box. Children cut out small
colorful pictures of birds, flowers, insects (pictures that are
appropriate for the child who is ill). These pictures are glued,
overlapping, on the box & its cover. Every surface of the box is
shellacked & allowed to dry. Wrap each of the following in a piece
of colorful tissue: sea shells, a magnifying glass, small interesting
rocks, a cocoon, a kaleidoscope, a small natural sponge & a
package of grass or clover seeds. Place gifts in box. The following
note is included with the packet of seeds: "You will find a sponge
in this Wonder Box. Soak the sponge in water. Roll it in these
seeds. Lay the sponge in a saucer of water & place it in a sunny
window. If you keep the sponge VERY WET you will have a
lovely green ball that's alive & growing." A get-well chain letter
written by the class may accompany the Wonder Box. A.F.S.C.

Language Arts

A classroom serial. If *you* are feeling creative here is an idea
to spark the new year, improve listening skills & stimulate creative
writing. Each day after lunch read an installment of a class serial
which you create. Incorporate occasionally into the story, names
of children in your room. You might make the serial in the form
of letters or the diary of someone caught in a time-machine or the
memoirs of a person held captive by pirates on an unknown island.
You may write in the 1st person. Include interesting science
information. Don't begin reading the serial until the children are
calmed down after re-entering the room after lunch. On days (&
these are naturally few) on which you haven't written the
continuation, you might bring in an old bottle with a note inside
that says, i.e., "Sorry, the next installment has been delayed in the
mails," or "Held up due to rain," etc. Once or twice when the
children are very involved in the story, let them write the next
installment themselves as a creative writing assignment.

Poetry. Let each student choose a color & then describe, in a
stream-of-consciousness manner, his impressions of that color. Let
him call to mind each of the sounds, smells, sensations, dreams,

memories that this color elicits. When sharing the finished pieces, the children should be reminded how poetry often does not rhyme, that a poem tells you something in a beautiful or unusual way, that a poem lets you hear someone's imagination at work.

My Black Friend

Black is a ship, pirates and fun.
Black is night.
Black is a storm.
Black is a tree falling.
Black is blood trickling. . . .
Black smells like a shark washed ashore
And it's rattling.
Black is a person with a knife in her.
Black is BLACK and there is nothing like it.
Black is a dead tree and the lovely aroma of
A rotten whale.*

—Benjie Viljoen (1964)

An interesting bulletin board display can be made of these poems. Have each child make an illustration or collage using ONLY the color (its shades, tones) of his poem.

Roodles of Riddles. One of a myriad of uses of riddles in the classroom. This one is good for filling in those 5 min. pockets of time before dismissal. It may also be a godsend for the substitute teacher. Print riddles in large letters on 8" x 24" pieces of sturdy paper. Children read silently as you hold each card up (answer appears on back). Raised hands are recognized for guessing of answers.

1. What questions can never be answered YES? (Are you asleep? Are you perfect? Are you dead? What does "No" spell?)
2. What questions *make* you answer "YES"? (Are you human? Are you alive? Are you being asked a question? What does Y-E-S spell? Are you awake? Are you reading this? Are you a child?)
3. A barrel weighed 20 lbs. A man put something in it & then it weighed 10 lbs. What did he put in it? (A hole.)
4. If a man is born in Australia, grows up in Africa, comes to America & dies in France, what is he? (Dead.)
5. What famous man in history didn't hang up his clothes at night? (Adam.)
6. What is the best butter in America? (A mountain goat.)

*Printed with the permission of the poet, Ben Viljoen, Jr.

7. What is the smallest bridge in the world? (The bridge of your nose.)
8. What 3 things does a woman look for, but never wants to find? (A run in her stocking, wrinkles, a gray hair.)
9. How many hard-boiled eggs could the giant Goliath eat on an empty stomach? (One, then it wouldn't be empty any more.)
10. Why isn't your nose 12 inches long? (Because then it would be a foot!)
11. How long is a string? (Twice as long as 1/2 its length.)
12. What is yours & yet it's used by others more than by yourself? (Your name.)
13. What goes up & *never* comes down? (Your age.)
14. When is a boy like a pony? (When he's a little hoarse.)
15. What room can you NEVER go into? (A mushroom.)
16. What trembles at each breath of air yet it can bear the heaviest burdens? (Water.)
17. What asks no questions but requires many answers? (The doorbell & the telephone.)
18. Who always goes to bed with his shoes on? (The horse.)
19. What names of people read the same forwards as backwards? (Eve, Anna, Otto, Ava, Hannah.)
20. Name 4 things that never use their teeth for eating? (A comb, a gear, a zipper, a saw.)
21. What has a mouth & never eats? (A river, a pitcher, a jar.)
22. What fruit, plants will not grow in good rich soil? (Taffy *apples*, caramel *corn, cotton* candy, jelly *beans*.)
23. What's a good place to go when you're broke? (To work.)
24. Unable to think, unable to speak, yet it tells the truth to the whole world. What is it? (A mirror, or good bathroom scales.)
25. What can you keep, even after you've given it to somebody else? (A smile, a promise, your name & address, a cold or the flu.)
26. What has never been felt, seen or heard—in fact, it's never existed & yet it has a name? ("Nothing.")
27. What can be written in 3 syllables, yet contains 26 letters? (The word "alphabet.")
28. What's invisible yet never out of sight? (The letter "i.")
29. What's the best way to carry water in a sieve? (Freeze it first.)
30. Add 10 to nothing & what kind of animal will it make (Ox.)
31. Why does a maroon car never pay a bridge toll? (Because the driver pays it!)

32. What stays **HOT** in the _refrigerator?_ (Horseradish, chilis, hot tamales, mustard, hot dogs, hot pastrami, chili sauce.)
33. What is the 1 thing you break when you say its name? (Silence.)
34. How many big men would you say have been born in *[the name of your city, town]* ? (None? only babies are born in_____.)

35. What's the easiest thing for a miser to part with? (A comb.)
36. Where can everyone always find "money" when he needs it? (In the dictionary.)
37. Where did Noah strike the 1st nail he put into the Ark? (On its head.)
38. What 3 letters will turn a girl into a woman? (A-G-E.)
39. What 8 letters will tell a girl named Ellen that she's pretty? (U-R-A-B-U-T-L-N.)
40. What 2 letters mean "not difficult"? (E-Z.)
41. What letter & number name an outdoor sport? (10-S.)
42. What are the 3 strongest letters in the alphabet? (N-R-G or TNT.)
43. What letter & number mean "conquered"? (B-10.)
44. What 2 letters spell "a wormlike fish"? (E-L.)
45. What 2 letters spell "to do better"? (X-L: excel.)
46. When a lady faints, what number will restore her? (You must bring her 2.)
47. Why is number 9 like a peacock? (Because without its tail it's nothing.)
48. What has 8 feet & sings? (A quartet.)
49. What animal never plays fair? (The cheetah.)
50. [Pull down the classroom wall map; point to it & ask:] Where are the Kings of England usually crowned?" (On the head.)
51. Name some times when a girl is not a girl. (When she's a dear [deer] or a bell [e] or a little pale [pail].)
52. What starts with a "t," ends with a "t," & in fact is full of "t"? (A teapot.)
53. What driver will *never* get a ticket? (A screwdriver.)
54. What does a person usually grow in his garden if he works very hard? (Tired.)
55. What word is usually pronounced incorrectly even by teachers? (The word "incorrectly," of course!)
56. What roof never keeps out the wet? (The roof of your mouth.)
57. What is the highest building in New York? (The N.Y.C. Public Library. It has, by far, the most stories!)
58. What man's business is best when it's dullest? (A knife & lawnmower sharpener.)
59. What is most remarkable about a yardstick? (Although it has neither a head nor a tail, it has a foot at either end & a third foot in its middle!)
60. What continent do you see when you look in the mirror in the morning? (You see Europe [you're up].)
61. What birds have 4 small feet & yellow feathers? (2 canaries.)
62. What kind of dog is a baseball dog? (Any dog that wears a muzzle, catches flies, chases fowls, & beats it home when he sees the catcher coming.)
63. Which is correct: "The yolk of an egg IS white" or "The yolk of an egg ARE white"? (Neither: the yolk of an egg is *yellow*!)

64. On which side of a church will you always find the cemetery? (On the outside.)
65. What 7 letters & a number did the Martian say when he met the little boy? (L-O-I-M-A-4-N-R.)
66. What Roman numeral can climb a wall? (I-V.)
67. What 4 letters would frighten a robber? (O-I-C-U.)
68. What has 100 legs & cannot walk? (50 pair of pants.)
69. I go out, but I can't come in; what am I? (A fire.)
70. What's the difference between an old dime & a brand new penny? (9¢.)
71. Why did the fly fly? ('Cause the spider spied her.)
72. What is ALWAYS behind time? (The back of a clock.)
73. How can you show that 1/2 of 12 = 7? (This way:)
74. Why is a man who runs a fish market likely to be stingy? (Because his business makes him sell fish [selfish].)
75. If butter is 50¢ a lb. in Chicago, what are window panes in Detroit? (Glass.)
76. If a mushroom is the smallest room in the world, what is the largest room in the world? (The room for improvement.)
77. Why is it dangerous to tell a secret on a farm? (Because the potatoes have eyes, the corn has ears & the beans talk [beanstalk]!)
78. What invention do we use to see through a wall? (A window.)
79. What is bigger when it's upside down? (The number 6.)
80. What is a bull called when it's sleeping? (A bulldozer.)
81. What did the jack say to the car? ("Can I give you a lift?")
82. What gallops down the road on its head? (A horseshoe nail.)
83. What starts with an E, ends with an E & only has 1 letter in it? (An envelope.)
84. What bird can lift the heaviest weights; (The crane.)
85. Name a liquid that *cannot* freeze? (Boiling water.)
86. What is the strongest creature for its size in the whole world? (The wasp: it can lift a 200 lb. man 3 feet off the ground.)
87. When is a ship at sea not on water? (When it's on fire.)
88. Why are fire engines red? (Fire engines are red because newspapers are read too and two & two are four; four times 3 is 12; 12 inches make a ruler; a famous ruler was Queen Elizabeth; The Queen Elizabeth sailed the ocean; the ocean is full of fish; fish have fins; the Finns fought the Russians; the Russians are Red—so fire engines are red because they're always rushin'!)
89. Why is a bad riddle like an unsharpened pencil? (Because it's dull & has no point.)
90. What in life is the end of everything? (The letter "g.")

Harder Riddles

1. An architect had a brother & the brother died; the man who died had no brother. Who was the architect? (A woman.)
2. What goes around a button? (A billy-goat. He goes around a' buttin'.')
3. What 2 good tunes make everybody happy? (Good cartoons & good fortunes.)
4. What's the difference between the sidewalk & a taxi? (Taxi-fare)
5. If your uncle's sister is not your aunt, what is she? (Your mother.)
6. Why is an empty purse always the same? (Because there's never any change in it.)
7. What has every person seen & will never see again? (Yesterday.)
8. What is put on the table, cut, but never eaten? (A deck of cards.)
9. [Pull down wall map & ask:] "Where does Thursday come before Wednesday?" (In the dictionary.)
10. Name the make of a car that tells what the woman said when she bought a hen. ("Chevrolet?" [She-ever-lay?])
11. Can you spell "happiness" in 3 letters? (X-T-C [ecstasy.])
12. Can you spell a funeral poem in 3 letters? (L-E-G [elegy].)
13. Can you spell a drug in 3 letters? (O-P-M [opium].)
14. What is skinny at the top, fat at the bottom & has ears? (Mountains.)
15. When is a sailor not a sailor? (When he's aboard ship.)
16. How can you show that 2/3 of 6 = 9? (This way: $\mathbf{SIX = IX}$.)
17. Why is a blotter like a lazy dog? (Because a blotter is an ink-lined plane, an inclined plane is a slope up, & a slow pup is a lazy dog!)
18. A father bought a ranch & presented it to his 3 sons. They planned to raise cattle for market, so they called the ranch "Focus." Why was this an appropriate name for their ranch? [*Note to teacher: Try to elicit the definition of "focus" from your group, i.e.,: It's the bringing of the rays of light together," etc.*] (Focus—That's where the sun's rays meet! [That's where the sons raise meat!])
19. Why didn't Moses take any bees into the Ark? (Because he hadn't been born yet; it was NOAH who took the creatures into the Ark.)
20. Can you think of a sentence in which all of these words are used: defeat, deduct, defense, detail? (Defeat of deduct went over defence before detail.)
21. What's the greatest riddle in the world? (Life: because in the end we all have to give up on it.)

Once shared with the class as a whole, the riddle cards might be stacked on a table at the back of the room where they may be re-read & shared during free time.

Science

Children can learn a good deal by watching the day-to-day growth of plants in their classroom; plants grow from different beginnings—seeds, cuttings, tubers, bulbs; but plants follow a definite pattern of growth. Baby plants will grow to be like the adult plants. Plants have different temperatures & require various amounts of water, sunshine, warmth & different types of soil. You can stock your classroom nursery with a variety of plants & at no expense; here's how.

Apple seeds. Seeds are not ready to be planted directly from the fruit. Put the seeds in a jar with damp moss. Refrigerate for 6 weeks (mark removal date on your classroom calendar). Turn them over periodically until they begin to sprout. Then fill a small pot with potting compost. Plant seed 1/2" down in compost. Keep in light, warm room. Keep moist.

Avocado pit. Place pit, round end down, in a small jar. Fill jar with water so that round end only is submerged. Then wait (for perhaps even 2-3 months). Keep adding water as it evaporates. When pit looks slimy & even moldy, do not despair; roots should appear any time. When root is 1/2" long, plant pit in a medium sized pot. Water it well when it is dry & give it food tablets from time to time.

Birdseed. Sprinkle on top of rich soil & then cover with 1/4" more of soil. Keep it moist!

Beet. Cut to within 1" of its top, retaining leaves. Trim foliage back. Plant beet top in sandy soil. Keep moist, not wet.

Broadbeans. Soak 2-3 hours until they swell. Cut & roll a piece of blotting paper & line a 1-2 lb. jam jar up to the mouth with the paper. Place bean about 1/2 way down between jar & paper. Pour 1" of water into jar. See that blotter remains WET. Place jar in dark cupboard until beans germinate, then bring jar into the light. (If you use 2 jars, placing 1 in cupboard & leaving 1 in the light, children will see which grows faster. Do they know why?) Lay sprouting beans on soil. Keep it moist.

Carrot. Cut, retaining 1" of foliage & 1" of root; set in a shallow dish filled with 1/2" of water. Add tiny pieces of charcoal to keep water sweet, or trim foliage; cut root 2" from top & hollow out center; hang upside down like a basket. Keep filled with water.

Corn. As a child in Illinois, my mother was taught to plant corn in this manner: "When sowing corn, plant 5 grains: 1 for the blackbird, 1 for the crow, 1 for the meal worm, & 1 won't grow."

Date Seeds. These need lots of room. Plant seed in sandy soil. When roots outgrow pot, break out bottom of pot & plant in a bigger pot.

Grapes. Dry seeds. Put 1/2" of clean pebbles in the bottom of a pot. Mix 1 part humus, 2 parts potting soil & a handful of vermiculite. Put in pot. Water, allowing soil to settle. Plant 12 seeds 1/2" deep. Keep soil damp. Place pot where it will get just 1-2 hrs. of direct sun each day—until vine is 7" tall. Put a re-enforcing stick beside vine for it to climb.

Grapefruit seeds. These do best if planted in February, I've read. You can use the grapefruit shell filled with potting soil & sand as the seed's initial holder. Soak seed overnight before planting. Sink soil down close about seed. Later transfer young plant to a sturdier container. The plant may grow for years. Keep earth moist by spraying with water every day. Also water twice a week.

Kumquats. (See lemon seeds.)

Lemon seeds. Cover with 1/2" sand & potting soil, after having soaked the seeds overnight. Keep earth moist (as described for *grapefruit*).

Lentils. Spread in single layer in a saucer. Moisten, but don't float lentils. Keep moist & in the sun. In 10 days they sprout & can be planted like beans.

Mango seeds. These are difficult to start as they, like the avocado, are slow in sprouting. Press seed into soil flat side down. Keep soil moist.

Oats. Can be started in the following way: Line the bottom of a pie tin with small stones. Add a layer of rich earth, then lay oats on top of earth. Cover oats with layer of fine soil. Cover entire top of pan with thin cloth (gauze); set in a sunny window. Sprinkle cloth with water each day. Oats should sprout on 3rd day. Remove cloth at this time. Keep soil moist.

Onion. Place pointed end up, in a small-mouthed jar. Cover 1/2 of onion with water. Add small amounts of charcoal to water.

Orange seeds. (See lemon seeds.)

Peach seeds. (See apple seeds.)

Pepper seeds. These seeds, from tiny red peppers in pickling spice, are spread out to dry on a paper towel. Punch small holes for drainage in the bottom of cottage cheese container. Fill container with soil. Barely cover seeds with soil. Keep soil moist.

Pineapple. Cut off 1 1/2"-2" from top of plant. Retain spiky foliage. Allow pineapple to dry for 3 days, then place in sandy soil. Water lightly. Keep as warm as possible. In about 2 weeks (if roots have grown), re-pot in good sterilized soil. Keep soil damp, warm & near light. Your plant won't bear, but it is attractive.

Potato Porcupine. Slice off the top of an Irish potato. Carve out a hole, leaving plenty of meat on the walls. Insert 4 toothpicks as legs. Make eyes by attaching two small white paper circles with black map tacks. Fill cavity with earth (or moist cotton) sprinkled with grass seed. Keep watered for 10 days until Porky's spines sprout.

Plum. (See apple seeds.)

Pumpkin. (See pepper seeds.)

Sweet potato. Some are heat-dried & won't grow so ask grocer for a *fresh* one. If possible choose one with a few whiskers. Cut potato in 1/2. Insert toothpicks around potato below cut surface. Place potato, tapered end down, in a jar, suspended by means of toothpicks. Fill jar with water. Put jar in closet until roots sprout, then bring plant into the light. Plant will sustain itself on water for a long while, or you may plant the potato in soil, allowing green sprouts to remain above earth.

Squash. Follow directions for pepper seeds, except press squash seeds down 3/4" into soil.

Watermelon seeds. Plant directly in soil. Sprinkle lightly & often with water. Seeds sprout quickly & plant has abundant foliage. Continue watering as mentioned.

White potato. Cut into sections, each section containing an eye or two. Plant in rich earth & keep moistened. Let it have lots of sun.

Yam. Choose one that has purple eyes. Then follow directions for sweet potato.

Free seed catalogs to help children become better acquainted with a variety of plants:

W. Atlee Burpee Co.   Wayside Gardens Co.
Riverside, Calif. 92502   Mentor, Ohio 44060
                             ($2.00, credited toward purchase)

Older children may enjoy learning about herbs & plants that are less common. Free catalogs are available from:

Nichols Herbs & Rare Seeds   Meadowbrook Herb Gardens
1190 N. Pacific Highway   Wyoming, R.I. 02898
Albany, Ore. 97321

Information on carnivorous plants & terrarium sets:

Armstrong Associates, Inc.
Box 127
Basking Ridge, N.J. 07920.

January Art

Printmaking. The most basic types of prints are made by applying ink to a flat surface (i.e., a carrot sliced in 1/2), & then pulling a print (see Page 42). Children could compile Print Samplers, experimenting, searching for unusual surface possibilities.

Rubbings. These are easy to execute. Tape or firmly hold a piece of lightweight strong paper atop a rough surface. Rub the entire piece of paper with a carpenter's pencil, crayon, or liquid shoe polish on a cotton wad in the toe of a child's sock. VARIATION: Apply a rich wash of diluted poster paint atop a crayon rubbing. VARIATION: Cut several rubbings into pieces. Make a collage of these pieces. Colored construction paper might also be used in this collage.

Monoprints. Prepare the materials for making monoprints & then hand out the following mimeos: (Let the children read these to themselves.)

"Clear off the desk (table) in front of you. Be sure you have enough room in which to work. Lay down a large piece of plastic wrap* and tape it smoothly to the desk. Get some starch** and pour 1/3 cup onto the plastic wrap. Return the starch. Decide on the color of paint you wish to use and *carefully* sprinkle a bit of dry powder paint onto your starch. Return the paint. Take some sheets of white paper to your desk. Now ──────────▶
Roll up your sleeves to the elbow. With *one* hand mix the starch

---

*Plastic produce bags, free at markets, may be slit, opened out flat & used in place of costly plastic wrap.

**This may be a commercial liquid starch (shake bottle WELL). Or you may prepare it at home the previous evening (from cornstarch) & bring it to class in plastic containers. (Keep starch quite dilute.)

& paint together. Try drawing in it. Use different parts of your hand & see what kinds of effects you can get. When you are happy with what you've done, take a sheet of paper (with your *dry* hand, of course) & lay it carefully on top of the starch-drawing. Pick up 1 corner of the paper & pull it sm-o-o-o-o-thly toward the opposite corner & off the starch. Turn the paper over & look at your results. Lay this print on the floor against the wall (where the newspapers are laid) at the back of the room. Try taking another print off the same starch by rubbing your hand in the starch and making a *new* picture or design. Or pull several prints off the same starch pattern.

When you're ready to clean up, untape the plastic wrap, roll it into a ball & place it in the waste can. Carefully wipe off the desk (and floor?) with a paper towel. Wash your hands & then read quietly or write a short story about an adventure that one of your monoprints might illustrate."

Linoleum block prints. (For older students.) Make an outline of linoleum block on tracing paper; draw your design within it. Turn your design over onto the linoleum surface of the block. Trace over the lines, pressing heavily so that the reverse of your design appears on block. Carve out all areas of block which you do not want to show on your finished print. Remember only the raised areas will take ink. Squeeze block-printing ink onto a small pane of glass. Roll brayer* back & forth through the ink until brayer is well coated. Roll brayer across face of block so that your design is fully inked. Carefully place paper on block; rub paper with spoonback or heel of hand to print design. Keep paper from moving. Starting at one corner, slowly peel the paper off toward the diagonally opposite corner. Allow ink to dry completely.

Prints from styro-foam meat trays. These are made by cutting or scratching design into foam tray. Ink is supplied & print taken as described above.

Veneer print-making. Described on page 37.

Felt block-printing. Children draw a basic design on paper. This is cut out & rubber cemented firmly to a piece of felt (from an old hat, etc.) & when dry, is carefully cut out with scissors. Trace around this basic design on the top of a scrap block of

---

*A brayer is a small hand roller used to spread ink thinly & evenly over surface of block.

wood. (Lumber yards are often happy to save such hand-sized blocks of scrap wood for you.) Apply rubber cement to *entire* paper-side of felt; apply glue or rubber cement to *entire* inner area of design drawn on wood block. When both rubber-cemented surfaces are dry, press felt to top of wood. Firmly attach felt to wood. Using a large (stencil) brush, apply poster-paint to felt design. Place paper to be printed atop a pad of newspapers. Then, holding paper in place, firmly press felt onto paper.

Foam-tape block-printing. Follow above instructions except use adhesive-backed foam-tape (used for weather-stripping). Child draws outline of a simple design on face of block; tape is pressed directly onto outline. Pour poster paint into flat cooky sheet; dip foam into paint & then stamp design onto paper. Child experiments with repetition of design & use of more than one color of paint at a time.

Silkscreen prints. Can be made by very young children in the following way: Purchase small (4"-6" in diameter) embroidery hoops. Cut old nylon hose into pieces & stretch these taut in the hoops. Each child either cuts from newsprint a simple shape smaller than the hoop itself or, with wax crayon, draws directly onto the nylon, being sure to press firmly enough so as to fill the mesh with crayon. A tiny scraper, a "squeegee" (that can easily fit within hoop), is cut from a heavy cardboard. Thick poster-paint (or a liquid starch & powdered tempera mixture) is applied to the screen with a spoon. Use the squeegee to firmly scrape the paint over the crayon drawing & through the mesh of the nylon. If a cut-out paper shape is used, place it between the nylon & the paper to be printed. The paint, when applied with the squeegee, will adhere the cut-out to the screen, producing a negative image on the paper.

Older children can use this more advanced type of screen: Cut a window in a cardboard box lid or base. Stretch & staple slightly dampened cotton organdy or an old marquisette curtain over the outside. Keep material taut, placing 1 staple in the center of each side before stapling all around. On the inside of box tape the edge of the window to the material. Seal all the edges with masking or paper tape. Coat all sides of the box with the shellac. Child makes a design no bigger than the window, then he places the screen over the design. He proceeds to block out with a wax crayon all areas that are not to receive paint: he does this by thoroughly filling in the fabric's mesh. (Or he may place a dampened cut-out of newsprint under the screen as described in the preceding paragraph.) Child places his screen on paper to be printed. At top of screen pour a generous amount of finger paint. Using a cardboard squeegee slightly smaller than the window, at a 45° angle, the child draws the paint firmly across the full length of the screen. If he wants a 2-color print, he marks guide lines on the paper being printed for registering the 2nd screen. He then prepares a 2nd screen, identical in size to the 1st. From a sheet of newsprint the size of the window, he cuts away that part of the design that he wants printed a 2nd color. Screen is registered over 1st print, & 2nd color (which holds newsprint to screen) is applied.

January P.E.

Indoor games for January. Often the weather this month doesn't permit outdoor play. Here are some games to be played indoors.

Memory. Put an assorted collection of objects on a table, i.e., scissors, cork, comb, spoon, thimble, pen. Children observe objects for 2 minutes, after which a cloth is spread over objects & children see how many objects they are now able to list. Additional credit may be given for correct spelling. After lists are completed & objects uncovered, discuss different methods children used in order to recall objects, what tricks (i.e., counting number of objects on display) help a person remember large groups of things?

Nursery Rhyme Charades. Divide class into "acting companies." Let each child decide on a nursery rhyme & then act it out for others to try to identify. Pantomime & dialogue may be used if necessary. VARIATION: A fairy tale is chosen & child acts out a portion of the story (not the entire tale).

Who's the Leader? Players stand in a circle. "It" leaves the room. A leader is chosen. All children begin clapping until "It" returns & goes to the center of the circle. "It" tries to discover who is leading the group in its actions. Children try to imitate the leader's frequent changes of action (hopping on 1 foot, turning around, patting his head, etc.). At the same time children try NOT to be caught obviously looking at the leader. Once the identity of the leader is discovered, he becomes "It" & leaves room. A new leader is chosen & game continues.

Macaroni-Baloney. Dump a bag of alphabet macaroni onto the middle of a table, or distribute tiny paper cups of macaroni, 1 to each child. A topic is announced (animals, fruits, people, places) & each child tries to spell a suitable answer. After a certain time, children share their answers. Originality & correct spelling are verbally rewarded. Spelling errors should be unobtrusively corrected.

Geometric Figure-Fun. Children are shown, on the chalkboard, geometric figures such as triangle, pentagon, circle, rectangle, octagon, square; children design animals & figures or objects using ONLY geometric figures. Whole landscapes or cities may develop; perhaps a chronicle of these new worlds might also be created.

Mix & Match. Children are given a list of 10 capitals, inventions, historic deeds, etc. Children write in the corresponding state, inventor or historic figure. Additional information given is worth extra points. Any logical answer is correct (i.e., S.F.B. Morse OR Arthur Vail might be written in to correspond with "the telegraph"). The out-of-the-ordinary answer demonstrates real creative thinking & should be encouraged at every turn.

Categories. Hold up a card on which 1 letter of the alphabet is printed. Call out a category (i.e., plant, animal, country). First person to name object with that 1st initial gets the card. If he can spell the word, he retains the card intact; if unable to spell the word, he gets 1/2 of card & child with correct spelling of word gets the remaining 1/2.

Headlines. (A game for older children.) Cut out several newspaper headlines. Separate words & mix them up in a pile. Divide children into groups of 4 or 5. Each group takes 3-5 words from pile & arranges these in any order as to form a kind of plot around which they develop a short (5 min.) play or pantomime. An "announcer" may give a brief build-up before the presentation. Emphasize that ANY usage of words is acceptable.

January Balloon Puppets

Blow up a balloon. Firmly tie knot in end. Tie a 2" string to balloon. Using liquid starch & thin strips of newspaper, cover balloon with papier mâché. Hang balloon by string to dry; this may take several days. When dry, tape cardboard or tagboard to balloon to build up features. Cover entire head with papier mâche, using paper toweling strips & liquid starch. Hang up to dry. When dry, paint with·poster paints. When these are dry, lightly spray with Varathane. Add hair, eyes, hat, etc. Deflate balloon. Simple 2-seamed cloth body is stapled or glued securely within neck of balloon puppet.

February

February brings the rain,
Thaws the frozen lake again.

1   1st Supreme Court Meeting, 1790.
    Victor Herbert (1859-1924), American composer of light
      operas.
2   Groundhog Day.
3   Felix Mendelssohn (1809-1847), German composer.
    Elizabeth Blackwell (1821-1910), 1st U.S. female doctor.
      She applied to 29 medical schools before being accepted.
4   Charles A. Lindbergh (1902-   ), American aviator: 1st to
      make solo transatlantic flight.
5   Roger Williams (1603 [?]-1683), American teacher; founder
      of Rhode Island.
6   George "Babe" Ruth (1895-1948), American baseball
      player.
7   Charles Dickens (1812-1870), English novelist.
    Sinclair Lewis (1885-1951), American novelist.
8   Jules Verne (1828-1905), French writer of science-fiction
      romances.
9   William H. Harrison (1773-1841), 9th U.S. President.
    U.S. Weather Service established: 1870.
10 Charles Lamb (1775-1834), English essayist.
    Boris Pasternak (1890-1960), Russian poet, novelist.
    Race Relations Sunday: 1st day in week in which we
      celebrate Lincoln's birthday.
11 Daniel Boone (1734-1820), American frontiersman.
    Thomas A. Ed son (1847-1931), American inventor; holder
        of   00 p tents.

12   Abraham Lincoln (1809-1865), 16th U.S. President.
      Charles Darwin (1809-1882), English naturalist.
13   Grant Wood (1892-1942), American painter.
14   St. Valentine's Day (the day of his death, more than 1700
         years ago).
15   Galileo Galilei (1564-1642), Italian scientist.
      Cyrus McCormick (1809-1884), American inventor of the
         reaper.
      Susan B. Anthony (1820-1906), American feminist.
16   Ulysses S. Grant (1822-1885) forced the surrender of Con-
         federate troops at Fort Donelson in 1862.
18   Alessandro Volta (1745-1827), Italian physicist.
      Planet Pluto discovered by Clyde Tombaugh on photo-
         graphs he took 1/23-1/29, 1930.
      National Brotherhood Week.
19   Nicolaus Copernicus (1473-1543), Polish astronomer.
      Thomas Edison patented the phonograph, 1878.
20   U.S. Mail Service established, 1792.
      Lt. Col John Glenn, in "Friendship," was 1st American to
         orbit Earth: 1960.
21   Constantin Brancusi (1876-1957), Rumanian abstract sculp-
         tor.
      W.H. Auden (1907-   ), Anglo-American poet.
      Malcolm X day.
22   George Washington (1732-1799), 1st U.S. President. His
         birthday is celebrated on the 3rd Mon. in Feb. as directed
         by the Mon. Holiday Bill.
      Frederic Chopin (1810-1849), Polish composer ("Butterfly
         Etude" & "Funeral March:" Sonata Opus 35, B flat
         minor).
23   George Frederick Handel (1685-1759), British composer
         ("The Cuckoo & the Nightingale").
      Winslow Homer (1836-1910), American marine artist.
24   Wilhelm Grimm (1786-1863), German writer of children's
         stories.
25   Pierre Auguste Renoir (1841-1919), French impressionist
         painter.
      U.S. Income Tax established 1913.
26   Wm. Cody [Buffalo Bill] (1846-1917), American scout.
      John Steinbeck (1902-1969), American writer: *East of
      Eden, Cannery Row.*

27   Gioacchino Rossini (1792-1868), Italian composer.
      Henry Wadsworth Longfellow (1807-1882), American poet:
         "Hiawatha," "Courtship of Miles Standish."
29   Leap Year Day: occurs every 4th year.
      Purim: The Feast of Lots (February or March). It is a
         celebration of the casting of the lots which showed
         Haman to be evil and Esther to be good. The children
         often give plays commemorating the story of Esther; they
         dress up as Queen Esther, her uncle Mordecai, the villain
         Haman and the good King Ahasveros.

February

The name comes from the Latin word *februa*, an instrument of
purification which was used by the ancient Romans on Feb. 15th. This
was a day of atonement & ceremonial feasting. Numa, the legendary
2nd King of Rome, is said to have introduced February into the Roman
calendar.

FEBRUARY QUOTATIONS

4   I saw a fleet of fishing boats . . . I flew down almost
      touching the craft and yelled at them asking if I was on the
      right road to Ireland. They just stared. Maybe they didn't
      hear me. Maybe I didn't hear them. Or maybe they
      thought I was a crazy fool. An hour later I saw land.—
      Charles Lindbergh

11   Results! Why, man, I have gotten a lot of results. I know
      several thousand things that won't work.

      I never did anything worth doing by accident, nor did any
      of my inventions come by accident, they came by work.
                                                    —T.A. Edison

12   No man has a good enough memory to be a good liar.

      To sin by silence, makes cowards of men.

      Die when I may, I want it said of me to those who knew me
      best, that I always plucked a thistle and planted a flower
      where I thought a flower would grow.
                                                    —A. Lincoln

13   The only good ideas I ever had I got while milking a
      cow.—Grant Wood.

15   Yet it *does* move. (Attributed to Galileo when being forced to recant his doctrine that the earth moves around the sun.)

Modern invention has banished the spinning wheel, & the same law of progress makes the woman of today different from her grandmother.

I am a full and firm believer in the revelation that it is through women that the race is to be redeemed.

(1875)—Susan B. Anthony

16   Everyone has his superstitions. One of mine has always been when I start to go anywhere, or to do anything, never to turn back or to stop until the thing intended is accomplished.—Ulysses S. Grant

18   (Nat'l. Brotherhood Week)

How wonderful it is, how pleasant for God's people to live together like brothers. (Psalms)

I am not an Athenian, nor a Greek, but a citizen of the world.—Socrates

The world is my country, all mankind are my brethren, and to do good is my religion.—Thomas Paine

Our true nationality is mankind.—H.G. Wells *(The Outline of History)*

20   Neither snow, nor rain, nor heat, nor gloom of night stays these couriers from the swift completion of their appointed rounds.—Herodotus (inscription on the N.Y.C. Post Office)

21   Mankind's history has proved from one era to another that the true criterion of leadership is spiritual. Men are attracted by spirit. By power, men are *forced.* Love is engendered by spirit. By power, anxieties are created.

I just want to read it [the manuscript of his autobiography] 1 more time because I don't expect to read it in finished form.

For the freedom of my 22,000,000 black brothers and sisters here in America, I do believe that I have fought the best that I knew how and the best that I could with the shortcomings that I have had.

—Malcolm X *(Autobiography of Malcolm X)*

22   Liberty, when it begins to take root, is a plant of rapid growth. (Letter to James Madison 3/2/1788)

     I hope I shall always possess firmness and virtue, enough to maintain that which I consider the most enviable of all titles, the character of an "Honest Man."

                   —G. Washington: *Moral Maxims*

27   The cares that infest the day
Shall fold their tents, like the Arabs,
And silently steal away.

                   —Henry W. Longfellow

     Give me a laundry-list and I'll set it to music.—Gioacchino Rossini

FEBRUARY EVENTS

• **Groundhog Day**   [2]

     The woodchuck, or groundhog, is a small, blackish-gray North American rodent. It was given this name by the Pilgrims when they arrived in America, as it lived in the woods & reminded them of the hedgehogs back in England. They also gave the groundhog the responsibility of the hedgehog on February 2nd—that of predicting the date of spring. Tradition dictates that on the morning of Feb. 2nd the groundhog comes up out of his hole & looks about. If the day is cold & cloudy, he decides that spring will be here soon & he emerges from his hole. If, however, it is a bright clear day, the sun will cause his shadow to be cast—& one look at his shadow sends the groundhog back into his hole & continued hibernation for 6 more weeks, at the end of which time it really *will* be spring.

     Discuss briefly with your class: How are traditions like this born? What are some probable reasons for such a tradition?

     Science. Does the groundhog really come out on Feb. 2nd? Research done at Pennsylvania State University over a period of 5 years & involving 4,000 groundhogs showed that a great number of groundhogs *were* seen out of their burrows on Jan. 31, Feb. 1st, 2nd, & 3rd. Other scientists state that Feb. 2nd is the middle of winter for a groundhog & so his hibernation should be at the deepest point. If he is seen above ground, it must be accidental, they say; he may have awakened to relieve himself. Scientists disagree on the answer, which indicates that more research on hibernation is in order.

• Birth of Jules Verne   [8]

In honor of the Father of Science Fiction, Jules Verne, let your class create fantastic stories based on 1 of the following topics. Emphasize how the inclusion of detailed descriptions is essential to any good science fiction story.

1. Make up a story surrounding the invention of some modern-day device (laser beam, atomic sub, rocket).

2. You have won a contest that allows you to travel FREE to any planet (known or unknown). Write about your choice, preparations (food, money, health precautions), take-off, weather, landing, the period of exploration, escape, rescue (capture), return trip, documentation of trip (samples of vegetation, soil; photographs), reception in America. This might be written in the form of a journal dated 2073 A.D.

3. Invent a country (or island, secret tower, room, attic, cave). Name it, after yourself, perhaps (i.e., Smithland or Smithtania). Describe its people, animals, plants, weather. What is of importance there? Do people live there? Why doesn't anyone else know of its existence? What do the people do? What do they believe? How are they similar to or different from Americans? Do they know about us? What do they think about us?

4. You have a friend from outer space. No one else knows about him (e.g., they can't see him, or they do not recognize him as an alien). You like each other very much. Tell about some adventures you have together. Tell how your friendship finally ends—if it *has* ended!

5. What discoveries (&/or inventions) would you most like to see by 2001 A.D.? Tell an imaginary story of how they came about.

• Birth of Sir Francis Beaufort   [9]

More than 150 years ago a British admiral, Sir Francis Beaufort, constructed the 1st practical anemometer & devised the Beaufort scale which appears below. An anemometer measures the force of wind which depends on the speed of air.

Beaufort Scale

No.	Description	Noticeable Effect on Land	Speed in m.p.h.
0	calm	smokes rises vertically	0
1	light air	wind direction shown by drift of smoke	1-3
2	slight breeze	wind felt on face: leaves rustle; flags stir	4-7

3	gentle breeze	leaves & twigs in constant motion: wind extends light flags	8-12
4	moderate "	dust & small branches moved; flags flap	13-18
5	fresh "	small trees in leaf begin to sway; flags ripple	19-24
6	strong "	large branches in motion: flags beat	25-31
7	moderate gale	whole trees in motion: flags extended	32-38
8	fresh "	twigs break off trees: walking is hindered	39-46
9	strong "	slight structural damage to houses	47-54
10	whole "	trees uprooted; much structural damage to houses	55-63
11	storm	widespread damage	64-75
12	hurricane	excessive damage	over 75

Word etymology. You know how a far-off hill can look like a cloud & clouds often have a hill-like quality. In Old English "cloud" was spelled "clud" & meant "a hill"! Typhoon comes from Chinese "tai-fong" which means "a great wind." Hurricane is from "huracan," a Caribbean word for "an evil spirit."

Science. Check with stores that carry balloons that are to be filled with helium. (Inquire at your local Army/Navy Surplus store to see if they have weather balloons available.) Have each child fill out an index card stating his name, age, date of launching & reason for launching. Have him ask who found the balloon, where, when, & how recovery was made. Have child put this card & a self-addressed (to school) postcard in a tiny plastic bag. Choose a day rating a No. 6 on the Beaufort Scale on which to launch your balloons. Obtain a tank of helium from a welding shop (look under "Gas-Industrial" in the yellow pages of your phone book). Each child gets a length of sturdy string. He ties his plastic package carefully & securely to one end of this string. As a balloon is filled, its end is tied in a firm knot & the free end of 1 of the children's strings is securely tied to the knot.

Bulletin board display. A fascinating display will develop as the post cards begin arriving. Thank-you notes can be written in which the children mention different places their balloons were found, mileage records, & what they have been learning in class about winds.

Information sources:

U.S. Weather Bureau
8060 13th St.
Silver Springs, Md. 20910

American Meteorological Society
45 Beacon St.
Boston, Mass. 02108

• Birth of Thomas A. Edison   [11]

Thomas Alva Edison was an inventor. He worked in his workshop. He worked in his laboratory. He worked in his mind. When he got an idea he looked at it from all sides. He never said, "That can't be done." When he was searching for the right material to burn in a light bulb, he tried *6,000* different things before he found the one he wanted! In addition to the electric light bulb, he invented the phonograph & motion pictures! Thomas Edison changed the world!

Word etymology. *Phonograph* is a Greek derivative meaning "sound-writing." ("Phonograph; *n.* A vibrating toy that restores life to dead noises." Ambrose Bierce, from his *Devil's Dictionary*.)

• Birth of Abraham Lincoln   [12]

Lincoln, six feet one in his stocking feet,
The lank man, knotty and tough as a hickory nail,
Whose hands were always too big for white-kid gloves,
Whose wit was a coonskin sack of dry, tall tales.
Whose weathered face was homely as a plowed field.
                                     —S.V. Benet*

Older students may enjoy this Lincoln's Day quiz:

How many of the following can you find on a Lincoln penny?

(1) a small animal (hair=hare); (2) a messenger (one sent=one sent); (3) a flower (two lips=tulips); (4) yourself (eye=I); (5) a drink (T=tea); (6) submarine (under the "C"=sea); (7) a snake (copperhead); (8) a fruit (date); (9) a part of a river (mouth); (10) a sacred building (temple); (11) long lines of soldiers (columns); (12) a part of the foot (arch); (13) result of game in which 2 teams have=score (tie); (14) an application of paint (coat); (15) a whole cob of corn (ear); (16) part of the mouth (roof); (17) a vehicle *(e pluriBUS unim);* (18) what Patrick Henry wanted (liberty); (19) a country (United States); (20) a statement of faith (In God we trust).

To assist them, you might explain that the answers to 1-6 are homonyms, 7-17 are nouns with more than 1 definition, 18-20 are straight (?) answers to the questions.

*From Rosemary Carr & Stephen Benet, *A Book of Americans* (383 Madison Ave., N.Y. 10017, Holt, Rinehart & Winston, Inc., 1933). © Holt Rinehart & Winston, Inc. Reprinted by permission of the publisher.

Etymology. Ancient Roman law prescribed a ceremony for the purchase of slaves: the new master laid his hand upon the slave's head. This was to fulfill the law of *mancipium:* "possession by the hand." Since *e* in Latin means "away," & *capio* means "taken," our word *emancipation* means "the master takes his hand off the emancipated slave."

"Freedom" comes from Old English & is related to a Norse word for "love & peace."

Information source: Lincoln Funeral Poster, Gettysburg Address in Lincoln's writing, Lincoln portrait formed from shading Emancipation Proclamation, & many other reproductions of Lincoln memorabilia are available from:

Pioneer Historical Society
Harriman, Tenn. 37748

The catalog, which costs 25¢, lists their many unusual, eccentric publications.

- **Birth of Darwin   [12]**

The Darwinian theory of evolution holds that "all species of plants & animals developed from earlier forms by hereditary transmission of slight variations in successive generations." Surviving forms are those best adapted to the environment, e.g., survival of the fittest, or natural selection.

Two boys once thought they'd play a trick on Darwin. They carefully glued together several parts of different insects; they attached the head of a bee to the body of a butterfly & they glued to this the legs of a grasshopper. They took it to the famous naturalist & asked, "Do you know what kind of a bug this is?" Darwin examined the creature for a moment & then he asked, "Did it hum when you caught it?" "Yes, yes," the boys answered, thinking they'd fooled the famous man. "It's just what I thought," Darwin replied, "a humbug!"

- **St. Valentine's Day   [14]**

Valentinus was a Christian priest during the days of the Roman Emperor Claudius II. It was a crime at that time to give aid or comfort to Christians. Valentinus was a good & kindly man, helping anyone in need. He was jailed by the Emperor & sentenced to death. Valentinus is credited with restoring the sight of the jailer's blind daughter, & according to legend & history, on the eve of his execution, Valentinus sent a farewell note to the little girl.

He signed it "From your Valentine." He was executed Feb. 14, 270 A.D. The practice of sending valentines grew out of an old belief extant even in Chaucer's day that birds began to mate on Feb. 14 & so this was an appropriate day for sending lovers' tokens. It is from Roman mythology that we have little Dan Cupid with his arrows dipped in love potion.

Bulletin board suggestions. A self-service post office makes a utilitarian display. Have each child paint a shoe box with white, pink, or red poster paints. Children stand shoe boxes upright & decorate them to look like mailboxes. Sturdy paper tabs for hanging are stapled to the insides of the top & bottom of box. A mail slit is cut in each box. Child's name appears near slit. Stapling these mailboxes in rows along a bulletin board facilitates the delivery of cards, cuts down on comparisons, & the bulletin board looks smashing!

Appropriate topics for bulletin boards this month include: "Valentine's Day Science" (information on the dove, the bluebird, flowers [forget-me-nots], the mechanics & function of the heart), "Let's Learn about Cupid" (historical, mythological background), "The Art of Archery" (examples of different types of quivers, arrows, bows, history of this sport, comic-relief by Dan Cupid shown making [in]appropriate remarks).

Language Arts

Ask older children to see how many compound words they, either individually or as a group, can list that incorporate the word "heart" (i.e., heartfelt, heartless, heartache, hearty, hearth).

Perhaps during your class party the students could try making words from the letters in the word "Valentine." Here are 89 possibilities:

vain, vale, valet, valiant, van, vane, vat, veal, veil, vein, vital, vine,
vie, vile, Vienne, Venetia, Venetian, venal, venial, vent, vial, a, ale,
ali, alien, aline, alit, Alvin, Ann, an, Anne, ant, Aventine, ate,
anvil, Lee, Lea, Lianne, let, late, lie, lone, Latin, lean, linen, lint,
enliven, let, live, alive, Elaine, Nat, Eve, Levi, Eli, Eva, Etna, net,
neat, nave, navel, native, naive, nail, evil, event, even, entail, elite,
elate; AND: ani, ante, Atli, len, Levant, lateen, lave, liane, lien,
linn, linnet, vail, vela, velate, vina, ventail, anile, anil.

With your class discuss St. Valentine & what a valentine
symbolizes (a message of love, laughter). Talk about the value of a
valentine as a form of communication (discuss making an appropriate one for your principal, Room Mother, etc.). With older
students you may criticize comic valentines, talk about their
probable origins, purposes they served (as a reaction to the
embarrassment at feeling affection for someone of the other sex,
or as an outlet for hostility). Ask older students when they feel
one should stop observing this day. Find out why they feel this
way.

An appropriate haiku (see pg. 171), written by her child,
would make a lovely valentine for Mother.

Convalescent patients, especially if they are elderly, would
appreciate receiving handmade cards today.

Word etymology. *"Cupid"* is from Latin *cupido* (desire,
passion). Our words *"friend"* & *"free"* probably both stem from
one Indo-European base which means "to be fond of, hold dear,"
as the basic sense of "free" is probably "dear to (i.e., akin to) the
chief" &, therefore, "not enslaved." The word *"flirt"* dates back
to the 16th century! The early Frisian word for "a giddy girl" was
"flirtje." It is also strongly influenced by the French word
"fleureter" which means "to touch lightly; to move from flower
to flower."

Vocabulary enrichment words: devotion, flirtatious,
betrothal, affectionate, quiver, amorous, passionate, friendship.

A riddle for Valentine's Day: Why is your heart like a policeman?
(Because it usually follows a regular beat.)

Poetry

My Valentine
I will make you brooches and toys
for your delight

Or bird song at morning and starshine at night.
I will make a palace fit for you and me,
  Of green days in forests
  And blue days at sea.

—Robert Louis Stevenson

Also appropriate:

A Red Red Rose: Robert Burns
How Do I Love Thee: Elizabeth Barrett Browning

Reading (To review rhyming words & give aural practice:)

"Where's Your Heart?" Pass out to each child in the reading group a paper heart. These have been made by pasting together 2 pink, orange, red or white hearts of equal size. Between the 2 hearts is placed a slip of paper on which is printed a simple request, i.e., "Act like a frog." The children sit in a circle & the 1st child says to the child on his right: "Tell me, where's your heart?" The 2nd child answers with any ending he likes, i.e., "My heart's in a deep blue lake." The 1st child must now give a response that rhymes with "lake," i.e., "Well, don't let it get eaten by a snake." Each questioner is allowed ample time to come up with a rhyme (use an egg-timer as a guide), & then if he cannot think of one, he is told that this must really "break his heart." Whereupon he tears open his heart shape, reads the request (to himself) & fulfills it. Game continues.

Valentine's Day Art

Room decorations. Valentine banners offer a pleasant change from the usual Feb. 14th room decor. Students may paint with water color directly onto long strips of rice paper. VARIATION: Printing stamps are cut from a sponge or a potato. These are dipped in liquid tempera & printed on white or colored lengths of tissue or newsprint paper. VARIATION: Very basic shapes are cut from a variety of finger-painted & construction papers. These may be glued atop one another & then to a length of rice or newsprint paper. VARIATION: Colored tissue paper shapes are cut out & pressed with a warm iron between 2 long narrow strips of wax paper. A short dowel is glued or stapled to top & bottom of each banner. A small copper tack is inserted into each end of the top dowel. A short string is tied from these. A longer dowel, or straight stick for carrying the banner, may be tied to the string as shown, or banners may simply be hung from the strings. Hang these banners so that the light will shine through them. Hang them in festive groupings or clusters when possible.

Why not let each child make a dove. These doves, as a group, can be suspended in flight from a corner of your room. Or you might use them about the border of an appropriate bulletin board or above the chalk board. Let the children study pictures of doves, pigeons; point out how & where the wings are attached to the body, the way in which the neck is shaped & how the tail grows. Then let children cut, from white paper, doves of their own design. The following might be used as a basis of construction, but let the *children* come up with their own solutions, variants.

OR

Valentines. In the 1st days of February, older children collect: several types of fern (clippings from a florist's), Queen Anne's lace, common clovers & any small leaves from bushes or trees that they may find available. These are pressed under heavy weights between sheets of waxpaper (which quickly accepts moisture) & then, in a week or so, are put between sheets of newsprint. Dilute milk glue with water. Apply it to backs of pressed

plants, using a wide brush & large strokes. Arrange plants appropriately on the center of a doily-backed heart, or inside a card that
carries a message on its cover.

Younger children make & collect flat materials that interest
them (tiny paper cut-outs, sequins, glitter, tin foil, feathers, leaves,
bits of fabric, lace, string). These are arranged in a pleasing manner
on a piece of wax paper. A 2nd piece of wax paper is put on top &
the 2 sheets are pressed together with a warm iron. Children cut a
large heart-shaped piece out of a card. Then an area of their wax
paper collage, chosen to go behind the heart-shaped hole, is cut
& glued in place.

Individual folders to hold (& in which to carry home) their
cards could be made in this way, too.

Traditionally, valentines had a lacy, almost fragile look.
Besides using the commercially made white or gold paper doilies,
the children can cut handmade doilies in the following ways:

(1) Fold square on dotted lines.

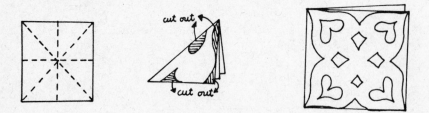

Paste doily onto card of a sharply contrasting color. Children may
want to slip tiny pieces of foil or colored tissue beneath cut-out
areas before doily is glued in place. This gives a more collage-like
freedom to the valentine.

(2) Fold rectangular piece of paper in 1/2 lengthwise & then
in 1/2 crosswise. Cut as shown; then fold diagonally & cut as
shown:

(3) Fold rectangular paper as described in #2. Cut as shown. Then open out & fold over each corner & cut as shown below.

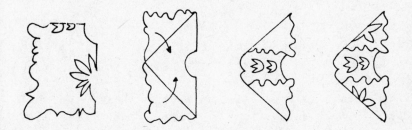

Doilies are opened out flat & carefully glued in place atop a folded card. The oval area in the centers of #2 & #3 is a perfect frame for a snapshot of the child, or for a tiny heart that opens revealing a secret, or as a space in which to print a message.

• U.S. Mail Established [20]

We get the word "mail" from the Old French "male," the leather pouch carried by postmen. This word came into the English language in the 17th century when it was still correct to say a "mail of letters." *Litera* in Latin means "letter"; its plural means "a message." So it is that when you form a group of letters, you've written a letter!

In the Middle Ages couriers of the king rode *post,* a chain of stations that supplied fresh horses & men to deliver royal messages to distant places. The word "post" comes from the Latin *posita,* placed, as the original posts were placed at regular intervals along the 1st mail routes. The 1st postmen delivered only royal mail!

Riddle: What word is this?

Take away my 1st letter, I remain unchanged.
Take away my 2nd letter, I remain the same.
Take away ALL my letters & I continue unchanged.
What am I?

(The postman.)

- **National Brotherhood Week: Information sources:**

Xerox Co. offers a series of booklets on Black History; these are sold by:

Xerox Educational Sciences
600 Madison Ave.
New York, N.Y. 10016

Nat'l. Conference of Christians & Jews
43 W. 57th St.
New York, N.Y.

- **Malcolm X Day**   [21]

A drop-out from school & an ex-convict, this man grew to become an American Black leader. Early in the 50's he joined the Black Muslims. After a decade of service he was suspended in 1963. An eloquent, provocative speaker, Malcolm X founded a new nationalist movement, "Afro-American Unity," in 1964. Hostility between the 2 groups developed & finally erupted into violence when Malcolm X was shot to death while addressing a rally of his followers.

Etymology. A martyr is a person who chooses to suffer or die rather than give up his beliefs or principles. We get this word from the Greek *martyr,* or *martys:* a "witness."

- **Birth of George Washington**   [22]

We learn from his biographers that Washington was a Virginia gentleman who wore dentures made of wood, wire & elk's teeth; he kept detailed records of the money he spent; known occasionally to swear, Washington was not noted for a sense of humor. But it is not for these oddities that he is called the Father of Our Country. His was the strength & perseverance that kept our men fighting in a Revolutionary War that practically demanded surrender. And without Washington's leadership during the formative years of our country, America might never have existed.

Bulletin board suggestion

After discussing with your class the story of Washington, cover a bulletin board with blue paper. Make waves at the top as shown. Have the title "ride" the waves. If possible get a reproduction of the painting "Washington Crossing the Delaware." Pin this to one side of the title, giving the illusion of a tiny boat atop the bulletin board waves. Print the following questions below the title:

Crossing the Delaware

What did Washington take across the Delaware, beginning with A?
What did he use to cross, beginning with B?
What day did he go on, beginning with C?
Whom were they looking for, beginning with E?
What did his men carry, beginning with F?
Whom did they fight, beginning with H?
What did Washington's soldiers take, beginning with P?

To the right of each question have a series of waves covering the answer. Children lift up the waves to read the answers: A-army; B-boat; C-Christmas; E-enemy; F-flags; H-Hessians; P-prisoners. Washington also took B-bullets; C-cannon; P-powder; S-supplies; S-soldiers. His men took M-muskets; S-swords. They fought the T-Tories.

Word etymology. "Hatchet" comes from the French word "hachette," the diminutive of "hache" (ax), & so "hatchet" means "little ax." According to Roman writers, the cherry is named after the city Cerasus which was in the ancient kingdom of Pontus on the Black Sea. A pie is made by filling a crust with a mixture, a collection of a variety of things. "Pie" comes from the same Latin word *pica,* as does the word "magpie." That's because a magpie has the habit of collecting oddments, a jumble or mixture of things! "President" comes from the word "preside" which we get from the Latin *praesidere. Prae* means "before" & *sedere* means "sit." So our President is a man who presides by "sitting before this nation"!

Vocabulary enrichment words: honorable, dedicated, tenacious, persistent, affluent, literate, equestrian, monarchy, republic.

Riddles: Name the flower that tells what George Washington was to his country. (Poppy.) We have very good telegraph service to Hong Kong & to Paris & to Rome. Then why is it awfully difficult to try to send a telegram to Washington today? (Washington died in 1799!)

A Game for Washington's Birthday: "Cherry Pie" This game for younger children helps improve coordination & running skills. Children form a circle, holding hands. This is "the pie" & each child is "a piece of pie." "It" runs around outside of circle & holds his arms together outstretched, pretending to be a knife. He brings his arms down quickly between 2 children & shouts "I cut the pie!" Then he stands with his hands at his sides. The two children "cut" go racing in opposite directions outside the circle. The one who gets back to his place 1st, cries "Here I am, Cherry Pie!" He becomes the new knife.

- **Leap Year Day**   [29]

Of unknown origin is the custom that in leap years women may take the initiative & propose. In 1288 an act of Scottish Parliament permitted a woman during leap year to propose to a man & if the woman were rejected (unless he could prove that he was already engaged), the man had to pay her 100 pounds. In a few years a similar law was passed in France; in the 15th century, the tradition was legalized in Italy. By 1600 the custom was a part of common law in England.

Riddle: What's the best day for a kangaroo? (Leap Year Day!)

FEBRUARY ACTIVITIES

A very informative bulletin board can be made by collecting the following: pictures of animals (native to your state), their tracks or track-casts, pictures of common wild birds, their nests, bird feathers, pictures of local trees, their leaves & their winter twigs. Number each item. Children try to locate the numbers of matching pairs. Although this display does take preparation, once the items are collected, you can save them & use them again another year.

Social Studies

If your class has an encyclopedia at its disposal, have a group of children compile a list of important place names that have been in the news recently. The group selects 5-10 names in such a way that different volumes of your encyclopedia may be in use at 1 time. An atlas, a world globe & wall maps will also be used. Divide the class into groups, 1 for each place name on the list. Each group then selects the proper volume of the encyclopedia, finds their place name on the map & then completes a mimeo-sheet which you have prepared & which is headed "Where on EARTH is it?" It asks the children to locate their place name on a map of the state, nation, or the continent; list the bordering lands & waters, find the exact longitude & latitude; estimate how far it is from their home town to this place name; decide how important this place name is to its state or nation; decide what kind of life style the people living there may have.

Language Arts

"A Letter to My Teacher." Set aside a time during which the children will each write you a letter. Ask them to carefully plan the things they would like to ask or tell you. Explain that these letters are strictly personal & will not be read aloud or displayed. You might answer each of their letters separately, or you may post an open letter to the class in reply to their missives.

Haiku. This verse form has been written since the 13th century. It is a little Japanese poem of 3 lines. The 1st & last lines always have 5 syllables; the middle line has 7 syllables. Haiku are usually nature poems describing the season or explaining the feelings of the poet. A haiku does not rhyme. It paints a small, often exquisite picture in your mind.

> The patting of rain
> Mist gently on my window
> Then a pounding! Hail.*

Have your class read this haiku aloud together, clapping in unison at each syllable. Ask the students to describe the mental images they had while reading this poem. Then give the children the 1st two lines of a haiku, i.e.:

> At this time of year
> I am always thinking how
> . . . . .

Let them supply the 3rd line. Discuss their responses. Now with the aid of Webster & Roget (the thesaurus helps immensely in finding a synonym with the right number of syllables), let your class begin composing their own haiku.

Reading. Young students will enjoy reading in their spare time from the *"Magic Readers."* These are made by 1st folding a mimeo mastersheet in 1/2, crosswise. On one 1/2 of the sheet print a short story that directs the child to do something. ("Get blue. Make a thing you use. We can all use it. We can paint it now. Color it blue. We can paint it blue. Guess what it is.") On the

---

*Used with permission of the author, Elisabeth Tracy.

remaining 1/2 sheet print a story that is a description. ("He is good. He is not old. He is brown & white. He is for me. He likes to play. He & I play.") Once these are run off, each mimeo is folded in 1/2, book-fashion, & a piece of newsprint folded in 1/2 is inserted in the middle of the mimeo. A colored paper cover states:

Name_____
Magic Reader Number_____

Cover & pages are stapled together. Any object that the child wishes to draw is acceptable, as long as it corresponds to the description given. This way each child's Magic Reader may have entirely different illustrations.

Secret Messages. Each child in the reading group is given a small card on which appears a set of instructions. You create specific cards for each child emphasizing those word analysis skills that he needs, or which the group has recently reviewed. Or you may simply have a stack of cards, each child choosing one card. The group silently reads their cards to themselves. Then each child acts out the instructions on his card:

Catch a big fish. Be a rabbit; eat cabbage. Act like a bee; act as if you are going to a flower; get some honey from the flower. Walk to the window; look out the window. Act like a bird. Stand under a light; stay there until I call your name. Walk; find a hat; put the hat on your head; sit. Act as if you have lost something; act as if you found what you lost.

Older children may have more complicated directives:

Let us see you creep like a black sheep in the deep green grass. Then you seem to hear a bad noise. It is a FOX! Scram! Don't hang around. You keep on fleeing, but the fox gets you. So all you can do is weep.

The others in the group try to figure out what is being pantomimed. Finally the actor reads his card aloud to the rest of his group.

Math enrichment activities

(The following information, or a portion of it, could make an interesting bulletin board display):

How we got our standards of length. These came about in a natural way from parts of the body: fingernails, arms, feet, fingers—each became a unit of length. The cubit, 1st known measurement (about 20"), was the length of an Egyptian's forearm from the tip of his elbow to the end of his middle finger. A digit (which is from .72 to .75 inch) was the breadth of a Sumerian's finger. Even today "digit" still means "finger." A foot to the Greeks could be subdivided into 12 thumbnail breadths. This foot-unit passed on to Rome & so the invaders brought it to Britain where its division of 1/12 (or *unciae*) became "inches." In Britain the Anglo-Saxons had a measurement called the "fathom"—the length across two arms outstretched. Cloth was the Norman's most important trade. Under them half a fathom, the length from the middle of the body to the end of 1 arm outstretched, was used for measuring fabric. And *that's* how we got the yard. King Henry the 1st, in the 11th century, decreed that the distance from the tip of his nose to the end of his thumb should be the lawful yard. In 1325 Edward II passed a law that 3 kernels of corn taken from the center of the ear & placed end to end equalled 1". (This meant that a foot could be from 9 3/4" to 19"!) In the 16th century the length of the left foot of 16 men who were lined up as they came out of church on Sunday morning became the lawful rod!

A big chart to give younger children experience with the sequence of numbers & the counting of money. On a large piece of tagboard measure off 3 rows & divide these into 4 spaces each. Repeat these measurements on a 2nd piece of tagboard. Into each space on 1 piece of tagboard paste the picture of an object & its actual cost. Make a few of these objects humorous if possible. On the remaining piece of tagboard, cut 3-sided flaps that will cover objects & their prices. Glue this piece of tagboard in place atop 1st piece. Put under weights until dry. Then provide class with a pile of play coins, post the chart, & instruct 1st child to "lift up the 2nd window in the 3rd row & tell us what you see. In what ways could you pay for this 19¢ object? Give the 'store keeper' the correct number of cents."

Science

Sound Exploration. These activities would offer fine preparation for organizing a bulletin board display:

1. Keep a record of every sound you hear in 3 minutes.
2. Make a list: "The Uses of Sound."
3. Experiment: How many sounds can you make with a pencil? a comb? 2 bobby pins? a glass of water? Write up a record describing these sounds.

4. An ode was originally a poem to be sung. Write an ode to an animal, insect, fish or bird.

5. Listen to a recording of sounds, i.e., Folkway record 6115, "Bird Calls"; 6120, "Sound of a Tropical Rain Forest"; 6122, "Sounds of the American Southwest"; & 6170 & 6180, featuring noise of machinery, street traffic, applause, New Year's Eve in N.Y.C.

6. Paint to music, i.e., Cage, Stockhausen or Samuel Barber's *Piano Concerto.*

7. Talk about the sounds of fear. How are these different from fearful sounds?

8. Tell a story with sounds.

9. Give the class a bag of bones & rubber bands. Make up a tribal chant & its accompaniment using these.

10. Talk about the sounds of anger, of playfulness & of distress.

11. Man makes instruments from objects he finds in his environment (e.g., seed pods in South America, shells in Fiji, bones in Africa). What objects specific to *our* culture suggest musical instruments to you? Make a drawing of several such instruments.

February Game

What to do when it's too cold to go out & play: One night ask the children to write as homework a group of 10 statements on any historical place, famous person, or form of nature. Each statement is to help in the identification of the object. Then ask them to arrange these statements in order from the most obscure to the most revealing. Check over these lists yourself, then return them to the students. Divide the class into teams. Each team decides on a list (from those of teammates) to use. Each team will in turn present its list of 10 statements. Team decides on 1 guess they will venture: ONLY 1 guess a time. If a team gets the right answer after 1 statement, they receive 10 points. One less point is earned after each additional statement.

February E-Z Puppet

Child measures the length of his index finger against a toilet-tissue tube. One inch is added. Cut around tube. Roll a piece of newspaper into a small ball. Put this in the center of a folded single sheet of newspaper. Stand the tube atop the ball. Bring the newspaper tightly up over the ball & tube. Tightly wind string around the length of the tube. Tie string where ball meets tube, forming neck of puppet. Cover head with a piece of sheet, leaving enough fabric to go past neck. Fasten sheet in place at neck with rubber band or string. Make features on the face by gluing on felt, or by painting them with poster paints or a felt-tip pen. Now child is ready to make the clothing. He measures a piece of colored fabric 2 1/2 x the length of his hand & 1 1/2 x the width of his hand when his fingers are outstretched. Locate the middle of this fabric. Make a tiny slit & cut shoulders. Glue the shoulder seams together with white glue. Also glue the side seams together. Carefully push the head through the slit in fabric. Glue the neck of clothing to the neck of puppet. Tie a little necktie, bow, or collar around neck to cover glued area.

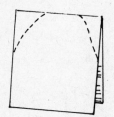

arch

March brings breezes loud and shrill,
Stirs the dancing daffodil.

1   1st U.S. bank established, 1780.
2   1st round world non-stop flight, 1949.
3   Alexander Graham Bell (1847-1922), American scientist, inventor of the telephone.
4   U.S. Constitution went into effect, 1789.
5   Howard Pyle (1853-1911), American writer, illustrator.
6   Magellan Day.
       Michelangelo Buonarroti (1475-1564) [commonly known by his 1st name, Michelangelo], Italian painter, sculptor, architect.
       Elizabeth Barrett Browning (1806-1861), English poet: *Sonnets from the Portugese.*
       Fall of the Alamo 1836; captured by Antonio Santa Ana. .
7   Luther Burbank (1849-1926), American horticulturist: developed over 200 plant varieties.
       Maurice Ravel (1875-1937), French composer: "Bolero."
       Alexander Bell patented telephone, 1876.
9   Amerigo Vespucci (1451-1512), Italian navigator after whom America is named.
10   Harriet Tubman (c. 1821, died on this day: 1913), American Negro abolitionist, called "Moses" by her people because she led 300 blacks to freedom (1850-1860).
       1st paper money issued in the U.S., 1862.
12   U.S. Post Office established, 1789.
13   tandard Time established in U.S., 1884.

14   Eli Whitney patented the cotton gin, 1794.

Johann Strauss (1825-1899), Austrian composer: "Blue Danube."

Albert Einstein (1870-1955), German-born American physicist, mathmetician.

1st transatlantic broadcast, 1925.

15   "The Ides of March" on which Julius Caesar was assassinated: 44 B.C.

Andrew Jackson (1767-1845), 7th U.S. President.

16   James Madison (1751-1836), 4th U.S. President.

George Ohm (1787-1854), German physicist.

17   St. Patrick's Day.

18   Grover Cleveland (1837-1908), 22nd & 24th U.S. President.

Nikolai Rimsky-Korsakov (1844-1908), Russian composer.

Rudolph Diesel (1858-1913), German engineer, invented the diesel engine.

20   Ovid [Publius Ovidius Naso] (43 B.C.-17 A.D.), Roman poet.

21   Spring equinox.

Johann Sebastian Bach (1685-1750), German composer.

Modest Mussorgski (1835-1881), Russian composer.

22   Anthony Van Dyck (1599-1641), Flemish painter.

Patrick Henry delivered his "liberty or death" speech, 1775 (see pg. 000).

24   Harry Houdini (1874-1926), American magician.

25   Gutzon Borglum (1871-1941), American sculptor, created Mt. Rushmore National Monument, S.D.

26   Robert Frost (1874-1963), American poet.

27   Nathaniel Currier (1813-1888), American lithographer, depicted manners, people of that time.

Wilhelm C. Roentgen (1845-1923), German physicist; discoverer of X-rays.

Mies van der Rohe (1886-1969), German architect.

29   John Tyler (1790-1862), 10th U.S. President.

30   Francisco Goya (1746-1828), Spanish painter.

Vincent van Gogh (1853-1890), Dutch painter.

31   Joseph Haydn (1732-1809), Austrian composer.

U.S. Daylight Savings Time began 1918 & lasted 2 years. It was repealed due to the violent protests from farmers that their cows gave milk an hour after the milk trains had passed. Following World War II it was re-established.

Holidays that may occur in March: Palm Sunday, Easter, Passover, Arbor Day.

Pesach: The Passover (springtime). It is a celebration of the freeing of the Israelites from Egypt. A traditional dinner, "seder," is preceded by the reading of the Haggadah which tells the story of the exodus.

March

In the Roman calendar, March was the 1st month of the year. This was the season for the waging of war & so the Romans named this month after Mars, the god of war. In 45 B.C. Caesar reformed the calendar & March became the 3rd month. The expression "mad as a March hare" evolved since "March is the mating season for hares & during this month they are supposedly 'full of whimsy.' "

MARCH QUOTATIONS

3   Mr. Watson, come here; I want you. (1st words spoken over telephone, March 10, 1876 by Alexander Bell.)

6   It is only well with me when I have a chisel in my hand.
     Trifles make perfection, but perfection is no trifle.
                                        —Michelangelo Buonarroti

14   Imagination is more important than knowledge. ("On Science")

     Sometimes one pays most for the things one gets for nothing.

     I never think of the future. It comes soon enough.

     My political ideal is democracy. Everyone should be respected as an individual, but no one idolized.

     When a man sits with a pretty girl for an hour, it seems like a minute. But let him sit on a hot stove for a minute—and it seems longer than any hour. *That's* relativity.
                                              —Albert Einstein

15   Et tu, Brute? (You also, Brutus?)—Alleged dying words of Caesar

     Our Federal Union: It must and shall be preserved; [Toast at Jefferson's birthday banquet, 1830]—Andrew Jackson

18   I believe our Great Maker is preparing the world, in His own good time, to become one nation, speaking one language. (Inaugural Address 1893)—Grover Cleveland

20   The crop always seems better in our neighbor's field, and our neighbor's cow gives more milk.—Ovid

21   (1st day of spring)

Grass is the forgiveness of nature—her constant benediction—Forests decay, harvests perish, flowers vanish, but grass is immortal. —Ingalls (Speech 1874)

27   (Speaking of architectural design:) "Less is more."—Mies van der Rohe

March Riddles: What is the worst month for a soldier? (A *long* March.) What can pass before the sun without leaving a shadow? (The winds of March!) What day is a command to move on? (March fourth.)

MARCH EVENTS

• **Birth of Alexander Graham Bell   [3]**

He knew the pattern of vibrations made by sound in the air, so he searched for an electric current that would follow the same pattern. It took several years of experimenting before he had refined his ideas & invented the 1st telephone.

"The History of Hello" may be used as a bulletin board display. Long ago people greeted one another by saying, "Hail." This became slurred to "hallo" & finally was pronounced "hello" in America. The French, German & Dutch still say "hallo" & the Spanish say "Hola."

In the early days of the telephone, people answered the phone by saying: "Are you there?" (This is still used in England.) It is said that Thomas A. Edison originated the practice of using the word "hello" as the opening greeting in telephone conversations.

Etymology: *Tele* is Greek for "far away" & *phone* means "sound."

Science. Mimeo-sheets are placed on a table along with objects & materials to be used in experimentation. Each sheet has space for child's name & the date, & is titled "Magnets." Beneath this is written:

1. What will a magnet attract? Check one: (Yes & No columns are at the right side of sheet). Brass, Copper, Cork, Glass, Iron, Nickel, Plastic, Rock, Rubber, Seashells, Silver, Steel, Wood.
2. Will a magnet attract another magnet? Will it attract both ends of the other magnet? Can you find out why?
3. How can you make a magnet of a needle that is here?
4. How are magnets useful in the world today?

● **Birth of Amerigo Vespucci   [9]**

America was named by a young German geographer, Martin Waldseemuller. He included in his book of 1503 a map showing a region he called "New World." He had been greatly impressed by the writing of Amerigo Vespucci, who had himself referred to these lands as "new," & so Waldseemuller designated part of the land as "America," mentioning in the margin why he had done so. This enraged the Spaniards, who, jealous for their Christopher Columbus, refused to use the name "America" until the 18th century.

● **Eli Whitney patented the cotton gin   [14]**

"The yankee Eli Whitney, by inventing the cotton gin, perhaps made inevitable the Civil War. The yankee Eli Whitney, by popularizing (if not inventing) the principle of interchangeable parts, contributed heavily to the winning of the war by the Union."*

● **Birth of Georg Ohm   [16]**

G.S. Ohm discovered a unit of electricity & it is named after him: an ohm is a unit of electrical resistance equal to the resistance of a circuit in which 1 volt contains a current of 1 ampere.

● **The Feast day of St. Patrick   [17]**

Born in Britain, Patrick, at the age of 16, was kidnapped by Irish pirates & enslaved in Ireland. For 6 miserable years he tended sheep on the cold hills of Ballymena. He escaped finally aboard a ship to France (then known as Gaul). There he studied for the priesthood & in 431 A.D. was named a bishop. The next year he was sent by the pope to teach the gospel to the people of Hibernia—the same wild Irish tribesmen who had kidnapped him as a boy. Patrick spent nearly 30 years trudging up & down the

*Reprinted by permission of the publisher, from Thomas A. Baily: *The American Pageant,* 2nd Edition Lexington, Mass.: D.C. Heath and Company, 1965).

Emerald Isle, teaching Christianity. Few people today actually know who he was, or what he did. The Irishmen who knew him when he was alive must have loved him dearly for they have transmitted their affection for him to their descendants for 1,500 years.

Bulletin board ideas. Display pictures & information under the heading: March Is a Good Month to Learn More About Snakes. Though it's a *legend* that St. Pat drove them out of Ireland, it's a *fact* that Ireland has NO snakes today. Why do you think this may be true?

Make a large leprechaun; divide him in 2. On 1 side pin green word cards, on the other side pin corresponding white cards. These cards should be changed every few days & may emphasize homonyms, synonyms, antonyms, abbreviations, or vocabulary words. Children match the appropriate words.

Etymology. In Irish "seamrog" is the diminutive of "seamar," a clover. So shamrock is "a little clover." Because of its 3 leaves, it was used by St. Patrick to illustrate the Trinity, & in this way it became the symbol of Ireland. The potato is a native of Peru. The Spanish conquistadores discovered it in the Andes Mts. & brought it back to Europe. The potato was introduced to America in 1719 by a group of Irishmen & so we have the "Irish potato."

Vocabulary enrichment words: chartreuse, emerald, Kelly green, forest green, verdant, blarney.

St. Patrick's Day Riddles: What was the trick in driving the snakes out of Ireland? (St. Patrick.) What's the name of an Irishman you'll find on every T.V. "talk" show? (Mike.) What kind of knee does an Irish traveling salesman like best? (Blarney.)

"Going to Dublin," a rainy-day reading game. Make a large chart like that shown.* Children sit in a line or semi-circle. The head seat is "Dublin" & all the players are trying to get there. Starting at the foot of the line, each child in turn spins the arrow. He reads his directions & follows them. Two or 3 turns per child can constitute a game.

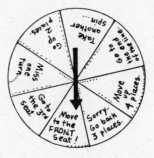

St. Patrick's Day Science. (For young children.) Bring a daisy for each child in your class. Put the flowers in a container of water to which the children add green food-coloring. As the daisies turn green, discuss how this happens (water travels to all parts of the flower, nourishing it). Let each child take a daisy home to Mother (& explain to her what has happened).

Try some starch detection experiments. Starch, a carbohydrate, is an important source of energy for humans. Starch is easily recognized by its reaction with iodine solution, when it turns blue. You will need: a medicine dropper, tincture of iodine, sugar, a slice of light & of dark bread, rice, beans, an apple, a lettuce leaf, corn, & an Irish potato. A hot plate & a pot may be used if you wish to cook the vegetables in the classroom. Boil uncooked food (rice, potato etc.) for a few minutes in order to release starch. Two or 3 drops of iodine are put on each food sample. See if the children can decide which foods will contain starch. Moisten cooked food (canned beans, corn) with a bit of water. See if the children can decide which foods will contain starch. Two or 3 drops of iodine are put on each food sample. When the dark brown iodine turns blue, this proves the presence of starch.

Help your class organize an Irish Rythm Band. (See pg.195 for instrument suggestions.) Teach them "Wearing of the Green" or "MacNamara's Band" so that they can really celebrate this day.

---

*If a small piece of corrugated cardboard is put between the arrow & the chart you may find that the arrow will spin more freely.

- **Birth of Johann Sebastian Bach   [21]**

    As a child, Bach had to copy music in secret by moonlight so that his jealous older brother would not find him. It was this brother who tried to prevent Johann from becoming too proficient on the organ. But Bach grew to become a famous organist, choir leader, & composer who influenced Beethoven, Mozart, Chopin & Brahms!

    Mention how at the same period in which Bach lived, Frederick the Great, Benjamin Franklin & George Frederick Handel were also alive. Indicate on the wall map the birthplace of Bach: Eisenach, Germany. Define & discuss the minuet; play "Minuet in G minor" by Bach; young children may enjoy improvising dance steps while the recording plays. The "Prelude" & the "Fugue" might be defined & presented in a similar manner.

- **Spring begins   [21] (Vernal Equinox)**

    On this day there are just 12 hours from sunrise to sunset & 12 hours from sunset to sunrise. This is called the day of the "equinox" because that word means equal (day & night). In Greek mythology, Demeter & Zeus had a daughter named Persephone. One day Hades, the ruler of the underworld, kidnapped Persephone & married her. When Persephone left the Earth, the flowers died & the wheat withered. Demeter begged the gods to send her daughter back; the gods agreed to let her return for 2/3 of each year. When Persephone returned to Earth, life began anew. She corresponds to the Corn Spirit (of the American Indians) which died & was re-born each year.

    Bulletin board ideas. Title: "A Collection of Fine Specimens." Display excellent papers done by children & intersperse these with 3-dimensional butterflies, the wings of which are cut from a variety of fingerpainted papers (*both* sides of which have color).

Two possible bulletin board titles (or writing assignment self-starters) for young children are: (1) "What did you see, touch, smell, hear on your way to school this morning?" (2) "What are the loveliest things you know (people not included)?"

As children have a tendency to grow restless at this time of year, plan a class walk to see pollywogs, pussywillows & to LOOK at spring's arrival. If your school is in a city, what signs of spring CAN be seen, heard? When you get back in the classroom suggest that each child make a drawing or painting that is "as fresh & new as spring" (which may be the title for the display of this artwork)!

A Spring Riddle: Why is it more dangerous to go out in spring than in any other time of the year? (Because in spring the grass has new blades, the flowers have pistils, the leaves shoot, the bean stalks, and the bulrushes [bull rushes] out!)

Spring Poetry

Now every field is clothed with grass,
And every tree with leaves;
Now the woods put forth their blossoms,
And the year assumes its gay attire.

—Virgil

For lo, the winter is past,
the rain is over and gone.
The flowers appear on the earth,
the time of singing has come,
and the voice of the turtledove
is heard in our land.
—The Song of Solomon, 2:11-12

Also appropriate:

"The Rain" by R.L. Stevenson
"The Wind" by Christina G. Rossetti
"Who Has Seen the Wind" by Christina G. Rossetti

Spring Science

The observation of nonpoisonous snakes can be an invaluable classroom experience. Snakes are clean, quiet & aesthetically pleasing. These reptiles are an important factor in the ecology of our land. Although a 1st hand study of snakes can do much to temper a generalized attitude of fear & suspicion, this classroom experience is not for every teacher.

First check with your principal to get his permission.

Talk with your students to learn how each of them feels about having a reptile in his classroom.

Then, if the reaction of the class is positive, set about choosing a snake with which you yourself feel at ease. It only perpetuates the cliche to present your students with an animal about which their teacher feels apprehensive.

Snakes can be collected in the spring months. They don't enjoy being handled, so children shouldn't over-do it. When handling a snake of less than 4 feet, let him move through your palms as you slowly go hand over hand along his length. This gives the snake the feeling that he is moving away. Grabbing a snake behind its head actually restricts the snake.

King snakes are the best snakes for classroom observation.* Adult gopher snakes are also good. Both are heavy-bodied, docile, eat well in captivity & are easy to handle. King snakes may lay eggs in captivity; gopher snakes over 3' long are of breeding age (3 years old), & gopher snakes breed well in captivity.

Keep snake in a cage that is as long as he is.

Using lots of hot water & Ajax, sterilize any commercially made cage & then put it out in the sun to kill mites (the sun dehydrates mites). A sterilized aquarium tank may be used, but don't use screening as a covering for its top as snake will rub his nose raw against wire screening. Instead, wrap a hardware cloth around a piece of screening cut to the size of top of tank. Snakes are natural escape artists, so any cage exits should be firmly secured.

Put a piece of slate, bark, or a small box into cage so that snake may hide beneath it. Don't put plants into a snake's cage as plants may carry mites.

A Few Suggestions About Keeping Toads, Lizards & Snakes in the Classroom

Toads may be kept in a gallon jar, the lid of which has holes punched in it.

Toads will eat common earthworms & most soft-bodied

---

*The common garter snake may bite, has an odor, & won't readily eat in captivity.

· insects (hairless caterpillars, meal-worms, adult & white crickets, termites & fly maggots). To obtain the latter, put some meat in a canning jar. When it is clear that flies have been there, screw on the rim, substituting wire screen for the metal disc. When flies hatch, dump the maggots, sans meat, into the toad's jar. (Adult toads will eat baby toads so they must be segregated.)

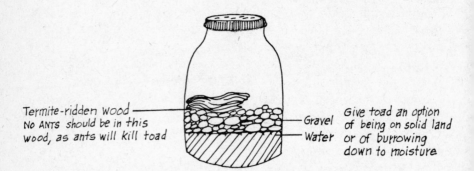

Termite-ridden wood — No ANTS should be in this wood, as ants will kill toad
Gravel — Water — Give toad an option of being on solid land or of burrowing down to moisture

Toads won't hibernate in the classroom as it is not cold enough there to trigger hibernation.

Some lizards require a lot of heat. Chameleons need 85°, & they may need their cages sprayed with water every day—& NO water dish left in the cage. Most other lizards need to have a water dish in their cages. Put a plastic vine in their cage for cover. Find out where your lizard came from & try to duplicate that environment.

Both snakes & lizards should have a coarse grade of gravel, NOT sand, in the bottom of their cages. Sand gets in their food & causes mouth rot. The aquarium gravel sold in pen shops is (as any gravel used *must* be) sterilized. After it has been used for several months, it can be re-sterilized by boiling it for a few hours or by baking it at 450° for 1 hour; this will save you the cost of purchasing new gravel every 2-3 months.

Give snakes water, but not enough to soak in (except during shedding period). If it gets too humid in cage, snake develops water blisters & starts cycle of ill health. Snakes periodically shed; 3-4 days before shedding, snake's eyes will turn blue. This is a good time to give him a bowl of water in which to soak.

Don't put 2 snakes in the same cage; it is an emotionally unhealthy environment for them. King snakes will eat 1 another, & infections can spread.

Don't place a snake's glass cage in sunlight. Glass blocks out the beneficial ultra-violet rays of sun & heat of direct sunlight will literally cook snake. The ideal temperature for snakes is 65°-85°. If the captive snake comes from the same general area as the school, there is no need to provide artificial heat. To heat a snake's cage do *not* dangle a bulb down into cage. A 15-25 watt bulb used as shown should work well. It's a good idea to have a thermometer to reassure one that temperature is 65°-85° within cage.

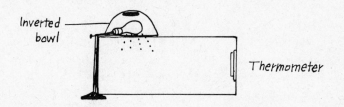

Feed snakes once a week. Most snakes will eat live mice, smooth-scaled lizards & *especially,* live frogs. If snake (especially a small one) doesn't eat for a month, set him free!

An easy way to differentiate between male & female: The tail of the male is longer & tapers more gradually. This is because the male sex organs are in the tail. The female's tail tapers suddenly to a point.

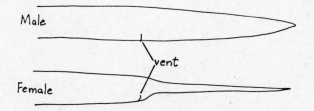

How to Recognize Dangerous Snakes & Lizards of the Continental U.S.A.

There are 5 different types of poisonous snakes: rattlesnakes, water moccasins, copperheads, coral snakes & rear-fanged snakes. *Rattlers, moccasins & copperheads* are all pit vipers, having broad heads & a pit under each nostril. (A rattlesnake has rattles at the end of its tail.) Rattlesnakes are found, mainly, in the mid & S.W. United States though they are still common in some areas of the

N.E. & S.E. Copperheads are found in the E. part of the U.S. & moccasins are found in the South.

Coral snakes have conspicuous rings of red, black & yellow. An old saying warns:

> When Red touches Yellow
> You'd better RUN, fellow!

(The beneficial Kingsnake has rings of *yellow*, black, *red*, black, *yellow*, black, *red*, black, etc.)

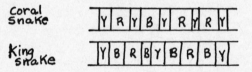

The coral snake is found in the South & Southwest.

Rear-fanged snakes are small, rare & secretive. Their venom is very mild (equivalent to a wasp's sting). They are found in the Western U.S.A.

The Gila Monster, found in Arizona, & its Mexican cousin, the Bearded Lizard, are the only poisonous lizards in the world.

Spring Clue Charts

Let the children make personalized clue charts for the identification of trees & flowers (similar to Bird Charts—see pg. 218). Seeds, leaves, insects, & *plentiful* nature specimens may be included.

Revisit the class tree & study all the life around it. Talk about the changes brought on by spring. Watch for the 1st flowers, the 1st leaves, the 1st insects, & record these dates. Changing cloud forms may also be noted.

• Birth of Harry Houdini   [24]

Bulletin board suggestion: Title—"In Honor of Houdini and National Magic Week":

> YOU'RE the Magician. Sometimes don't you wish you could change things to suit YOURSELF? Well, here's your chance! Let's see how you'd change THESE things: What would you make bigger so that it would be more fun? What would you make slower so you could use it more often? What would you make sparkle so it would be more helpful? etc.

These might be answered on a mimeo-sheet or as a Creative Writing assignment.

Word etymology. The priests of ancient Persia had a word *magus* that meant "priest" or "fireworshipper." This word later became *magos,* meaning "a wizard" or "a juggler." From this came the word *magikos* which became "magic." Our "magicians" have generally retained all the original meanings implied by their name.

Reading for older students. None of the instructions are given orally; they are all written prior to class on large sheets of newsprint, or on the chalk board, in the following manner:

The Ashes Can Speak!

I am a mind reader! I have a few slips of paper to write numbers on. As I call you, come up & whisper a number for me to write down. I will fold each slip & put it in the tall can. Then I will ask someone to come up & pull out 1 slip of paper. He must not tell its number. The rest of the slips will be set on fire & burned up. Then I will read the ashes!

After slips have been burned in a tall metal can (wastebasket),* sift through the ashes slowly. Then announce that it's easy for you to read the remaining slip held by the student! Announce it (since you wrote down the 1st number you were told on *every* single slip of paper you can't go wrong). Pass out a mimeographed sheet that explains how & why the trick worked. This way the class *reads* the answer. Mention on the mimeo (& verbally impress upon the class) that this trick has *got* to be done in a tall metal can & with their mother's or father's O.K.!

Math enrichment

Number tricks. Ask each child to choose a number & keep it secret. "Double your number. Now multiply it by 5 & tell me the total." (Knock off final digit & you will have their secret number.) Why does it work? Children have actually multiplied numbers by 10. VARIATION: "Take a number. Double it. Now add 9. Subtract 3. Divide by 2. Subtract the number you started with. The answer you now have is 3!" (It will always be 3, because

$$\frac{2X + (9-3)}{2} - X \rightarrow \frac{2X}{2} + \frac{6}{2} - X \rightarrow X + 3 - X = 3.)$$

---

*Have a wet towel handy—just in case—to impress the class with your feelings about safety measures!

"Scientific" Magic Tricks

Magic Candle. Offer to light a candle without touching fire to its wick. First light a candle as you are explaining that *anyone* can light a candle *this* way. Blow it out. Light a 2nd candle & let it burn a minute. Hold 1st candle 3" above lighted candle in path of rising smoke. Flame travels up smoke & lights candle.

Magic Milk Bottle. Set bottle on table & drop a lighted match inside bottle. Place the small end of a peeled soft (but firm) boiled egg in mouth of bottle. Hold it there. The heat has created a partial vacuum & this sucks the egg inside. Once the egg is in, hold the bottle to your mouth with the small end of the egg in the neck of the bottle. Force all the air you can into the bottle by blowing, using the egg as a valve to let air in & to keep it there. When mouth is released from bottle, egg is forced out by air pressure.

Magic Needle. Drop a needle slantwise into a glass of water; needle sinks. Retrieve needle; dry it. Grasp needle at its middle & gently lower it to surface of water; needle floats. Explain how surface tension of water is supporting needle.

Information source:

> The Society of American Magicians
> 93 Central St.
> Forestville, Conn.

• Birth of Mies van der Rohe   [27]

Here is an art project that uses architectural forms as a basis: Each child is given a large sheet of 1/8" thick corrugated cardboard, the type that has a somewhat rough surface. Children draw their basically linear compositions on cardboard with pencil or chalk. Toothpicks are then glued to follow the general outline of the drawing. Thin balsawood (in sheets or sticks, available at hobby stores) is cut into appropriate lengths & used for outlining tiny areas & for giving a variety of textures. When glue is absolutely dry, a thin mixture of plaster of Paris is prepared & this is applied to the entire surface of the cardboard with the use of old, clean, wide brushes & various sponges; these last are used, again, for textural effects. Wherever toothpicks have been glued closely together, plaster must be applied with care so as not to clog area & make composition imprecise. Once surface is set, color is applied. Let the children experiment, using diluted poster paint applied with soft big brushes. A deep color, emphasizing the linear element, is applied, lastly, by brayer.

MARCH ACTIVITIES

Bulletin board suggestions. "March was named for Mars, the Roman god of War. Mars is also the name of a planet, 4th in distance from the sun. Let's learn some more about this planet. Mars is famous for its red light. Its circumference is 4,230 miles. (The earth's is 24,830 miles at the equator.) Its year is 686.9 days.

(Ours is 365 days.) ⚥ is the symbol of MARS (and also the symbol for MAN)."

Title: "It Happened in_____." Divide your class into the same number of groups. Each group decides on a historical date & place with which to complete the title. *Any* historical event (discussed in class this year) may be used. Each group works privately to complete their section. The completed display can be very interesting visually, & informative.

Title: "The Origin of the Umbrella." The umbrella or parasol originated in Asian countries* where it was used as protection against the glaring sun. "Parasol" actually means "for sun" (*para* = for + *sol* = sun)! It was introduced into England from Italy in the 18th c. Englishmen shunned it as being "women's wear" until Jonas Hanway, an English traveler, demonstrated its usefulness against rain. In 1740 when it was 1st used in America at Windsor, Conn., it was ridiculed; the townspeople made a line behind its poor owner & they paraded along carrying sieves attached to broomsticks!

Social Studies

A Biographic Movie. A group of these make an intriguing display for Public Schools Week. Have the children bring sturdy small boxes (shoe boxes are good). A rectangular hole for the "movie screen" is cut in the bottom of each box. Hole should not be cut right up to edge of bottom; a bit of bottom should remain as a frame. Cut a long strip of white butcher paper, a bit narrower than the width of the box (i.e., 10" x 24" long). Children choose a famous person in history. They divide paper into sections (leaving

---

*Umbrellas appear in Assyrian friezes of the 7th century B.C.

several inches free at top & bottom of strip) according to the number of "frames" they want in their "film." Titles for the film & an appropriate closing are designed. Balloons from the characters may be used or commentary may be printed atop each frame. Encourage ingenuity in the illustration of the films. The variety should be most appealing. Perhaps making a draft on news print 1st will save butcher paper & patience. Once the movie is finished, it is taped from its topmost edge to the wooden dowel (or if the box is big, to the paper-toweling tube). Dowel is then carefully inserted into 2 holes which have been made (& reenforced) in the sides of the box somewhat above the top of the movie screen. By turning the protruding ends of the dowel, movie is rolled up until bottom edge is exposed. This is taped to the lower dowel (or tube) which has already been inserted in the lower 2 holes shown. Wooden spools or beads may be glued to the ends of dowels to facilitate turning of film.

Language Arts

Older children may enjoy the challenge of making "Lion" into "Lamb" by changing 1 letter at a time, forming a new word at each step: Lion, Loon, Lorn, Lore, Lone, Line, Lime, Limb, LAMB!

Cinquain. An unrhymed 5-line verse, Cinquain is a form of Japanese poetry. The youngest student can have success with this writing form:

> The 1st line is 1 word, the title.   Kitten
> The 2nd line is 2 words & describes the subject.   Brown cat

The 3rd line has 3 words, expressing action.	Runs in circles
The 4th line has 4 words expressing feeling, emotion.	Good to play with
The 5th line is 1 word, a synonym for the title word.	Pet*

Here's one way to help your class learn to be concise in what it writes. Discuss newspaper want-ads: what they are designed to do, why they must be concise. Then each child writes an appropriate newspaper ad for some inventor who has been discussed since fall (e.g., Edison, da Vinci, Watts, Bell, Carver, Franklin). These ads may be composed as though the inventor were trying to sell his patent or as if the invention had just been discovered today.

Weather indicators. March is a month of varied weather. Have the children observe natural change-of-weather indicators & make a collection of these (over a weekend). Such lists, when thoughtful & detailed, are usually also quite poetic. Here is such a list as found in a 19th century reference book:

> "Weather Indicators, Animal Creation: Rain is sure to come when the cattle snuff the air and gather together in a corner of the field with their heads to leeward; when sheep leave their pastures with reluctance; when goats go to sheltered spots; when dogs lie much about the fireside and appear drowsy; when cats turn their backs to the fire and wash their faces; when pigs cover themselves more than usual in litter; when cocks crow at unusual hours and flap their wings much; when hens chant; when ducks and geese are unusually clamorous; when pigeons wash themselves; when swallows fly low and skim their wings on account of flies upon which they feed having descended toward the ground; when toads creep out in numbers; when frogs croak; when singing birds take shelter; when bees leave their hives with caution and fly short distances; when ants carry their eggs busily; when flies bite severely and become troublesome in numbers; when earthworms appear on the surface of the earth."

Rebus. This is a kind of puzzle, the meaning of which is indicated by *things* rather than by *words*. Rebus offers a way to occasionally "candy-coat" review information or a homework assignment for your class. Rebus helps children analyze the written word in a new way. It's fun to try to invent new rebus symbols. Here is a good start on a Rebus Dictionary for your students' use!

---

*Written by a twelve-year-old student, Malcolm Garrard.

ab EXIT⟩ **about**

🌑 mire **admire**

ap 🐒 **appear**

R **are**

💬 th **bath**

🔪 4 **before**

b 🪺 **beg**

b 🧨 **bring**

🪓 d **build**

🥫 **can**

🌳 **country**

d 🚂 **dark**

🦌 **dear**

D 💡 **delight**

ever E 📅 **everyday**

4 **for**

🚦 ing **going**

🤚 8 **great**

h 📋 **had**

🌀 I

I 🪧 **learn**

l 👁 k **like**

m 👁 **my**

n 🏠 **nice**

O'c 🔒 **o'clock**

OFF **10** **often**

✕ **or**

🎻 **pair**

✂ choor **picture**

📦 T **safety**

⚠ 🤵 **salesman**

🪚 **saw**

〰〰〰 **see**

⚖ **someway**

☆t (or) st ♥ **start**

str 8 **straight**

sud 🦁 LEE **suddenly**

t 👒 **that**

t 🐔 **then**

t 〜〜 **those**

👔 m **time**

👔 🎀 **tiny**

t 🏆 d **turned**

un 💰 **until**

w 🛖 **what**

🧙 **which**

Y **why**

📜 **will**

March Music

These instruments may be made by the teacher, by older students for a younger group, or by the students themselves:

Bass viol. Prepare a *large* tin can (an oil can from a gas station) by removing 1 end with a can opener. In the middle of the remaining end punch a small hole. Take a long piece of cord & thread it through the hole. Secure it in place by tying a button to it on the outside of the can. Tie a large button to the other end of the cord. Oil cord well with a candle stub. To play, child sits in a chair, grasps can between feet, holding cord taut by button with 1 hand & strumming cord with remaining hand.

Bongo drums. Stretch heavy plastic taut across open mouth of coffee can. Secure plastic in place with strip of inner tube or rubber sheet. Repeat with a 2nd coffee can. Bind 2 cans side by side with rope or masking tape.

Bell sticks. Saw 3/4"-1" dowel sticks (or an old broomstick) into 6" lengths. Nail (or staple) large jingle bell onto either end of stick.

Bottle xylophone. Fill 8 identical bottles with varying amounts of water to reproduce (approximate?) the 8 notes of a musical scale. Bottles are struck with pencil.

Cigarbox guee-tar. Stretch 4 rubber bands of varying widths & lengths over an open cigar box. Pick or strum bands.

Drums. Bases may be: #10 cans, nail-kegs, automatic transmission fluid cans, coffee cans, chopping bowls. Heads may be: heavy oilcloth or canvas which is coated, after attachment with clear Dope. Inner tube drumheads are more resonant; after attaching, hold tubing firmly to base by overlapping 6 (1 1/2") inner tube strips. Heads are attached to metal bases by strips of inner tubing & to wooden bases by tacking head all along 1 edge, pulling tight on the opposite side & tacking. Repeat until tacks are placed every 1" or 2". Child may hold smaller drum under 1 arm to play.

Ersatz bells. Have children collect & bring old keys to class. These or curtain rings strung on a string simulate, when shaken, the sound of bells.

Gongs. A bent metal rod or a heavy pot cover suspended from a pole is held aloft & struck with a wooden spoon.

Hand bells. Cut 2 pieces of elastic, 8" each in length. Make a loop of each & sew its ends firmly together. Sew bells onto that section of each elastic which will cover backs of hands. (Child slips hand into loop & shakes or claps hands to play bells.)

Kazoo. Cut several small holes in the middle of a paper-toweling tube. Cover 1 end of tube with a large piece of wax paper taped in place. Child places fingers on varying holes & hums or sings into open end. Of course, this instrument must, by its nature, be played by just 1 student. If several bazookas are made, children's names may be printed on each.

Knockers. Nail flat block of wood to dowel rod handle. Or drive nail down through center of wooden spool (handle) into 4" x 6" wooden block. Make 2 of each knocker.

Nail chimes. Hang nails from thick dowel & strike with small metal pipe.

Raspers. Staple sandpaper on underside of a set of knockers. Or notch the length of 2 thick dowel rods. These are then rubbed against 1 another.

Rattles. Scrub 6-8 ring-shaped bones of lamb shoulder or lamb chops. Dry well. String. Or nail a wooden dowel handle to a frozen orange juice can; put pebbles inside & cover top of can with vinyl & a rubber band. Or use small boxes or cans with snap-in lids (e.g., baking powder) & put rice or buttons inside. Or papier mache *heavily* over a large used light bulb: once covering is thoroughly dry, break bulb within.

Tambourine. Make tiny slits every inch or 2 along the edge of the round top of a cardboard container. Insert loop of sleigh bell through slit & secure in place from behind with a safety pin. Or cut 2 (1/4") circles of plywood (5" in diameter). Enamel the edges. Mark off the edges into 1/8" divisions. Flatten a number of soda pop bottle caps & punch a hole through each. Hammer a nail through each of the 1/8" marks in 1 circle. Place 4 flattened caps on each nail so that they may move freely up & down. Place 2nd circle atop nail points & hammer gently & firmly in place.

Tom-tom. Get a large hatbox or round wooden cheese box. Cut its lid in 1/2. Glue 1/2 of lid securely in place atop box. With string secure a 3" long flat stick to the middle of lid as shown. Tap on free end of stick to produce a tom-tom-like beat.

Xylophone. This affords a good lesson in fractions. Have the children collect cardboard mailing tubes. You will need strong cord & 2 wooden lathes. The proportions are: 1, 8/9, 4/5, 3/4, 2/3, 3/5, 8/15, 1/2. Tubes are struck with a dowel that has a cork nailed to its end.

March Games

Flowers in the Wind. Divide children into 2 equal groups, one being "the Wind" & the other "Flowers." The Flower group gets together & secretly chooses a specific flower as their group name. Either end of the playing area is "Home"; the middle field is neutral. The members of the Wind spread out along their Home line. The Flowers walk up near to the Wind who, 1 child after another down the line, calls out the name of a different flower (pausing after each name), trying to guess the name that has been chosen by the Flowers. Once the correct flower is called out, all the Flower children race for Home, the Wind at their heels! Any Flower caught joins the Wind. Remaining Flowers choose a new name & game continues until every flower is captured.

Whip-Lash. Children form a circle except for 4 who stand in a line inside circle, with their hands on the shoulders of the child in front of them. The children in the circle have a ball & try to hit the final child in the line. Of course the line whips about protecting this player. When last child *is* struck, he goes & joins circle, & child who succeeded in hitting him becomes the new head of the line.

March Puppet: Shadow puppets & theatre

Figures (drawn in profile) are cut from tagboard or card-stock. An extra 4" or 5" is left at the bottom of the figure. Color is of no importance but detailed outline or cut-out areas add much to these puppets. Thumbtacks may also be punched into the figures, leaving tiny holes (textural areas) for light to come through. The extra inches at the bottom are folded over a dowel or stick & stapled in place. Let the children use their ingenuity to come up with solutions for how to show clouds, rain, wind, lightning.

Theatre is made from a large refrigerator box, the back side of which you have removed. Cut a large rectangular opening in the front leaving a 3" frame. Opening should be twice as tall as puppets. Staple a large piece of sheet (taut) to the inside of frame. Lay box, on its side, on top of a table. (Make sure that table is near a wall socket.) Set heavy-based lamp with a strong bulb inside box. Make sure cord is long enough to easily reach outlet. With masking tape adhere cord to floor to prevent any accidents. Place several bricks inside box to stabilize it, if necessary. Puppets may be inserted through a long opening cut on underside of box, in which case children will sit on floor beneath table & box front will slightly overlap table. Or long openings cut on either side of box will admit puppets held by students who stand beside theatre. Darken room. Children insert puppets behind screen & move them as they speak.

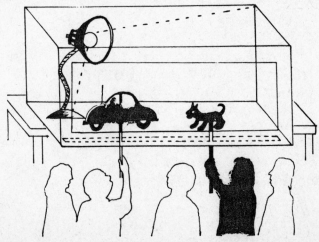

pril

April brings the primrose sweet,
Scatters daisies at our feet.

1   April Fools' Day.
2   First U.S. Mint established, 1792.
     Hans Christian Andersen (1805-1875), Danish writer, collector of fairy tales.
     Sergei Rachmaninoff (1873-1943), Russian composer.
3   Washington Irving (1783-1859), American author: *Rip Van Winkle, The Legend of Sleepy Hollow.*
     John Burroughs (1837-1921), American naturalist.
     Pony Express began: 1860.
     Dorothea Dix (1802-1877), American humanitarian, reformer.
4   American flag adopted, 1818.
     Pocahontas married John Rolf, 1614.
5   Booker T. Washington (1856-1915), American educator.
6   Peary set foot on the North Pole, 1909.
7   William Wordsworth (1770-1850), English poet.
10   Beginning of U.S. Patent System, 1790.
12   Henry Clay (1777-1852), American statesman.
     U.S. Civil War began at Fort Sumter, 1861.
     Soviet Major Yuri A. Gagarin orbited earth, 1961.
13   Thomas Jefferson (1743-1826), 3rd U.S. President.
14   Lincoln fatally wounded by J.W. Booth; 1865. (Lincoln died at 7:22 the following morning.)
15   Leonardo da Vinci (1452-1519), Italian artist, inventor.
     Henry James (1843-1916), American writer.

16   Wilbur Wright (1867-1912), American inventor.
Earth Week.
18   Paul Revere's ride, 1775.
19   Patriots Day, commemorating the Battle of Lexington, 1775.
U.S. Revolutionary War began, 1775.
Adolph Hitler (1889-1945), German dictator.
20   Mohammed (570-632 A.D.), founder of the Moslem religion.
Curies discovered the weight and properties of radium, 1902.
21   Legendary founding of Rome, 753 B.C.
John Muir (1838-1914), American naturalist, writer; born in Scotland.
Spanish-American War began, 1898
Birth of Queen Elizabeth II 1926; Queen of England since 1952.
National Library Week.
22   Arbor Day (date varies in different states).
Earth Day (Friends of the Earth).
23   William Shakespeare (1564 [disputed date]−1616).
James Buchanan (1791-1868), 15th U.S. President.
Sergei Prokofiev (1891-1953), Russian composer.
24   Guglielmo Marconi (1874-1937), Italian inventor.
Wilhelm de Kooning (1904-   ,), American abstract painter.
26   John James Audobon (1785-1851), American ornithologist and artist.
Walter de la Mare (1873-1956), English poet, writer.
27   Samuel Morse (1791-1872), American inventor.
Ulysses S. Grant (1822-1885), 18th U.S. President.
28   James Monroe (1758-1831), 5th U.S. President.
30   President George Washington inaugurated, 1789.
Louisiana Purchase (1803). Napoleon sold La. Territory to the U.S. for $15,000,000.

Palm Sunday, Good Friday, Easter, Passover are movable Feasts; Easter occurs on the 1st Sunday following the full moon that falls on or after March 21st.

Public School Week and Arbor Day may occur in other months; different states have different dates.

pril

No one knows for certain how our 4th month, April, got its name. Some sources state that it may have been named after Aphrodite, the Greek goddess of love. Webster's New World Dictionary (World Pub. Co.) says that April is akin to Latin *aprilis* which probably comes from the Indo-European root *apero*, "latter, 2nd," as April's original meaning was more than likely "the 2nd month." Other sources say that "April" may come from a Latin verb meaning "the opening." It is a fact that the Greeks called this season of spring "the opening."

APRIL QUOTATIONS

5 We are crawling up, working up, yea, bursting up. . . . There is no power on earth that can permanently stay our progress. *(The American Standard)*

No race can prosper till it learns that there is as much dignity in tilling a field as in writing a poem. *(Up from Slavery)*

—Booker T. Washington

6 The Eskimo had his own explanation. Said he, "The devil is asleep or having trouble with his wife, or we should never have come back so easily." —Admiral R. E. Peary (On his successful return from the North Pole)

7 The child is father of the man.

My heart leaps up when I behold
A rainbow in the sky.

I wandered lonely as a cloud
That floats on high o'er vales and hills,
When all at once I saw a crowd,
A host of golden daffodils.
    ("I Wandered Lonely as a Cloud")

—William Wordsworth

12 I would rather be right than be President! (Speech, 1850)—Henry Clay

13 The whole of government consists in the art of being honest.

Eternal vigilance is the price of victory.

If a nation expects to be ignorant and free, in a state of civilization, it expects what never was and never will be.

We hold these truths to be self-evident; that all men are created equal; that they are endowed by their creator with certain unalienable rights; that among these are life, liberty and the pursuit of happiness.

(Declaration of Independence)–Thomas Jefferson

14   *Sic semper tyrannis!* The South is avenged! (Spoken after he shot Lincoln, April 14, 1865. The translation of the Latin is "Thus always to tyrants!")–John Wilkes Booth

15   Iron rusts from disuse; stagnated water loses its purity and in cold weather becomes frozen; even so does inaction sap the vigors of the mind.–Leonardo da Vinci

16   I do not believe [the airplane] will surplant surface transportation. I believe it will always be limited to special purposes. It will be a factor in war. It may have a future as a carrier of mail. (Interview: March, 1906)–Wilbur Wright

18   Listen, my children, and you shall hear
Of the midnight ride of Paul Revere.

("Paul Revere's Ride": H.W. Longfellow)

19   Here once the embattled farmers stood
And fired the shot heard round the world.

("Concord Hymn": R.W. Emerson)

23   Suspicion always haunts the guilty mind.

There's nothing either good or bad, but thinking makes it so.

All the world's a stage,
And all the men and women merely players:
They have their exits and their entrances;
And one man in his time plays many parts. (*As You Like It*)
–William Shakespeare

If you are as happy, my dear sir, on entering this house, as I am in leaving it and returning home, you are the happiest man in this country. (Said to Lincoln, 1861)–James Buchanan

27   What hath God wrought! (1st message sent by Morse code: May 24, 1844)

28   The American continents ... are henceforth not to be considered as subjects for future colonization by any European powers. (From his message to Congress, December 2, 1823)—James Monroe

April Riddles: Why should soldiers be tired on the first of April? (They've just finished a March of 31 days!)

How is a crown prince like an April day? (It's very likely he will reign [rain].)

Which is the worst month for rodents such as rats and mice? (April: because it's always raining cats and dogs.)

Why can it never rain in April for 2 *days straight?* (Because there's always a night in between.)

APRIL EVENTS

• April Fools' Day   [1]

Traditionally, on this day Noah sent the dove from the ark & it returned, unable to find land. Some sources say that April Fools' Day is a relic of an old Celtic heathen festival In any case, there are 18th century records of April Fools' Day celebrations being held throughout Europe. In Scotland, if you're tricked today, you're a "gowk" (Scottish for "cuckoo"); in France, you become "un poisson d'Avril" ("an April fish"). In other words, you're a person who's easily caught.

Some general suggestions. Write the date on the chalkboard: "August 1, 197 " or "April 1, 1983"; asterisk the date & at the foot of the board, in tiny letters, print: "April Fool." Set the clock ahead (or back) & when this is discovered, use the opportunity to emphasize time-telling. Prepare a bulletin board or a mimeographed worksheet titled: "Don't be April-fooled! Answer the question & define the word!" Beneath this appears: "Would you feel flattered if someone called you arrogant? enthralling? vociferous? facetious? eccentric? insipid? rapacious? valorous?"

Another bulletin board suggestion. Display photos that are greatly blown-up shots of portions of familiar objects or aerial shots of the earth. These pictures have been collected by the teacher from magazines & should be untitled; it is up to the children to try to identify each photo. Listen as they say *how* they came to identify each one; what types of clues they found; what methods of deduction were used.

Language Arts. Point out the differences between a lie, a playful joke & a practical joke. Which is funny? The sense of (what is) humor(ous) differs from people to people: humor is partly a matter of culture. Talk about the role of jester in medieval times & his present day equivalent. Ask the children: *"Why* do we laugh?" Some possible answers: We laugh to release tension, anger, embarrassment, aggression, fear. We laugh to experience a sense of "togetherness," being a part of a group. Older children might give examples of different types of situations that illustrate different types of laughter.

Read aloud some Aesop's Fables in which animals get fooled. Then let the children write fables about creatures who get fooled.

Nonsense Stories, a card game. There are 4 piles of cards (green: nouns; red: verbs; blue: adjectives; yellow: adverbs). Each child picks (receives) 1 card from each pile. These cards are made into a nonsense sentence & upon this sentence the children build a nonsense story. Once the stories have been written, they can be read aloud &/or exchanged & read silently (& illustrated).

Word etymology. The Latin word *follis* from which we get "fool" means "a bag of wind"! Ambrose Bierce, in his *Devil's Dictionary,** defines April Fool as: "noun. The March fool with another month added to his folly." Vocabulary enrichment words: gullible, deceptive, fraudulent, ingenuous, guile, equanimity.

April Fools' Day Poetry.

> *Just As He Feared*
>
> There was an old man with a beard
> Who said, "It is just as I feared!
> Two Owls and a Hen, four Larks and a Wren
> Have all built their nests in my beard.
> —Edward Lear: *Book of Nonsense*

Also appropriate: "Old Quin Queribus": Nancy Byrd Turner (from *Zodiac Town:* Little, Brown & Co.)

Reading

April Fool Tachistoscope. Ask the children in the reading group, "Can you tell what the jester says? Watch him speak!" or ("Take the words right out of his mouth!")

---

*Ambrose Bierce, *The Devil's Dictionary* (180 Varick St., New York, N.Y. 10014: Dover Publishing Co., 1958). © by Dover Pub. Co., Inc.

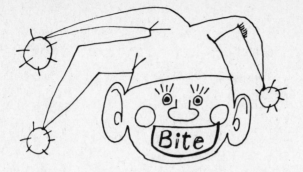

To help your class practice word analysis (& as a method of quick check-up), have each child fold his paper into 8 squares. (Teacher draws a similar pattern on the chalkboard & in each square prints a word that has an emotional connotation, i.e., furious, elated, astounded, etc.) Children draw a face in each square to reflect the word that appears in the corresponding square on the board.

Fishing with Simple Simon. Discuss the old rhyme: "Simple Simon went a-fishing, For to catch a whale; All the water he had got—Was in his mother's pail." Introduce a class fishpond (complete with bamboo or dowel fishing poles) to the reading group. Pond may be made from a large cardboard box painted blue with poster paints. Colorful cutouts of sea life are glued to the sides of box. Each child in the group goes fishing with his pole (to which a magnet on a string is tied); he tries to catch a new word (or a riddle or joke to be read aloud). Each card in the pond is made in the form of a fish (or octopus or jellyfish or old shoe) & has its message clearly printed on 1 side; the magnet on the fishing line is attracted by the large paper clip which is attached to each card. (Teachers' or Helpers' names might also be selected in this manner.)

Science

The following may be presented in the form of a mimeo sheet (to be done in free-time or as a part of homework):

"Your Personal Science Experiments." (Be careful: don't be fooled!)

1 Make a tube out of a piece of paper. Hold your left hand up in front of your eyes, about 6'' from your nose. Put the paper tube up to your right eye & rest the tube against the side of your left hand. Keep both eyes open and stare through the tube. What seems to happen to your left hand? Do you understand why?

2 How many pencils do you have? Tightly cross your 1st & 2nd fingers. Close your eyes. Now rub a pencil along the length between your crossed fingers. How many pencils do you think you feel? (Here's why: Under normal circumstances, the opposite edges of BOTH your index & middle fingers would not be touched at 1 time by a single object, so when such a sensation occurs, it is interpreted by your brain as coming from 2 objects.)

3 Your ♥ pumps the blood through your veins. With each "pump," the vein stretches a little. This stretching causes your "pulse." The rate of your pulse tells us how fast your ♥ is beating. You know that you can *feel* your pulse; well, here's how you can *see* how fast your heart's beating! Break a wooden matchstick or toothpick in 1/2. Stick the point of a thumbtack up into the end of the broken toothpick. It should look like this: Find your pulse: place the fingers of 1 hand along the wrist (below the thumb) of your other hand. With a felt-tip pen make a dot on the place where you feel a strong pulse. Now rest your arm on a desk or table. Place the head of the thumbtack on the dot on your wrist. Sit quietly. You should see the toothpick move with each beat of your pulsing ♥ !

The Mysterious Shoe-box. At some convenient place in your room, post the following sign & beside it place the esoteric box. "NOTICE!! You cannot IMAGINE what is in this box. You've never seen these things inside any box in your WHOLE life. But—beware! Once you look inside this box I will have April-FOOLED you! *[Signed]* Your teacher." Here's how to make the box: Tape a small hand mirror to the inside (end) wall of a shoe box. At the opposite end of the box, cut 2 small round eye-holes.

Cut a slit in the top of the box above the wall where the mirror is. Put lid on box & look through 2 round holes; if no adjustments to slit are necessary, firmly glue top of box onto bottom.

• **The date on which Peary set foot on the North Pole   [6]**

Word etymology. The Greek word *arktos* meant "bear." The Great Bear Constellation, which revolves about the northern part of the earth, is referred to as "arktikos." From this we get our word "arctic." The word "Eskimo" is said to be derived from the American Indian (Labrador-Algonquian) "eskimantik," eater of raw fish.

• **Birth of Thomas Jefferson   [13]**

He was described by his biographer, James Parton, as "The gentleman of 32 who could calculate an eclipse, survey an estate, tie an artery, plan an edifice, try a cause, break a horse, dance a minuet and play the violin."

Jefferson himself wrote this epitaph for his grave: "Here was buried Thomas Jefferson, author of Declaration of American Independence, of the statute of Virginia for religious freedom, and father of the University of Virginia."

• **Birth of Leonardo da Vinci   [15]**

In order to protect his scientific discoveries, da Vinci described his inventions in his notebooks by the use of this "code": he reversed each letter & wrote his sentences from right to left. Your class may enjoy experimenting with mirror writing or you may occasionally write their homework assignment (on a mimeo sheet) using this technique: Print words in reverse order with each word spelled backwards & each letter reversed. Message is held up to mirror to be read. Up-side down mirror writing is produced by printing words in reverse order, each word spelled backwards & each letter printed upside down; only "s" will have to be reversed. Pocket mirror is held at right angle to message in order to "break this code."

• **The date of Paul Revere's ride   [18]**

Bulletin board suggestion. Title: "Straight from the Horse's Mouth." (Perhaps title & the race-track origination of this expression should be discussed with class.*) Children list or write (in the 1st person) the impressions that Paul's horse gathered from that long night. What did he see, smell? Did anything frighten him? How did Paul speak to him? Was he tempted at any time to discontinue his mission? What were his after-thoughts? How did the other animals treat him after that night?

• **Quotations for National Library Week**

A Book is a Garden carried in the Pocket.—Arabian

Reading is to the mind what exercise is to the body.—J. Addison

Books are ships which pass through the vast seas of time.—Bacon

Few are better than the books they read.—Anonymous

A man only learns in two ways; one by reading and the other by associating with smarter people.

—Will Rogers

To acquire the habit of reading is to construct for yourself a refuge from all the miseries of life.—Somerset Maugham

Except a living man there is nothing more wonderful than a book! A message to us from . . . human souls we never saw. . . books arouse us, terrify us, teach us, comfort us, open their hearts to us as brothers.—Kingsley

"Little Theatre" constructions. Once his little theatre is built, each child peoples each of the 4 stages with the characters, scenery of 4 of his favorite books or 4 different events in 1 of his favorite books. These constructions can also be used for the dramatization of (reading) stories. To construct little theatres, each student gets 2 (8" x 16") pieces of cardboard & 1 (16" x 16") piece of cardboard. A slit is made to the middle of each of the 2 smaller pieces & they are then inserted into 1 another forming the 4 walls of the theatre; the slits may be reinforced with tape. The larger piece of cardboard is glued or masking-taped to the walls & the

---

*Presumably bettors at a race track like to feel that they are getting advice from people intimately involved with the stables; horses would, therefore, be the ultimate sources of authority.

construction is complete. Scenery may be painted, pasted on walls, & clay or paper figures moved about within it. Free-standing trees, buildings, etc., are possible. These theatres make an interesting exhibit on a table in the classroom.

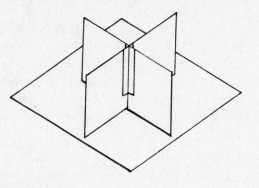

• **Arbor Day** [22]

J. Sterling Morton proposed to the Nebraska legislature the establishment of an Arbor Day to be observed on April 10, 1872. The date, in many states, is now fixed at April 22, coinciding with Morton's date of birth.

Math enrichment. To measure the diameter of a tree: with a tape, measure the girth of a tree. Divide this number by 3 (for an estimated measurement), or by 3.1416 (for a more exact measurement). To measure the height of a tree: with a piece of chalk, mark the trunk of the tree at 4 feet from the ground. Holding a ruler outstretched *at arm's length* before you, step back from tree. Close 1 eye & continue stepping back until the 1/2" mark on your ruler covers the area from the ground to the chalkmark on the trunk. From this exact distance measure the entire tree on your ruler. Multiply the number of 1/2" by 4 to get the height of the tree.

Sources of information:

Sierra Club
Mills Tower
San Francisco, Calif. 94104

U.S. Environmental Commission
Washington, D.C. 20460

American Forestry Association
919 17th Street, N.W.
Washington, D.C.

U.S. Forestry Service,
South Building
14th Street & Independence
Avenue, S.W.
Washington, D.C.

● **Easter**

The 3 principal events celebrated by those of Christian faith are the birth of Christ, His crucifixion & His resurrection. Easter commemorates the latter two.

Easter falls on the 1st Sunday following the full moon of, or after, the spring equinox (March 21). Its name & time of celebration indicate that it was originally a festival of ancient times celebrating the death of winter & the resurrection of the sun. Early Germanic peoples honored "Ostern," the goddess of spring, at this time of year; her name was also related to the East—in which the dawn appears.

Easter eggs. From earliest times the egg has been the symbol of the universe. It also stands for fertility; ancient Babylonians exchanged eggs at the beginning of each spring. Colored eggs symbolize re-birth; the Persians, Egyptians & ancient Chinese dyed eggs for their spring festivals. The origin of the *Easter egg hunt* is unclear. One source states that a noble woman was the 1st to hide colored eggs for the children.

Easter bunny. Our Easter bunny is related to the ancient Egyptian belief that the rabbit is the symbol of spring, the beginning of a new life.

Easter lily. There is also an original American Easter symbol! Towards the end of the last century, churches in America began having special Sunday services to help console those who had lost loved ones in the Civil War. The churches were filled with flowers, one of these being a Bermuda lily which was used in such profusion as to become associated with this season & which therefore has been named the Easter lily.

Vocabulary enrichment words: confections, apocalypse, resurrection, transfiguration, renaissance, crucifixion, Calvary.

Easter Rabbit Riddles: (These may be presented in the form of 3-4 Easter Rabbit Riddle Books, simply illustrated with colored felt tips, the answer appearing on the back of each riddle's page. Children may read these books during their free time.) How can you find the Easter Bunny when he gets lost? (Make a noise like a BIG carrot.) How can you buy eggs and be *sure* there are no baby chicks inside? (Buy duck eggs.) What kind of bush does the Easter Bunny hide under on a rainy day? (He hides under a wet bush.) What's the difference between a crazy rabbit & a phony dollar bill? (One's a mad bunny & the other's bad money.) There were 9 ears of corn in a field & a rabbit came each night & took away 3. How many nights did it take him to get *all* the ears? (Nine nights: each night he took his *own* ears when he left the field.) What goes up pink & comes down pink & white & yellow? (An Easter egg.) Which is correct: the yolk of an Easter egg *is* white or the yolk of an Easter egg *are* white? (Neither, because the yolk of any egg is YELLOW!)

Reading

Mimeos can be prepared using bunnies to emphasize words & word-skills appropriate to your group, e.g., "Circle the word that does NOT begin like the other 2 words in each bunny."

Using the puppet described on pg. 174 as a basis, add ears, tail & broom bristles for whiskers, to make a Reading Rabbit who will help introduce new words to your reading groups.

Easter Science

Science topics include the study of clouds, nests, rainbows, flowers & eggs.

Some Egg Experiments. "Can you tell which egg is the boiled egg?" Put a hard boiled egg on 1 saucer & an uncooked egg on a 2nd saucer. Place these on a table in front of the class. Ask if anyone knows how to tell which egg is the boiled egg. Spin each egg (sideways) on its saucer; the uncooked egg wobbles noticeably while the boiled egg spins smoothly. This is because the uncooked egg is filled with liquid. When spun, the contents of this egg, due to inertia, can't follow rapid motion smoothly. The inner part of the white of the egg slides over the outer layers of white, causing such friction that the egg wobbles & comes to a stop. Now spin the eggs again & this time quickly stop each one, immediately letting go of them. The uncooked egg will continue to spin for a bit; this is because its inner layers of white are still in motion.

"Can you suspend an egg in water?" Here's how: dissolve a great deal of salt into a jar that you 1/2-fill with water. Try putting an egg in this water; when enough salt has been dissolved, the egg will float on top of the water. Then carefully pour fresh tap water down the side of the jar until the jar is filled. The egg should remain suspended in the middle of the jar. This is because the salt water is heavier (it has a greater specific gravity) than an equal amount of fresh water. An egg (or any object) will float on top of the water only when it is exactly the same weight as the amount of water it is displacing. Between the fresh & salt water is an invisible boundary at which the egg will remain suspended.

"Do you know how to change a white egg to SILVER?" Completely blacken a hard-boiled egg with a heavy coat of soot from a candle. Carefully lower the egg into a glass filled with water. Suddenly the egg becomes a dull silver! This is due to the way that the light waves are reflected off the egg & through the water.

Easter Art

Cards. Supply each student with 2 or 3 buttons & a little piece of ribbon. They use these as the basis for an Easter bunny. The buttons are glued to the front of a folded sheet of colored paper & the rabbit is drawn around them. *Any* placement of the buttons is acceptable, e.g., buttons need not be used as shown.

VARIATION: Each child draws the side view of a *large* rabbit on the front of his card. A small slit is made in the upper torso (teachers may go around & make slits with razor blade; slip a small square of cardboard between cover & inside page of card in order to protect the latter). An arm is inserted as shown. A brad holds arm in place & allows rabbit to nibble at carrot or an Easter egg.

NOTE: Certain Christmas display suggestions (i.e., see pg. 103: stained glass window) are also appropriate for the class to make at this time of year.

Easter baskets (see pg. 226, May baskets, for further ideas). Mimeograph an enlargement of this basic outline onto sheets of construction paper or tagboard. Children add design of *their invention*. You might discuss how basket's sides could be a rabbit's head, a brooding hen, a basket with decorated eggs showing, etc. Then children cut out baskets & glue or staple sides in place.

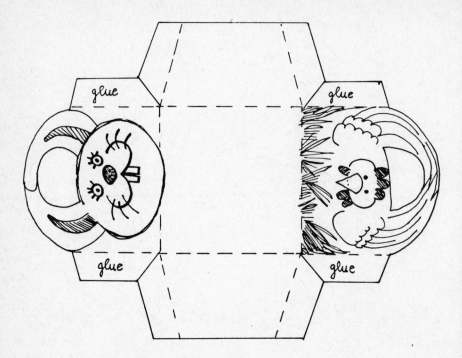

Easter eggs. Pioneer children dyed their eggs in the following way: with thread, they bound the outer gold or purple skins of onions to eggs which were then boiled. Bits of log wood bark were boiled with eggs to produce lilac, deep purple; vinegar was added to water to produce red. Once colored, these eggs were rubbed with butter or sweet oil & then polished to a bright glow.

It is not always practical to use hard-boiled eggs in the classroom. You may want to show your students how to blow out eggs & ask them to collect these empty eggs for use during class time.

Easter egg characters. Egg is dyed an appropriate basic color. Paper appendages are designed, cut out & glued in place. Tiny glass (seed) beads may be used for eyes or noses, brush bristles glued to eggs for whiskers, & yarn glued in place for a mouth or tail. Four burnt match sticks glued to egg become legs of animal. Let the children use a myriad of scraps of felt, trim, beads, sequins, papers, glitter, plastic to invent their own characters. Here are some ideas:

Eggs are made to stand by the use of a tube of construction paper as with bunny, or by sticking a small piece of modeling clay to underside of egg as with fish, mouse, octopus, frog & mermaid.

Collage eggs. By gluing overlapping tiny pieces of colored tissue, children cover egg's surface. Final effect should be almost like stained glass.

Older students will be able to produce eggs like those made in Poland & Yugoslavia. *Polish Easter Eggs:* Tiny long strips of glazed paper are folded in accordian pleats & cut to produce a chain design effect, i.e.,

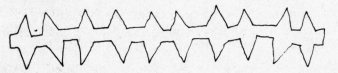

or tiny squares of glazed paper are folded & cut to make geometric shapes, i.e.,

These are carefully covered with rubber cement, as is area where they will be on egg. When all cement is dry, tiny shapes are secured to egg's surface. Excess cement is *gently* rubbed off egg.

Yugoslavian Easter eggs: Using kitchen tongs, blown egg is immersed in pan of melted paraffin. Entire surface of egg is covered with wax & this is allowed to dry. Children use orange sticks (toothpicks) to incise designs with lines wide enough to accept dye. Egg is dyed & allowed to dry. (If more than 1 color is desired, 1st color must be a water-proof ink, applied heavily.) Wax is washed off with very hot water. Finished egg is oiled & polished.

• **Public School Week**

Some suggestions for preparation of your room: Display the children's work by subject matter but *don't* label groups as "Our Best Work" unless *all* the students have papers exhibited. Every child should have several examples of his efforts on display; some papers can be taped to windows if these are at eye level.

There can be a *large* book of drawings & stories covering many subjects. Classroom plants can have little signs noting dates seeds were planted. Try emphasizing the foreign language taught (if any) by labeling all the common objects about the room with the foreign names which the children have learned. Post examples of comparative writing efforts (Sept. & April); include 1 sentence that is the same, if possible (i.e., "This is my very best penmanship"), or short paragraphs written especially for this display ("What I Love About My Parents," "The Funniest Day in 4th Grade," "Why I Think I Want to_____When I Grow Up"). Display many different types of artwork, labeled as to medium used: tempera, collage, silkscreen, rubbings, etc. Have a small group of photographs taken each month covering as many subject areas as you can. Set out the microscope with slides THEY'VE made.* On the Science table have an experiments display: list purpose, materials, procedure, results, conclusions; have the experiment's materials set up in the center of the table.

Have a pile of mimeographed sheets for parents to take home; these might cover: Characteristics of the (i.e., 4th) Grader—physical, emotional, intellectual, etc. Enliven presentation of learning projects, study materials & students' work with tape recordings (at a labeled "Listening Post"), or by having an

---

*Boxes of unprepared slides (& directions for their preparation) are available through scientific supply houses.

automatic cartridge of slides shown in one corner of your room. Post this proverb & discuss it with your class: "Remember: it was the North Wind that made the Vikings."

For parents of older students, prepare a mimeographed sheet of objectives for each subject covered at your grade-level. Word these concisely; avoid using educational jargon, generalizations. Note areas to be covered, projects & enrichment work, e.g.:

> *Reading:* Continuation of the developmental reading program. In addition to this, a study of vocabulary, root words, structural & phonetic analysis is emphasized. Recreational reading ("reading for fun & profit") is encouraged through the library program. Subject matter reading is stimulated through assignment of projects in Science, Social Studies & other academic areas. Your child will be encouraged in many ways this year to develop a life-long interest in reading!

- **Birth of James Buchanan   [23]**

While studying law, James became engaged to a beautiful young woman who was sensitive & shy. She heard some gossip about her sweetheart & wrote him, breaking their engagement. Shortly after, she died. Many years later he told a friend that he had only gone into politics to distract him from his grief. Buchanan, who wanted to be a married lawyer, lived to become a lonely, childless man & 15th President of the United States.

- **Date of baptism of William Shakespeare   [26]**

The actual birthdate of Shakespeare is unknown. However, his baptism took place at Stratford-on-Avon on April 26, 1564.

Bulletin board suggestion. Mount a picture of Shakespeare on a brilliant piece of paper; cut from white paper a large comic-strip balloon which will connect with Shakespeare's mouth & will have printed within it the title: "What's in a Name?" (A 2nd balloon might state: "A rose by any other name is STILL a rose." Yet our names do link us to our ancestors & tell us something about them: the *work* they did, *where* they *lived,* or how they *looked!*) Spot about the board, brightly backed papers that tell the derivations of the surnames of every student in your class. A book of name origins will be a help; give the derivation of the given name, if the surname cannot be traced. Older children might do their own research. Here is a start:

> *Archer, Bowmen:* a man who used arrows to do battle. *Chester,—cester:* from Latin *Castra* (camp); means your ancestors lived near

a fortified Roman site in England. *Crump:* round-shouldered. *Dexter, Dyer:* A man who teased the wool before it was made into yarn. *Fitz–:* "son of," dates back to Norman invasion of England. *Fletcher:* a man who made or sold arrows. *Hill, Dale, Moore:* described the land he lived on. *Latimer:* from "Latiner," one who could translate a strange tongue into a universally understood language. *Lightfoot, Ambler, Trotter:* described the way a man walked. *Mac–:* Scottish, "son of." *O'–:* Irish, "son of." *Pollard:* a bald man. *Quincey:* you are the descendant of the Normans who invaded England 900 years ago! *Scrivener, Scriver:* a scholar. *Schearer, Sherman:* a man who worked on the nap of the wool cloth (13th c). *Smith:* not all were blacksmiths; many worked in gold, silver, copper, tin; or it may refer to a man who lived *near* the forge. *Tailor* (and *Taylor*), *Weaver, Webster, Webb:* weavers of wool: 13th c.

- **Birth of John James Audubon   [26]**

Audubon spent his life painstakingly recording, in beautiful watercolors, the wild birds of 19th c. America. Many states celebrate Audubon's birthday; in some places Audubon Day & Arbor Day (see pg. 209) are celebrated as one.

Have the children observe birds. Help them learn to discriminate as to size (relative to the robin, starling, & sparrow), color (markings), & shape of body & bill. With experience, children will learn to make finer discriminations. (How does it fly? How does it get its food? Does it run or hop? What are its nesting habits? Of what value are these birds, ecologically?)

Science

Have each child accumulate clues for his own personal bird chart; each child's chart should be completely different from the other children's. Divide large sheets of tagboard into sections entitled: Size, Shape, Color & Markings, Special Characteristics, Location Where Seen, Flight Pattern, Song, & finally, NAME. Children may illustrate any section with a drawing; "the song" should be in terms of how it impresses the *child;* the size section should compare each bird to a robin, starling, & sparrow.

Sources of information:

Nat. Audubon Society (Jr. Program)
1130 Fifth Ave.
New York, N.Y. 10028 (free materials & information)

"The Community of Living Things": a set of 5 books written

with cooperation of National Audubon Society ($6 each; $30 for set). Write for information to: Creative Educational Society, Inc., Mankato, Minn. 56001

- Birth of James Monroe   [28]

Word etymology. "Doctrine" comes from the Latin word *docere,* to teach. A doctrine is a theory based on carefully worked out principles & *taught* by its adherents. The Monroe Doctrine stated that the U.S.A. would regard as an unfriendly act any attempt by European powers to interfere with American affairs or to increase their possessions on the American continents.

APRIL ACTIVITIES

Bulletin Board Lettering Suggestions. In order to attract attention to displays try making titles from unusual materials, i.e., bent cellophane straws glued to a vivid background color, fabric remnants cut with pinking shears, aluminum foil letters glued to a color that is in strong contrast to silver. One important (& at the same time short) word in the title can be spelled from toy building blocks; you may wish to re-paint each of these letters in a bright poster paint.

Title: FACE IT! Teacher &/or children collect all kinds of pictures of faces. From these each child chooses 1 & writes a history of this person: where he is, what he's doing now, what he wants from life, etc. Each theory, part of the history may be proven by details noted in the photograph, e.g., worry-lines, make-up, expression, hair-style. Children hypothesize what each face is thinking at the moment it was photographed. These compositions & their corresponding photos make fascinating reading & an intriguing display.

Language Arts: Creative Writing "Self-Starters"

1. One dark night an owl flew by your house. He landed on the window ledge & looked into your living room. Describe *every* thing he might have seen.
2. Take a simple human interest (animal) story from a newspaper or the S.P.C.A. Newsletter (i.e., involving the rescue of a wild animal). Have the children write, speculating as to how the animal got into its predicament, what might be done to help it & then what becomes of it & why.
3. If you could take a trip to any place in the world, describe your

itinerary, activities, possible adventures, how this trip might change your life. This could be written as a satirical Baedecker or "_____on $____a Day."

4. You find a bottle on the beach. A note is in it. What does the message say? Because of the note, what do you do? What finally happens to the bottle & its contents? How has finding this bottle changed your life?

5. Teacher holds up a large sheet of newsprint on which is written: "One day I got up & went & looked at my face in the mirror. I let out a LOUD cry because I was so surprised & upset. . . . "

6. Children write an autobiography of an animal, vegetable or mineral, e.g., "My Life as a Hunk of Coal."

7. Display 3 large random photos (of persons, animals, objects) in the chalk tray. Children are to write a sentence incorporating the 3, i.e., "The dog stopped beside a stream because he thought he heard a fish calling his name." Children are asked to complete the stories which these sentences introduce.

8. Without identifying them by name, describe the largest &/or smallest thing(s) you noticed during recess.

9. Discuss the term "x-ray." Emphasize how details are essential to a good adventure story. Ask the children to write about: "If I had X-ray Eyes (Vision)."

10. "My Most Popular Day Dream."

11. "I was a Caveman in 40000 B.C."

12. "Lost and Found (and Lost Again)."

13. Teacher brings to class a good reproduction of a famous painting. Children are asked to write, answering "What kind of person do you think made this painting? How did he happen to paint it? Did he like it? What did other people say about it? What became of it after the artist died? How did it get to be recognized as a masterpiece?" (After children finish writing, teacher might tell them, via mimeo sheets, the actual historical answers to these questions about the painting.)

14. Let each child choose a new name for himself & tell *why* he likes it, what it makes him think of, why he would (would not) like to *legally* have this name, how it might make his life different.

15. Ask each child to choose an emotion or state of mind. Then have him put it in the blank space & finish the sentence with a story: "I feel _____when(ever) _____."

16. "I Wish Grown-ups Would STOP _____."

17. "The _____Person I Know."

18. Think about something that really scares you. Try to think back to the very 1st time you got scared by it. How did it happen? Why did you feel that way? In what ways does(n't) it make sense to be afraid? How would you handle this fear in your *own* child?

April Poetry

Sweet April showers
Do bring May flowers.

—Tosser: "500 Points of Good Husbandry"

For as the rain cometh down, and the snow from heaven, and returneth not thither, but watereth the earth, and maketh it bring forth and bud, that it may give seed to the sower, and bread to the eater.

—Isaiah 55-10

Be still, sad heart, and cease repining;
Behind the clouds is the sun still shining;
Thy fate is the common fate of all,
Into each life some rain must fall,
Some days must be dark and dreary.

—Longfellow: "The Rainy Day"

April P.E.

Mystery Man: Children line up along the home base line. They close their eyes & keep their hands behind them. Teacher goes down the line, behind the children, pretending to deposit a penny in each child's hands. Children immediately clench fists when teacher has passed them. Child who actually receives coin does not let this be known. When entire line has been covered, children open their eyes & begin to move out onto playground. After a few minutes the teacher calls out, "Mysteryman! Mysteryman! Catch them all if you can!" Everyone runs for the home base line. Child with the coin calls, "I will! I can! I'm the Mysteryman!" & he tags as many children as he can before they cross home base line. Once everyone has gotten to safety, "Mysteryman" counts up the number of his victims, just to get the record straight. Children form line & "Mysteryman" goes behind it, depositing the coin in some unsuspecting person's hands. And so game continues. *VARIATION:* Children stand in a circle, hands extended in front of them. "It," who is inside the circle, goes to each child & pretends to put a penny into his extended hands. Each child acts as if he *may* have penny. Child who actually gets penny breaks away from circle & runs to cross a goal line. Whoever catches him becomes the new "It." If no one catches him, he is then "It."

April Puppet: Very Simple Hand-Puppets
Made from Rubber Gloves

A black rubber glove with cut-out paper features quickly becomes a spider. A pink rubber glove, treated in a like manner, becomes an octopus. Features are attached with rubber cement. To make a butterfly or snail, cut out a set of cardboard wings (or a cardboard snail shell); staple to it a wide elastic band that slips over a gloved hand. The 1st 2 fingers are entended, becoming antennae, & thumb grasps remaining fingers beneath puppet. Eye spots or a face may be painted on antennae or glove. A curtain secured to either side of a doorway becomes an adequate "stage" in lieu of an actual puppet theatre. These puppets, while limited in their range of actions, are appropriate for reading group practice sessions or as a little something special for a rainy day.

ay

May brings flocks of pretty lambs,
Skipping by their fleecy dams.

1   May Day.
2   Catherine the Great (1729-1796), German-born empress of Russia.
3   Niccolo Machiavelli (1469-1527), Italian statesman, author.
5   Karl Marx (1818-1883), German philosopher.
    1st U.S. sub-orbital space flight by Alan B. Shepard, 1961.
6   1st postage stamp, "the penny black," issued in England, 1840.
    Sigmund Freud (1856-1939), founder of psychoanalysis.
    Robert E. Peary (1856-1920), American arctic explorer.
7   Robert Browning (1812-1889), English poet, husband of Elizabeth Barrett.
    Johannes Brahms (1833-1897), German composer.
    Peter Ilich Tchaikovsky (1840-1893), Russian composer.
8   Harry S. Truman (1884-   ), 33rd U.S. President.
9   Capt. Kidd was tried for piracy, 1701.
10   Completion of the railroad across the U.S., 1869.
    Mother's Day: 2nd Sunday in May.
12   Florence Nightingale (1820-1910), English nurse; regarded as the founder of modern nursing.
13   1st permanent U.S. settlement (by English): Jamestown, Va., 1607.
14   Gabriel Fahrenheit (1686-1736), German physicist.
15   Pierre Curie (1859-1906), co-discoverer of radium.

17   Dr. Edward Jenner (1749-1823), discoverer of vaccination against smallpox.

18   Walter Gropius (1883-1969), German-born American architect.

19   1st Ringling Bros. Circus: 1884 at Baraboo, Wisc.

20   Dolly Madison (1768-1849), official hostess at the White House for widowed Pres. Jefferson & later for her husband, Pres. Madison.
      Charles Lindbergh's flight: 1st non-stop transatlantic solo, 1927.

21   Albrecht Durer (1471-1528), German painter, engraver.
      1st bicycles imported to U.S. from England: 1819. These were called "swift-walkers"; when pedals were invented, the name changed to "bone-crushers."
      Clara Barton (1821-1912), founder of American Red Cross.

22   Alexander Pope (1688-1744), English poet.
      Richard Wagner (1813-1883), German composer (Wedding March from *Lohengrin*).

23   Franz Kline (1910-1962), American abstract-expressionist painter.

25   Ralph Waldo Emerson (1803-1882), American poet.

26   1st steamship to cross the Atlantic: U.S.S. Savannah, 1819. (She made it largely with the help of her sails.)

29   Patrick Henry (1736-1799), American statesman.
      John F. Kennedy (1917-1963), 35th U.S. President.
      Memorial Day (the 1st one was in 1869), 4th Monday in May: Monday Holiday Bill.

30   Joan of Arc burned at the stake in Rouen, France, 1431.
      Hernando de Soto, Spanish explorer, landed on Fla., 1539.

31   Walt Whitman (1819-1892), American poet ("Leaves of Grass," "Song of the Open Road," "I Hear America Singing").
      May is "Be Kind to Animals Month."
      Shabuoth: The Festival of Weeks or Pentecost (end of May, seven weeks after Passover). It is in commemoration of the bringing of the Torah to the Hebrews by Moses & is also in celebration of the beginning of the grain harvest.

May

Probably named for Mai Majesta, the Roman goddess of spring, May

was also dedicated to the goddess of grain, Ceres. In the N. Hemisphere, corn, the favorite grain of Ceres, is planted in May. The corn-growing Navajo Indians of N. America called May "the month of tiny & tall leaves."

MAY QUOTATIONS

5   From each according to his ability, to each according to his need. —Karl Marx

7   Words break no bones; hearts, though, sometimes.

The year's at the spring
And day's at the morn;
Morning's at seven;
The hillside's dew-pearled;
The lark's on the wing;
The snail's on the thorn:
God's in His Heaven—
All's right with the world.
(*Pippa Passes,* Part I)
—Robert Browning

8   Sixteen hours ago an American airplane dropped one bomb on Hiroshima. . . . It is a harnessing of the basic power of the universe. The force from which the sun draws its powers has been loosed against those who brought war to the Far East. (Aug. 6, 1945)—Harry S. Truman

12   Too kind—too kind. (When handed the insignia of the Order of Merit on her death bed)—Florence Nightingale

22   Fools rush in where angels fear to tread.—Alexander Pope

25   The reward of a thing well done is to have done it.

Fear always springs from ignorance.

Life is short but there is always time for courtesy.

A friend is a person with whom I may be sincere. Before him I may think aloud. ("Friendship")

Write it on your heart that everyday is the best day in the year. He only is rich who owns the day and no one owns the day who allows it to be invaded by worry, fret and anxiety. Finish every day and be done with it. You have done what you could.
                                        —Ralph Waldo Emerson

29   Ask not what your country can do for you; ask what you
      can do for your country. (Inaugural Address: 1/20/61)
      If we all can persevere, if we can in every land and office
      look beyond our own shores and ambitions, then surely
      the age will dawn in which the strong are just and the
      weak secure and the peace preserved. (Address to U.N.
      9/25/61)

                                                      —John F. Kennedy

      Is life so dear or peace so sweet as to be purchased at the
      price of chains and slavery? Forbid it, Almighty God. I
      know not what course others may take, but as for me,
      give me liberty or give me death! (2nd Va. Convention:
      3/22/1775)—Patrick Henry

31   And the narrowest hinge in my hand puts to scorn all
      machinery—Walt Whitman

   May Riddle: If April showers bring May flowers, what do May
   flowers bring? (The Pilgrims.)

MAY EVENTS

• May Day   [1]

This is 1 of our oldest holidays. Over 2000 years ago
the Romans honored Flora, the goddess of flowers on this day.
The tall marble columns in Flora's temple were twined with
garlands & the children danced about them praising the goddess;
such is the history of *the May pole.* The Pilgrims brought from
Europe the custom of giving *May baskets,* which are a secret
message of friendship & celebrate the arrival of spring.

Language Arts

With older children discuss the relative importance of this
day in relation to other holidays; why has it lost importance
through the years?

May Art

Baskets: Quickie. Make a slit at the center of each end of a
rectangle of construction paper. Lap over ends & staple or glue.
Attach handle.

Paper doily. Doily is folded in 1/2 & rolled into a cone. Glue edges together & let dry thoroughly. Attach handle of pink construction paper. *Fruit basket* may be painted, if it is wooden, with colorful stripes of poster paint. If basket is plastic, strips of a contrasting color of paper are woven in & out between slats of basket. Staple handle in place. *Tiny paper basket* may hold a few flowers & a haiku, or a few pieces of candy made in class. Each child folds an 8" square of paper in 1/2 horizontally & then in 1/2 vertically. This is then folded in 1/2 along a diagonal line. Cut as shown. Fold across tip. Open out & overlap each section with the 1 next to it. Rubber cement sections in place. Add handle.

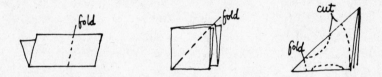

A Conservationist's May basket. Using 6" x 9" pieces of paper, children design their own flowers to fill this basket. Once colored (or painted or cut & glued), basket of flowers is cut out & paper is formed into a circle & glued. A 1/2" x 13" strip of paper becomes handle. A variety of leaf & flower shapes help this to become a very pleasant & personal May basket.

Completed baskets may hold cookies made in class (see suggested recipes at back of book) & "delivered" to an older person or a shut-in. Teacher might arrange in advance to give baskets to a local convalescent or rest home.

• **1st U.S. Sub-orbital Space Flight   [5]**

Language Arts

As a class effort, a Space Age Dictionary is compiled; children collect both pictures & terminology & draw illustrations when they cannot find appropriate photos. A large inexpensive scrapbook may be used & its edges indexed to speed location of words.

Reading. "Man in Space" is a game for reviewing facts. Students are told that each of them represents "a man in space." At the front of class is a globe representing the Earth, & the teacher represents "Houston" (or "Controls" or "Cape Kennedy"). Each time teacher holds up a drill card, she waits a moment before calling the name of one of the men in space; this commands attention of class & allows each child to prepare an answer. When his name is called & he answers incorrectly, child leaves his seat & "returns to Earth where he is quarantined" (goes to stand by globe). When teacher next calls out the name of a man in space, the earthbound student attempts to answer 1st; should he succeed & also give the correct answer, he returns to space & the other student becomes quarantined. Game continues this way.

Information sources (for Free Air Age teaching materials, pictures, bulletins):

Lockheed Aircraft Corp.
Public Relations Director
Burbank, Calif.

Aerospace Industries Assoc. of
America
1275 DeSales St., N.W.
Washington, D.C.

American Institute of Aeronautics & Astronautics
1290 Avenue of the Americas
New York, N.Y.

Nat. Aeronautics & Space
Administration
400 Maryland Ave., S.W.
Washington, D.C.

- **Birth of Sigmund Freud** [6]

Psyche is a Greek word meaning "breath, soul, or spirit." *Psycho-* is a combining form meaning "the mind." *-Logy* is a combining form coming from the Greek *-logia* & meaning "a theory of, a science, or study of." From these we derive our word "psychology." "Psychoanalysis," developed by S. Freud, is a method of studying a person's "mental life" in order to help treat disorders of the mind.

• Mother's Day

President Woodrow Wilson proclaimed this day as a national observance on May 9, 1914, but it has roots far back in history. In pre-Christian times the people of Asia Minor worshipped Rhea, the great mother of the gods, as she was called. When Christianity took the place of these ancient rites, the Virgin Mary became "the Mother of the Roman Catholic Faith" & the "Mother Church" idea developed. During the Middle Ages in England this Mid-Lent Sunday was called "Mothering Sunday." It was the custom for each person to return to the place of his birth & attend his mother church. As everyone was in his home town, after church services people would go & visit their parents, bringing cakes & gifts to their mothers.

Language Arts

Have the children, as a group, dictate sentences (which you quickly record) based on their ideas & feelings about "Mothers." The teacher organizes these & prints them, in large letters, on a piece of butcher paper that nearly covers a bulletin board. A colorful paper border outlines the composition for which the class should choose a title. This is also an appropriate time for improving public relations by writing your Room Mothers notes of thanks; perhaps you might organize a small party for all the mothers of your students.

Mother's Day Cards

Pop-up card. Make by folding a piece of 8" x 10" paper in 1/2 lengthwise & cutting out a 3" x 3" notch as shown. The portion that is left jutting out from card is folded inside & pops up when card is opened. Children modify pop-up shape (oval, heart) or draw a face, a bouquet or a jack-in-the-box on it. Cover of card is designed so as to accommodate "cut-off" top left-hand corner.

Talking card. Each child cuts a small (2"-4") square of white paper in 1/2, diagonally. Each triangle is then folded as shown. Finally, a rectangular piece of white paper for the card itself is folded in 1/2 lengthwise, the 2 modified triangles are placed at the center of the inside fold, & flaps 1 & 2 are glued down to card. Child draws a face around these "lips": it may be a self-portrait that answers "ME" as his mother opens the card. Message on front of card might then be: "Who wishes you a HAPPY MOTHER'S DAY?"

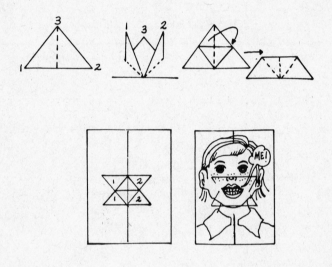

Mother's Day Gift

Suggestions. A plant grown in class from a seed or carrot top, class-made cookies or other sweets (see recipes at back of book).

A decorative tile. This can be made by using the encaustic technique: Heat unglazed tile on a hot-plate or in an oven. Apply a line drawing or decorative pattern with wax crayons, or scatter shavings from wax crayons on heated surface. VARIATION: Dissolve crayons in Amaco Brand Glaze Surfacer* (or *turpentine*) & apply to *un*heated bisque tile as you would tempera. Spray (or brush) design finally (once design is dry) with glaze surfacer or a fixative for a semi-gloss protective coating.

Clay slab dish. Each child finds & brings to class a 3"-8" smooth oval stone; these are scrubbed clean. On a table across

---

*Available from the American Art Clay Co., Indianapolis, Ind. 46222.

which an old sheet has been stretched & tacked in place, children 1st pound clay to "wedge" it, breaking up any locked-in air bubbles. Wedged clay is pushed down with the heel of the hand until surface of clay is 1" thick. Then, using rolling pins, cut-down broom handles or sturdy mailing tubes, children roll out clay into a smooth slab. Each of these is placed over a stone & molded to fit snugly. Keep top edges wide, erase any cracks by smoothing clay with moistened fingers. Sturdy feet or a cube base may be added by 1st scratching area on dish where feet will be & *then* attaching them. This scratching helps prevent the breaking off of appendages. Large dishes are removed from stones when clay is sufficiently dry to retain its shape. Clay edges, when leather hard, are smoothed with fingers. When completely dry, edges may be gently sanded, if you like. If there are no facilities available for firing clay, "Marblex," a product of the American Art Clay Co. (Indianapolis, Ind., 46222), may be used by the students. This self-hardening clay dries firm & durable without being fired in a kiln. (See "December Gifts" for other ideas.)

Lavendar Sachets. Students mix the following ingredients & put them in cambric bags, tied with pretty little bows: 2 oz. dried thyme, 2 oz. table salt, 1 oz. ground cloves, 1 oz. caraway seeds, 2 oz. dried & ground mint, & 1 lb. dried lavender flowers.

Clove

An East Indian evergreen tree (Eugenia aromatica), the unopened flowerbud of which is dried & used as a spice. The oil from clove trees is used in medicine & perfumery.

• Birth of Gabriel Fahrenheit   [14]

Most inventions are the products of the labors of many men. For instance, both Galileo & Sir Isaac Newton experimented with thermometers, using water & alcohol with some success. But it was a manufacturer of weather instruments who built the 1st mercurial thermometer that allowed temperature changes to be seen & recorded. Gabriel Fahrenheit was German & yet the Germans do not use the fahrenheit thermometer. Instead, they use the centigrade thermometer, which is named after Celsius, its Swedish inventor!

● **Memorial Day**

This was originally called Decoration Day & had its 1st formal observance on May 30, 1868. In the South, after the Civil War, mourning friends & relatives of slain soldiers put flowers on the graves of both Southern & Northern soldiers. The news of this gesture traveled north & soon most of the states honored the war dead on this day.

● **May is "Be Kind to Animals Month"**

> "Animals are such agreeable friends; they ask no questions, pass no criticisms."—George Eliot

Science

Let each child make an Animal Chart (similar in lay-out to the Bird Chart described in "Science," pg. 218). These charts may be based on any 1 of the following groups of mammals: Farm, Zoo, Forest, Jungle, Arctic, Local, or Household Pets. Categories would cover: Comparative Size, Shape, Coloration, Track Prints, Food, Habits, Family to Which It Belongs, & Ecological Value (how it fits into the "Web of Life").

Information sources:

Nat. Wildlife Federation	American S.P.C.A.
1412 16th St., N.W.	441 E. 92nd St.
Washington, D.C.	New York, N.Y. 10028
American Humane Assoc.	Publishers of *Nat. Humane Jr. News*,
P.O. Box 1266	a newsletter for children; free copy
Denver, Colo., 80201	for teacher

MAY ACTIVITIES

Bulletin board title: "What kind of May flower will grow, if you plant": Beneath title are listed a dozen "exotic seeds" & following each of these is a large flap beneath which appears a full color photo (from a seed catalog) with its identity printed clearly under it. Children, in attempting to answer riddles, will familiarize themselves at the same time with a variety of May flora. These are the 12 unknowns: (1) "A couple" plus "part of your face"? (Tulip.) (2) A vehicle & all the people of a country? (Carnation.) (3) "The expensive spread" & "a drinking vessel"? (Buttercup.) (4) A whole lot of sheep? (Phlox.) (5) A liquid & an Easter decoration? (Water lily.) (6) The name of a man & a part of a feather? (Jonquil.) (7) A word that means "just fine" & the king of all beasts? (Dandelion.) (8) Anger & the singular form of the verb "to be"? (Iris.) (9) A Xmas decoration & a part of a pig's leg (or a word that means "to leave something at the pawnshop")? (Hollyhock.) (10) A fib & a word that means "not having enough"? (Lilac.) (11) A bird & something a cowboy wears? (Larkspur.) (12) The opposite of "sour" & a common green vegetable? (Sweet peas.)

Lettering suggestions. Cut letters from unwanted finger-painted papers. Make simple letters in a short title from toy plastic clothespins glued to a contrasting color of background paper.

May Social Studies

In honor of Florence Nightingale, whose birthday is May 12, invite a nurse to visit your class. Before she actually arrives, talk over with the children types of questions that *they* would be interested in asking her. Help them to cover a wide range of topics; encourage them to take full advantage of this opportunity to interview a professional in the field of medicine. (Just for fun to help break down pre-conceptions, you might sometime invite a male nurse.)

At the front of the class, display a long line to which is tied a variety of kitchen utensils (e.g., wooden spoon, pancake flipper, egg timer, vegetable grater, pastry brush, kitchen shears, rubber spatula, etc.). Ask each child to choose a utensil & to keep its identity a secret. Now ask the students to thoughtfully outline the probable history of this utensil, describing how it may have been (& looked when it was) invented. Were equivalent utensils used by cavemen, ancient Mayans, Egyptians, early Christians, etc.? What famous people in history probably used an ancestor of this utensil? Describe 1 such historical incident. Each child might anthropomorphize his utensil & have it tell of its birth, youth, complaints, desires, attitudes now. Encourage students to cite as much historical data as they can in writing these papers.

Language Arts

"When it is dark enough, men see the stars" (Ralph Waldo Emerson): discuss this quotation with the children. This month affords many opportunities for short talks about thoughts, ideas of famous men (e.g., Whitman, Browning, Kennedy, Patrick Henry).

May words. Pass out to each child a mimeo sheet of May words: mayor, maybe, Mayflower, Maypole, mayhem, mayhap, May Day, May Queen, Maying, Mayflowers, Maynard, mayonnaise, dismay, manger, mail, maiden, male, make, maze, Mabel, mate, matron, mason, mane, main, maple, maniac. Discuss any word on the list which seems unfamiliar to a student. Then ask children to write a story or poem incorporating as many of these May words as they can.

The literary forms include: adaptation (condensed version), adventure fiction, allegory, autobiography, ballad, biography, essay, fable, feature article, folk tale, haiku, historical fiction, legend, limerick, mystery story, myth, parody, picture story (i.e., *Life* magazine), poetry, satire, science fiction. Ask the children to identify, describe those with which they are familiar. Then ask the students to list for each style 3 types of experiences that would provide good backgrounds for an author wishing to write in each these styles.

Vocabulary enrichment words. Maternal, bouquet, beneficent, compassionate, protective, magnanimous.

May Poetry:

           May
May be chill, may be mild,
May pour, may snow,
May be still, may be wild,
May lower, may glow,
May freeze, may burn,
May be gold, may be gray,
May do all these in turn—
May May.

                         —Justin Richardson, in "The Countryman"*

---

*Quoted in *New York Herald Tribune* & subsequently in *The Reader's Digest.*

(He is) as fresh as the month of May

Chaucer 1340?-1400 *(Canterbury Tales)*

Reading

Ask each child in a reading group to outline in 5-6 sentences the life history of a famous person (or the historical background of a holiday) about which they have learned this year. Once these sentences have been checked for accuracy & grammar, they are carefully printed on sheets of tagboard. Each group of sentences is cut apart & placed in an envelope on which is written: "These sentences are mixed up. Arrange them to make a story." Envelopes are used by class during periods of free time.

May Science

An informative bulletin board may be made based on the following: "A mosquito & a bee make different noises. What causes the difference?" "The wings of a mosquito are much smaller than the wings of a bee. The mosquito's wings go up & down much faster than the bee's. The faster a thing goes up & down, the higher the sound it makes. And so a mosquito makes a higher sound than a bee!"

Word etymology. *Entomology* is the study of insects. This word comes from the Greek *entomos* which means "cut-up." Insects have segmented or "cut-up" bodies. Our word "insect" comes from the Latin *insectum* which means "cut up." It is simply the Roman word for the Greek *entomos! Metamorphosis* is from the Greek; *meta-* means "changing" & *morphe* means "form." Metamorphosis means "a change of form or shape."

The Study of Insects. This study can be introduced by taking the class for a walk to a nearby vacant lot, if 1 is extant. Pencils, paper, sticks & string are taken along. There each child stakes out a 1-foot square claim of earth; he may even drive 4 ice cream sticks into the 4 corners & bind it round by a piece of string. Then he examines every inch of his claim, recording every single thing he finds; he may even dig into the earth if he wishes. When they're back in class, students compare notes, see who had the richest claims & who they feel "struck it rich." A bulletin board record of this walk may be titled: "Have you ever really seen a *vacant* lot?"

Before collecting or exhibiting any insects, ask the class one day during an art period to draw or make a butterfly. Then ask them to make a moth. Elicit answers to such questions as "How are moths & butterflies different?" The children may not look at any photos in books but they may ask questions that can be answered by "yes" or "no." These drawings should be kept for a few weeks & then returned to the children who, by then, should have a much clearer idea of how each insect looks. The children will, additionally, be able to see how they have improved their scientific knowledge.

Once the class has begun collecting insects, the following sign might be posted: Do you get moths & butterflies confused? Here are some ways to tell them apart:

Moths	*Butterflies*
night-flyers	day-flyers
thin, hairy feelers	club-shaped feelers
short, fat bodies	thin bodies
spread out wings when lit	fold up wings when lit

Trapping insects. Lay towel or open out umbrella beneath bush; beat bush with stick. At night collect moths from about neon signs. The grills of cars sometimes afford undamaged insects. Bury a topless tin can, its upper edge flush with the soil; pour a little molasses into bottom of can. Place a large stone *over* can (but *not interfering* with access to *rim* of can); beetles should crawl toward sweet smell & be trapped in can. Lightly bury a cookie sheet in soil; put a dead mouse or baby chick (some pet shops sell these frozen) on top of the soil-covered sheet. Scavenger insects should appear beneath animal after a few days.

Rearing insects. Children can experiment with raising various sorts of insects:

Beetles are kept in large gal. mayonnaise jar that is fairly high in humidity (see De-nested & Mealworm).

Butterflies can be raised from *larvae*, from *pupae* or from *eggs*.

Crickets are raised in a 1 gal. jar, the bottom of which has 2" of soil spread on it. Put a watch glass* (or plastic container lid), filled with water, on top of the soil. Mouth of jar is covered with wire mesh. Make certain that watch glass keeps filled with water. Crickets eat old mashed potatoes, tiny shreds of lettuce, corn meal

---

*A 1/2"-1" deep glass receptacle used in science studies.

mush or bread soaked in milk; once in a while give them a little library paste or peanut butter for a special treat!

De-nested beetles are caught as they are attracted by a piece of cheese children have left outdoors in warm weather.* Placed in a screen-covered jar, they are given the dried carcass of a dead mouse. Class may study *osteology* at the same time ("Osteon" is Greek for "bone") as beetles clean off carcasses, exposing skeletons beneath.

Grasshoppers are raised in a 1 gal. jar, the bottom of which has been lined with a 2" sod of grass. This is watered from time to time & provides food & an egg-depository place for grasshoppers.

Larvae (caterpillars) are raised in a wooden crate that has its bottom knocked out & its sides covered with screening. Box is stood on end & potted "feedplant"** with larvae on it is placed in box; or line bottom of aquarium with 2" of moist soil into which are planted "feed plants," (or jars of water with stalks of "feed plants" are placed in tank). Put larvae on "feed plant." Cover top of aquarium with "Stretch & Seal." The more airtight the larvae's cage, the longer his food supply will remain fresh, edible. There's little chance of suffocating larvae as they use very little air to live.

Mealworm beetles cultures can be obtained from a biological supply house if no one is able to find any in seldom-used box of cereal, corn meal or flour. Fill gal. jar 1/2 full of All-Bran, atop which you lay a piece of crumpled newspaper. Put 1/2 a potato on top of the newspaper; this affords moisture & food. Place culture in jar & cover jar's mouth with screening. Put jar in a warm place. Replace potato when it dries up.

Moths can be reared from larvae, from pupae or from eggs.

Praying Mantises are carnivorous & eat live insects; give a baby mantis aphids to eat, while an adult mantis will eat houseflies, roaches; if not fed enough the mantis will turn cannibalistic. Spear tiny piece of liver on a toothpick if no live ·

---

*Beetle cultures may be purchased from a Biological Supply House (i.e., Scientific Center, Santa Clara, Calif.). Cricket cultures are available from Wards Natural Science Estab., Inc., 316 Cannery Row, Monterey, Calif. 13940.

**The real secret to successful rearing of larvae is to keep them well-supplied with their "food plant": each adult female lays her eggs on a specific plant which will provide the food for emerging larvae. These larvae will usually *not* eat *any other* plant & so most captive larvae in the classroom starve to death amidst heaps of grass & green leaves. So it is essential to identify the "food plant" of larvae, e.g., either take note of plant on which larvae is found & get it & keep it fresh for larvae or use Frank Lutz's book: *Field Book of Insects of U.S. & Canada* (New York: G.P. Putnam's Sons, 1948) to help identify food source.

insect food is available. Eggcases must be collected in the fall or winter,* brought indoors & placed in jar (as described under Roaches). Babies emerge in 2-4 weeks.

Pupae: Larvae will molt several times & then stop eating. They may go beneath soil in jar to pupate. Don't bother them. Keep pupae to watch adult emerge (or children may collect cocoons & bring them & branches of the "food plant" to class). Put 1" soil in bottom of large jar; stick branches in soil & with a few drops of glue attach cocoons to sticks. Cover mouth of jar with screening. Once a week spray soil & pupae with water to keep air in jar humid (but never to the point of producing mold or mildew). If kept in a warm room, cocoons will produce adults in a few months; these will die if their host plants are not in leaf & available. If you wish to raise eggs & larvae from the adults, you must prevent their emergence until the spring. To do this, place jar between regular window & storm window on northern side of the school building. (To make certain that you get fertile eggs, you'll need both sexes of moth from pupae. A newly emerged female attracts males, so just put her in a cheesecloth covered jar & set this outside of an evening—males should arrive any time!

Insect-inspired art. Ask children to make a *painting* from a "bug's-eye view" (i.e., the huge, slightly transparent leaves overhead, etc.). Have children create an imaginary environment (& a *written description* of it) for an imaginary insect. Use an insect's wing to inspire a *stabile;* use the segmented body, legs to point out *balance in designs.* Use insect markings or microscopic view of insect to inspire an *all-over design* or an *abstract cut-out:* fold piece of newsprint from insect to edges of paper. Keep paper folded & cut out insect; open out paper & mount on contrasting paper.

Yarn pictures. Ask younger children to make a large pencil outline of a moth or butterfly on cardboard. Glue is applied to

---

*Or you may purchase praying mantis cocoons (3 for $2, 5 for $3) from Bio-Control, Route 2, Box 2397, Auburn, Calif. 95603. Each cocoon contains *many* young insects.

entire inside of this drawing & yarn is carefully laid in place, wound about, always touching edge of previously placed yarn, & coiled in this way until entire area of insect is made of yarn. Wax paper is put over picture & heavy book put on top to insure adherence of yarn to board. Different colors, textures of yarn should be used. Background may be filled in carefully with poster paint.

May Art

This month freshen up your room by developing a Creative Corner in the classroom. Here children, when they have free time & the inclination, may sit quietly & experiment, inventing new toys, games, constructions, ways of seeing things. The Creative Corner should be functional but not elaborate, containing a table, chairs & a *few* of the following objects. (As the days pass, objects will be changed; specific areas of interest shown should be noted & capitalized upon when new objects are added): tiny boxes, scraps of Lucite or colored plexiglass, film-tins, a large magnifying glass, colored toothpicks, Styrofoam, geometric wooden shapes (scraps from lumber yard), Plasticene (modeling clay), interesting buttons & seeds, a small flannel board & colorful felt scraps, scissors, a small piece of pegboard & yarns & Mexican hemp, golf tees, a broken alarm clock, sea shells, negative & positive shapes cut from cardboard (some reproductions of Arp),* durable toys from different countries & made of different materials, small wheels of different sizes, organic materials (i.e., blown-out egg shells). From time to time a book might also be put on the table (e.g., a book of African masks, mythical creatures, folk art etc.). After a while children may decide on a special name of their own for this corner, in which case it could be printed in large bright letters on a sign that is posted above table. Experimentation of all types should be allowed; what might appear to be dawdling can often lead to the most inventive results &, of course, not all results will be material.

---

*Jean Arp (1887-1966), French painter & sculptor.

May P.E.

Paper-cup relay: Divide class into teams of equal numbers. Each team forms a line. At a distance from each team is a chair on which stand 2 paper cups, 1 of which is filled with water. (Each team's cup holds the *same* amount of water initially.) At a given signal, the 1st player on each team runs to the chair, carefully pours water into empty cup, replaces cup on chair, runs back & tags 2nd player, who repeats this procedure. The team who finishes 1st, retaining the most water in a cup, is the winner.

Spiders & Flies.* A game for young children. The "spiders" stand in a long line facing away from the "flies" who creep softly up on them, until teacher calls out "Look out or the spiders will get you!" at which the spiders whirl about in pursuit of the fleeing flies. Any flies caught before reaching safety are taken back to the web & become a new arachnid. Now flies turn *their* backs & spiders creep up on them, etc.

May Finger Puppets

Child places his hand on a sheet of paper, fingers touching the edge, & 1st 2 fingers slightly apart. He draws around the 1st 2 fingers. The rest of the figure is drawn in proportion to these 2 "legs"; distance from tip of finger (foot) to middle knuckle (knee) is equal to distance between "knee" & "hip," "hip" & "shoulders," & "shoulders" & top of "head." A circle is drawn & cut out at base of each leg to allow entrance of fingers. At least 3/4" margin is left beneath these 2 openings. A gathered fabric or crepe paper skirt may be glued to waistband to heighten effect. Tiny modeling clay slippers or little bows tied on 2 fingers complete the illusion.

---

*From Doris Anderson, *The ENCYCLOPEDIA of Games* (1415 Lake Dr. S.E., Grand Rapids, Mich. 49506: Zondervan Pub. House). Copyright © 1955 by Zondervan Publishing House. Reprinted by permission of the publisher.

June

June brings tulips, lilies, roses,
Fills the children's hands with posies.

2   Thomas Hardy (1840-1928), English author: *Far from the Madding Crowd.*

3   Jefferson Davis (1808-1889), American statesman, President of the Confederacy.

       Dr. Charles R. Drew (1904-1950), "Father of Blood Plasma."

4   Henry Ford drove 1st successful Ford down streets of Detroit, 1896.

5   Socrates (469 B.C.-399 B.C.), Greek philosopher.

       Adam Smith (1723-1790), Scottish author, economist: *Wealth of Nations.*

       1st public ascent of a balloon, France, 1783.

6   Nathan Hale (1755-1776), American patriot.

7   Mohammed died, 632 A.D.

       Gwendolyn Brooks (1917-   ), 1st Negro to receive Pulitzer Prize, 1950 *(Annie Allen).*

       Children's Day.

8   Diego Valasquez (1599-1660), Spanish painter.

       Robert Schumann (1810-1856), German composer.

       1st vacuum cleaner patented by Ives W. McGuffrey, 1869.

       Frank Lloyd Wright (1869-1959), American architect.

9   Peter the Great (1672-1725), Czar of Russia, responsible for the westernization of Russia.

       1st ballistic missile submarine launched, 1959.

11   John Constable (1776-1837), English painter.

Richard Strauss (1864-1949), German composer: *Der Rosenkavalier.*

12   Henry David Thoreau (1817-1862), New England author: *Walden.*

14   Flag Day: Continental Congress adopted official American flag, 1777.

15   Magna Carta granted, 1215.

Rembrandt (Harmensoon van Rÿn) (1606-1669), Dutch painter.

Edward Grieg (1843-1907), Norwegian composer: *Peer Gynt Suite.*

16   1st extra-terrestrial flight by a woman, Jr. Lt. Valentina Vladimirovna Tereshkova; orbited Earth 48 times in 2 days, 22 hrs. & 50 min., 1963.

Father's Day (the 3rd Sunday in June).

17   Discovery of Mississippi River by Louis Jolliet & Father Marquette, 1673.

Bunker Hill Day, 1775.

18   Igor Stravinsky (1882-1971), Russian composer in America: *The Rites of Spring.*

19   Blaise Pascal (1623-1662), French philosopher.

Arrival of the Statue of Liberty in N.Y.C., 1885.

20   Adoption of design of Great Seal of U.S. by Congress, 1782.

21   Jacques Offenbach (1819-1880), German-French composer: *The Tales of Hoffman.*

Summer begins.

23   Treaty with Indians signed by William Penn, 1683.

U.S. Secret Service established, 1860.

Henry Hudson died after 6/23/1611: set adrift, without food or water, by a mutinous crew, Hudson wasn't seen again after that date.

25   Custer's Last Stand, 1876.

26   U.N. Charter signed by 50 nations, 1945.

27   Helen Keller (1880-1968), American author, speaker; blind & deaf since infancy.

1st demonstration of color television, 1929.

28   King Henry VIII (1491-1547), established Church of England.

Peter Paul Rubens (1577-1640), Flemish painter.

John Wesley (1703-1791), English minister, founder of Methodism.

Battle of Monmouth, Revolutionary War, 1778.

30   1st demonstration of transistors, 1948.

June

May have been named for the great goddess Juno, protectress of women, although some Romans felt that its name came from the Latin *iuniores,* in which case June would be a month dedicated to the young. Some scholars believe that "June" is derived from Junius, a Latin family to which the murderers of Julius Caesar belonged.

JUNE QUOTATIONS

3   All we ask is to be let alone. (Inaugural Address as President of the Confederate States of America, 1861)—Jefferson Davis

5   Know thyself.

Courage is knowing what not to fear.

Nothing can harm a good man, either in life or after death.

The nearest way to glory is to strive to be what you wish to be thought to be.

—Socrates

6   I only regret that I have but one life to lose for my country. (Last words, 9/22/1776)—Nathan Hale

8   The physician can bury his mistakes, but the architect can only advise his clients to plant vines. *(New York Times* magazine, 10/4/53).—Frank Lloyd Wright

12   In the long run you hit only what you aim at. Therefore though you should fail immediately you had better aim at something high.

Our life is frittered away by detail. . . . Simplify, Simplify. ("Where I Lived and What I Lived For")

—Henry David Thoreau

19   Man is but a reed, the weakest in nature, but he is a thinking reed.—Pascal

Give me your tired, your poor,

Your huddled masses yearning to breathe free,
The wretched refuse of your teeming shore,
Send these, the homeless, tempest-tossed to me:
I lift my lamp beside the golden door.
    (*The New Colossus,* inscription for the Statue of Liberty)
    —Emma Lazarus

27   Security is mostly a superstition. It does not exist in nature,
      nor do the children of men as a whole experience it.
      Avoiding danger is no safer in the long run than outright
      exposure. Life is either a daring adventure or nothing.—
      Helen Keller

28   (About Rubens): "The fellow mixes blood with his
      colors."—Guido Reni

      Cleanliness is next to Godliness.—John Wesley

June Riddle: What's a good thing to keep in summertime? (Cool.)

JUNE EVENTS

A few words about June: Try to plan these last weeks of school so that the inevitable restlessness of the children will not be compounded. Let the children work with the encyclopedia, tracking down answers to questions the class raises as a group. Bring in large, sturdy puzzles of the U.S.A. or of the world. Bring to class a set of wildlife books for free time reading. Construction paper scraps need to be used up so encourage the making of collages, torn paper compositions, or a scrapbook of magazine & student-made pictures for a hospital children's ward. The classroom will have to be cleaned (on the last day of school). This may be facilitated by dividing older children into 4 groups, each assigned the responsibility of thoroughly cleaning 1 side of the classroom. Make sure that all things to be accomplished in each area are clearly noted (where to put old papers, etc.) before you announce (by blowing a whistle) the beginning of house cleaning. First group successfully finished is rewarded in some small way. This may mean 5-10 minutes of noise but at the end of this time your room should sparkle!

- **1st successful drive by Ford of his car   [4]**

    Many people believe that Henry Ford invented the automobile. This is incorrect. Karl Benz, a German, built the 1st Benz, a 3-wheeler, in Mannheim. Although it was greatly ridiculed, he was driving this car down the "autobahn" in the fall of 1885—11 years before Henry drove his Ford through the streets of Detroit.

Information sources:

Automobile Mfrs. Assoc.	Am. Auto. Assoc.
320 New Center Bldg.	1712 G Street, N.W.
Detroit, Mich 48202	Washington, D.C. 20006
Society of Automotive Engineers	Museum of History & Technology
485 Lexington Ave.	nology
New York, N.Y. 10017	Washington, D.C.

• Patriots Day   [6]

The ancient Greek term *patrios* meant "founded by the forefathers" (*pater*=father). For this reason *patriotism* is the quality of one devoted to his family, who is prepared to defend the country of his forefathers at any cost.

• Flag Day   [14]

When he taught in Wisconsin in the early years of this century, Dr. Bernard J. Cigrand, each June 14th (in honor of the anniversary of the day in 1777 when the U.S. flag was adopted), would fly the American flag over his school. In 1916 President Wilson officially designated June 14th as Flag Day.

Bulletin board suggestions. Paper chains of red & white are made by the class. These are alternated to fill an entire board. The deep blue rectangle is filled with 50 stars also designed & cut out by the children.

Creative writing topic: "What America (My Flag) Means to Me."

Vocabulary enrichment words; halyard, pennant, flagstaff, banner, hoist.

History. Each day as the children salute the flag, they should understand the true meaning of the words they speak. Why not (with the assistance of the children & their dictionaries) paraphrase the salute to the flag, e.g., "I promise (myself) that I'll be loyal to the American flag & to the United States, whose power belongs to the voters, a country which, believing in God, cannot be divided & offers liberty & justice to everyone."

Occasionally set aside 5-10 minutes prior to the pledge, in which you discuss a topic such as: how are flags made commercially? Who wrote the Pledge of Allegiance? What is the Flag

Code? (June, 1942, U.S. Congress.) Who were Barbara Frietchie, Betsy Ross?

Flag Day relay race. At the opposite end of the playing area are 2 chairs. On each chair is a lump of clay in which is stuck a tiny American flag. Class is divided into 2 equal teams. First child of each team runs to chair, snatches flag, bringing it back to 2nd child who takes it & runs back to chair & sticks flag into clay again. Throughout relay flag is *always* held upright. 2nd child runs back to line, tags 3rd player who repeats procedure until 1 team finishes.

● **Birth of Rembrandt   [15]**

A painter of the Dutch school, he produced many remarkable portraits & figure paintings outstanding for their masterly technique. He was also an etcher of high ability.

Information source:

Publications Distribution Section
Smithsonian Institution Press
Washington, D.C. 20560

(Free catalogs & papers, Rembrandt's etching technique: an example, by Peter Morsel, is #61)

● **Bunker Hill Day   [17]**

Read to the class the long narrative poem "Grandmother's Story of Bunker Hill," by Oliver Wendell Holmes. (It can be found in *The Golden Treasure of Poetry,* edited by Louis Untermeyer & published by Golden Press, New York, N.Y., in 1959.)

● **Father's Day (the 3rd Sunday in June)**

Mrs. John B. Dodd & her 5 brothers & sisters had been raised by their father after their mother's death. One spring day in 1919, while listening to the Mother's Day sermon, Mrs. Dodd had an idea. She thought how she would like to honor her father & other men like him, & so, after the sermon, she spoke to her minister. He agreed with Mrs. Dodd & drew up a resolution for her, proposing that June 10, 1919, be set aside as Father's Day. Three years later, on the 3rd Sunday of June, America celebrated the 1st national Father's Day.

Although Father's Day usually falls after the closing of school, a small gift made in advance would undoubtedly be welcomed by Daddy. (See December: Christmas Gifts, pg. 114, for suggestions.)

Ask the children to finish: "My Daddy is. . . . . . ." & illustrate these pages.

Combed finger paintings. These afford an unusual, colorful gift wrap for Father's gift. Cut a notched comb from cardboard 2½ x 4"-8". Comb is drawn through application of wet dark-colored finger paint. Variation in notches (wide, deep, shallow) will vary texture of patterns produced.

● **Summer Solstice   [21] or [22]**

In the Northern Hemisphere, the sun appears at its highest point in the sky on June 21. On this day the sun's rays shine directly on the Tropic of Cancer, an imaginary line north of the equator, which encircles the globe. This line goes through Havana, Cuba; Calcutta, India; & Hong Kong, China. People living in these 3 cities see the sun directly overhead on June 21.

● **The Battle of Monmouth during U.S. Revolutionary War [28]**

Read aloud to the class "Molly Pitcher" by Kate Brownlee Sherwood (also found in *The Golden Treasury of Poetry*, Golden Press, New York, N.Y., 1959). Older students may read poem silently.

JUNE ACTIVITIES

Bulletin board lettering suggestions. Cut letters from corrugated cardboard; use these themselves, or cut letters in reverse from corrugated cardboard, paint these &, while wet, stamp letters of title on a long strip of white paper.

Title: Who Are We? What Are We Doing? A manipulative bulletin board. Children mix & match pictures of famous people & balloons with quotations in them. Quotations & dates of historical events might also be used.

Game of Presidents. Write (can be a mimeo-sheet)—*What President* was called: Tippecanoe? (Harrison); was the son of a President? (John Quincy Adams); said "I do not choose to run"? (Coolidge); was called Old Hickory? (Jackson); was called "the Sage of Monticello"? (Jefferson); outlined a foreign policy with S. America? (Monroe). What 2 Presidents died on the same day? (Jefferson & John Adams.) What 4 Presidents were assassinated? (Lincoln, Garfield, McKinley, Kennedy.)

A blown-up balloon is tied to the end of a slender stick of balsa wood which is anchored by a lump of clay beneath the paper figure. Felt pen lettering on balloon directs children to read books on table in their free time.

Language: want ads. Have children bring last night's paper (the same edition) to class. Study the classified section for wording, abbreviations, prices. Have children compose want ads for historical figures; ads may advertise for something to rent, lease or swap; may describe a lost/found object; may be in the category of "personals" or services-to-be-rendered. These ads are printed up on the primary typewriter for an interesting bulletin board or as a mimeo which the children will read to themselves. VARIATION: Hand out pictures of inventions you've mentioned in class during the year & ask each child to describe his in an ad (e.g., an almanac, reaper, phonograph, balloon, sewing machine, movie camera, tank, steamboat, telephone). VARIATION: Older students design full-page magazine lay-outs incorporating photos, lettering, border.

Penmanship practice—imaginary postcard correspondence: Each child is given a piece of tagboard cut in the shape of a postcard. He is asked to pretend that he is already on vacation & that he is sending the teacher a picture postcard. On 1 side he draws or pastes a collage of a picture of a vacation spot; he may show himself in the picture. On the reverse side he writes a note to the teacher & her address (which is clearly printed on the front chalkboard). Humor & ingenuity are encouraged.

At the end of the school year have the children write a class letter thanking the Room Mother. Each child designs & cuts out of colored paper a tiny bird, flower, butterfly, heart or angel & these

are pasted all around the letter, in its margins. Letter is rolled up &
tied with a pretty ribbon, each tail of which each has

a pasted on it.

Poetry

> And what is so rare as a day in June?
> Then, if ever, come perfect days;
> ... We may shut our eyes, but we cannot help knowing
> That skies are clear and grass is growing.
> —James Russell Lowell (19th c.)

Also appropriate is "The Seed Shop," by Muriel Stuart.

Reading

Pictorial review. Make a large book with cover & pages of
tagboard. On the left hand pages draw or paste 2-4 pictures
depicting famous people, historical events discussed in class during
the last few months. These pictures may also stress sequential
order. On the right hand pages cut slits to hold oaktag sentence
slips which describe pictures. Children insert slips (which, initially,
appear as a group in front of book) in correct positions throughout book.

A wheel of fortune. This helps break the routine of drill
sessions in the reading group. Pointer of tagboard wheel is spun &
number designates pile of cards from which "fortune" is chosen.
This card is read aloud by child & may indicate small prize, poem,
puzzle or penalty. (Reading instruction may be involved in
"deciphering" of fortune.)

On finishing a reader. Ask the children to think back over the
stories they have read & choose 1, giving it a different ending

(beginning)? Ask how each character might have behaved differently in that case. VARIATION: Go through the reader & choose sentences at random from different stories. On slips of tagboard print 2-3 sentences that might begin or end a story. These slips are drawn from a box by children. Each child thinks for a few moments & then tells his original story, based on these sentences, to his group. Children may enjoy trying to identify the story in reader from which sentences were actually taken.

End of the year reading mimeo for older students. This may be done on the last day of classes; its vocabulary should be adjusted to the children who will be using the mimeo

1. If blackberries are still green when they are red, write *H* in the left hand margin. If not, write *Z*.
2. If brown cows give white milk which makes yellow butter, write *A* in the left hand margin. If not, write *W*.
3. If paper can be made out of wood, write *V* at the left. If not, write *3*.
4. If Leap Year has 366 days, write *E* at the left. If not, write *A*.
5. If a ground hog is a pig that lives in the earth, put an *8* at the left. If not, write *A* there.
6. If the letter "M" comes before the letter "K" in the alphabet, write *R* at the left. If not, write *G*.
7. If the Atlantic Ocean is the largest ocean in the world, write *P* at the left. If not, write *O*.
8. If Beethoven was deaf the last years of his life, write *O* at the left. If not, write *T*.
9. If basketball is a major sport, write *D* at the left. If not, write *S*.
10. If the 1st day of summer is called the Spring Equinox, write *K* at the left. If it is called Summer Solstice, write *S*.
11. If seventy is larger than seventeen, write *U* in the left margin. If not, write *T*.
12. If Edison invented electricity, write *P* in the left margin. If not, write *M*.
13. If Francis Scott Key wrote our national anthem, put an *M* in the left margin. If he didn't, put an *X*.
14. If Mr. Gettysburg wrote the Gettysburg Address, put *B* in the left margin. If not, put *E*.
15. If the Pilgrims had never seen corn until they came to America, put *R* at the left. If they *had*, put *Z*.
16. If this is the final question in this quiz, put *!* at the left. If not, put a *?*

When children have correctly answered each question, "HAVE A GOOD SUMMER!" appears in the margin.

June Science

Grasses are among the most useful of all plants. They flower in summer but do not ripen until late July, August or September. Wild grasses include timothy, rye grass, meadow foxtail, cock's foot & common quaking grass. Cultivated grasses include wheat, barley & oats. The flower-head of grass is called the "ear" or "panicle." The flowers that develop are called "spikelets."

Classroom cacti may flower in June. Give them a bit of water once a week if the weather is dry.

Nature Quiz. This may be used for Classroom Baseball, which is played as follows: Divide class into 2 equal teams. Players come to bat as in regular baseball. They tell the pitcher (teacher) the type of "ball" they want. Teacher pitches that type question at batter. If batter answers correctly, he makes a hit & gets on base (designated on blackboard or elsewhere in room) & 2nd player comes up to bat. A team completes an inning when it has missed 3 questions. According to their difficulty, questions are labeled as being singles, doubles, or triples, or a home-run. For older children, extremely easy questions could be called "double-play balls"; if any men are on base, 2 outs are made if batter answers incorrectly. Teacher will evaluate questions according to the ability of the class. Prior to "pitching" question, teacher announces type of question involved, i.e., "This question is for a home run!"

1. What does "equinox" mean? (Equal night & day.)
2. What planet, discovered in 1930, is named after the god of the lower world? (Pluto.)
3. Who discovered the Pacific Ocean? (Vasco Nuñez de Balboa.)
4. How does a deciduous tree differ from a non-deciduous tree? (A deciduous tree sheds its leaves annually, while a non-deciduous tree is "evergreen.")
5. Who invented the telescope? (Galileo.)
6. Explain why the whale is a mammal & NOT a fish. (It is warm-blooded, breathes air, bears its young alive & feeds them milk.)
7. How many legs has a spider? (8.)
8. Do snakes close their eyes when they sleep? (No.)
9. Why don't they? (Snakes have no eyelids.)
10. What do sugar, sand, salt & snowflakes all have in common? (They are all crystals.)

11. What planet, discovered in 1846, is named after the Greek god of the sea? (Neptune.)
12. How long would it take to drown a grasshopper by holding its head under water? (It would starve to death 1st, as a grasshopper breathes through apertures on its sides.)
13. How long is a year on the planet Mercury? (3 months.)
14. Explain how it rains. (Water from the earth evaporates into the atmosphere where it is condensed & falls back to Earth as rain.)
15. Name a marsupial found in the U.S.A. (The opossum).
16. Who invented the phonograph? (Thomas Alva Edison.)
17. Name the 1st man to walk on the moon. (Neil Armstrong.)
18. When Wilson Bentley photographed 1000s of snowflakes, what 2 discoveries did he make? (Each snowflake has a hexagonal pattern. No 2 snowflakes have the exact same pattern!)

History Culmination

Help the children learn to draw conclusions by giving them some "problems" to discuss & answer, e.g.: I think Henry David Thoreau was a great man because _____; If I had come on the Mayflower, I would have brought _____, etc.; If Franklin (Lincoln, Booker T. Washington) had never lived, the world today would be different in these ways _____.

June P.E.

Relay Races (See November P.E. for organization suggestions.)

Hopping. The trip to goal is made by hopping 1st on 1 foot & then the other OR by taking 5 hops on 1 foot & 5 on the other.

Hurdle Relay. Divide each team into couples. Have the couples line up 1 behind the other at arm's distance between pairs. The 1st 2 children of each team are given a broomstick (yardstick). Holding this near the ground as they go, they run down the length of their team. Each couple must jump the hurdle as it passes. When the end of the line is reached, the 2 children who are now at the head of the line run back, grab the broomstick, run up to head of the line & continue the race until every couple has held the stick.

Jump rope Relay. At a given signal, 1st child of each team begins jumping rope toward goal line 40 feet away. Once there he turns around & continues jumping rope back to the starting line where he gives rope to the 2nd child on his team, who repeats procedure.

Run and POP Relay. Brown paper bags (1 for each player) are laid on 2 chairs at goal line. A wastepaper basket stands between the chairs. 1st child of each team runs to his chair, takes bag, blows it up, pops it (with his fist), throws burst bag INTO wastebasket & runs back & tags 2nd child, who may *not* leave starting line until he is tagged.

Cottonball Relay. Each player is given a soda straw. At goal line is a bowl with 2 little cotton balls in it. 1st child of each of the 2 teams runs up to bowl. Holding his soda straw in his mouth & sucking in, he causes a cotton ball to adhere to his straw. In this way the ball is taken from bowl & child runs back & deposits ball into a bowl that is on a chair next to his team. 2nd child repeats procedure. NO HANDS are allowed throughout relay; should cotton ball fall en route to destination, it must be rescued without aid of hands.

Pea-picker Relay. Children are divided into equal teams. 1st child of each team is given a round-ended plastic picnic knife (or butter knife or tongue depressor). Near each team is a bowl filled with a given number of dried peas (or beans). At the goal line are empty bowls, 1 for each team. At a signal, 1st player of each team goes to his bowl, scoops up as many peas on his knife as he can & proceeds to goal line where he empties peas into his team's bowl. (Warn children not to run with upheld knives as speed is NOT the idea of this relay!) He then tags 2nd player who repeats procedure. Dropped peas are not counted or retrieved. Team with most peas in bowl at goal line is the winner.

Summer Vacation Mimeo

A summer vacation mimeo for parents might be extremely helpful. This mimeo could include suggestions for how to make a summer trip educational; the selection of educational souvenirs; reminders about vaccinations, swimming lessons, poison oak prevention. You could list suggestions for use of free time: local hobby shops, educational films, T.V. shows to watch for, recreational facilities. You might list games that can be played without equipment, activities that can be done alone, short trips the family could take together, summer art lessons offered (by a local museum). Instructions for simple hand crafts, i.e., Spool Knitting which can be done by 6 yr. olds, might be included:

> Four finishing nails are hammered into top of spool. Thin yarn is threaded up through spool & wound about nails as shown. Loop A is picked up & drawn over B & top of nail. Repeat at each nail in turn. Long knitted roll develops. This roll can be handstitched to form purse, doll clothes, a mat.

Summer vacation mimeo to parents might also include a list of appropriate summertime reading suggestions, summaries of things accomplished during the year, e.g., "Math Facts I Know," "Words I Know How to Read," "Words I Can Spell." Review of these pages during the summer will provide materials for playing school & will help children retain their skills over vacation months.

A list of activities which children may enjoy while traveling in a car might be appreciated.

Prepare a recipe box of suggestion cards from which the children will draw when they can think of nothing to do. Only 1 card at a time should be drawn from the box, & once selected, the suggestion should be followed. Suggestions should not include things the children would normally think of themselves. A few suggestions:

—Act out a favorite story.
—Make & cut out a set of paper dolls.
—Make a hat from an old newspaper & become a pirate hunting for treasure.
—Make a sampler by using a big needle & bright yarn on a piece of burlap.
—Draw a picture of your entire family.
—Make a clay model of your right foot.
—Make a hand (finger) puppet from a piece of an old sheet, felt-tip pens, felt & feathers, & then give a puppet show.
—Play doctor & pretend that you are making a round of house calls.
—Tell Indian legends around a make-believe bonfire.
—Make a map of your neighborhood, including buildings, plants & main landmarks.

—Close your eyes & feel the things around you; make a list of the different textural qualities you feel.

—Design a perfect bedroom for yourself.

—Using a stack of old magazines, go through them & collect an entire alphabet of capital letters & objects illustrating each; use these to make an alphabet book.

—Using tagboard, a big needle & yarn, make a sunglasses holder similar to the one shown here.

Classroom Cookery

During their Social Studies reading, the children may learn of unusual or interesting foods prepared in other countries or areas. As these foods are mentioned, the teacher could prepare some for the students to taste. This allows the children an opportunity to see the food in a raw form as well as in its cooked state. Tortillas, succotash, poi, maple sugar are a few possibilities.

Six of the following recipes require no cooking. The few utensils necessary can be kept in a classroom cupboard: wooden spoons, plastic or metal measuring cups, measuring spoons (which have been separated one from another), a plastic wash basin for mixing ingredients (preferable to glass bowls which are awkward for children to handle & can accommodate only one child at a time), cooky sheets & wax paper. A sponge & a 2 lb. coffee can of warm water will facilitate quick clean-ups. Several men's shirts, worn buttoned down the back, will make excellent aprons.

Each recipe can be so organized as to involve each of the children (in the reading group) in some aspect of the preparation. This preparation of food in the classroom will give the children experience with volumetric measures & will impress upon them (as nothing else may) the importance of careful reading. After clean-up, children may be asked questions based on the set of directions which a recipe represents.

Classroom cooking also offers a chance to break down the stereotyped idea which children may have that it is only *women* who belong in (or more subtly, can function in) the kitchen.

If a hot plate is available for classroom use, many other creative cooking experiences, including the making of art supplies, are possible. With the addition of a double-boiler & a candy thermometer to their store of cooking utensils, the children will be able to prepare any of the following recipes.

Culinary Word Etymologies

For many centuries Latin words have poured into our language. One of hundreds which we have adopted without even a spelling change is "recipe."

It is from *dactylus,* the Latin word for "finger," that we get our word "date," as that fruit was once thought to resemble a human finger.

In 496 B.C. a terrible drought afflicted the Roman countryside. The priests brought forth a new goddess, Ceres, & the people were told that if they immediately made sacrifices to her, rain would fall. Because Ceres was successful in ending the drought, she became "the protector of the crops." The Latin word *cerealis* meant "of Ceres," & gave us our word "cereal."

"Currants" were named for the corrupt city of ancient Greece, Corinth.

In the first century before Christ the Roman legions were in Germany. Whenever anything was sold to the semi-savage tribes found living there, the Latin name for the object went with it. In this way many Latin words found their way into German. Some centuries later German invaders brought nearly a hundred Latin derivatives into Britain—& into English; "butter" was one of these.

"Walnuts" means "foreign nuts." The Anglo-Saxons called them *wealhhnutu* (*wealh*="foreigner" & *hnutu*="nuts"), as these nuts were unknown to England before the arrival of invading armies.

"Yolk" is a derivative of a Middle English word *yolke* or *yelke*, through an Old English word *geolea,* from *geolu,* all of these words meaning "yellow."

Sometime in the year 850 A.D. a goatherd named Kaldi became puzzled by the strange actions of his goats. He noticed that they were nibbling at the berries of a certain bush. When Kaldi tried some of these berries himself he was amazed at the feeling of exhilaration he experienced. He rushed off & told the other goatherds of his discovery. The Arabs learned to boil the berries of these bushes, calling the brew "gahve." The Turks introduced it to the French who called it "cafe," & in this way we got our English word, "coffee."

Coffee

Trees of the genus Caffea, native to Africa & E. Asia, bearing fruit containing beans used in making coffee. The green coffee bean is freed from the pulp & dried in the sun.

"Vinegar" is actually *vyn egre* meaning "sour wine," & comes from Old French.

The Latin word *gelo* means "to freeze" or "to congeal," & it led to the French word *gelee*, "a jelly," & in English this became "gelatine."

Under William the Conqueror, in 1066, the Normans (Northmen) conquered the Germanic tribes who, in turn, became their servants. The vocabulary of these conquered peoples was of the field & kitchen & from it we get such words as "house," "hearth," "oven," "pot," "stone," "wheat" & "milk."

The Mexican Indians called the tree from which the cacao seed comes, "caucauatl." The invading Spanish had difficulty pronouncing this Indian word & shortened it to "cacao." In English it became "cocoa." Another Mexican Indian word, "chocolatl," meaning "bitter water," gave us "chocolate."

The word *"coconut"* (also spelled "cocoanut," thanks to an error by Dr. Samuel Johnson in his dictionary), comes from the Spanish & Portugese word *coco* which means "a grimace." The three holes in the bottom of the coconut were thought to resemble a grimacing face & so "coconut" actually means "funny-face nut."

Candy Recipes:

(All starred recipes require no cooking whatsoever.)
Egyptian hieroglyphics show that in 1566 B.C. candies made of honey, flour, almonds & figs were being sold in the market places.

*Greek Candy: Karridakia (makes 20)

1 c. dried figs
1 c. pitted dates, apricots
   or raisins

1 c. shelled walnuts
1/2 c. powdered or granulated
   sugar
1 t. cinnamon

Chop figs, dates, walnuts (by running them through a meat-grinder). Mix thoroughly. Roll into balls 1" in diameter. Mix sugar & cinnamon. Roll balls in this mixture until well coated. Store in tight jars. ("Hi Neighbor": Book III UNICEF U.N. New York, N.Y.)

*Algerian Lemon Fondant

1/3 c. soft margarine
1/3 c. light syrup
1/2 t. salt

1 t. lemon extract
4-1/2 c. sifted confectioner's
   sugar
yellow food coloring

Blend margarine, syrup, salt & extract. Add sugar all at once. Then add a few drops of food coloring. Stir. Knead. Turn out onto a wax-papered surface. Knead until smooth. Shape into cherry-sized balls. ("Days of Discovery" packet: American Friends Service Committee, 160 N. 15th St., Phila., Pa. 19102.)

*Orange Fondant Balls

2 egg whites
1 T. cold water

1-1/2 T. orange flavoring
4 c. sifted confectioner's
   sugar
orange food coloring

Beat egg whites & water until well-blended. Add sugar gradually until mixture becomes stiff. Add flavoring & coloring. Knead until smooth; then shape into balls. (Ibid. American Friends Service Committee.)

Ann G.'s Recipe

2 c. sugar	dash of salt
1/2 c. milk	1/2 c. peanut butter
1/4 lb. margarine	1 t. vanilla
3 T. cocoa	4 c. oatmeal, uncooked

Put sugar, milk, margarine, cocoa, salt in a pan; bring to a rolling boil. Remove from heat. Add peanut butter & vanilla. Pour this mixture over oatmeal. Drop by teaspoonfuls onto wax paper lined cookie sheet. Cool. Enjoy.

Simple Crispies

corn flakes or crisp rice cereal	(coconut or chopped nuts) cupcake liners
milk chocolate candy bars	

Put candy bars in pan & place over hot water until melted. Stir cereal (& coconut or nuts, if desired) into chocolate until cereal is completely coated. Place a spoonful of mixture in each cupcake liner. Let stand 5 minutes.

Fudge-in-a-Minute (makes 18)

8 squares semi-sweet chocolate	1t. vanilla 1/4 t. salt
2/3 c. sweetened condensed milk	

Melt chocolate in milk over low heat, stirring to blend. Add vanilla & salt. Spread into an oiled 4 x 8 pan. Chill until firm. Cut into squares. (Simple yet satisfying.)

Fantastic Fudge (makes 30)

2-1/4 c. white sugar	1/4 c. butter
3/4 c. canned milk	1/4 t. salt
4 c. tiny marshmallows*	1 c. chocolate bits
1 c. chopped nuts	1 t. vanilla

In a pan mix sugar, milk, butter & salt. Bring to a boil, *stirring constantly.* Don't let it stick on the bottom of the pan! Boil & stir for 5 minutes. Stir in chocolate bits. Stir until melted. Stir in nuts & vanilla. Pour mixture onto an oiled plate. Cool. Cut.

(This is wording that can be read by young students themselves. A good recipe.)

*Or 16 marshmallows cut up into little pieces.

*No-Bake Chocolate Walnut Balls (makes 40)

36 chocolate wafers, crushed fine
1/2 c. finely chopped chocolate
   bits
3 T. corn syrup

1 c. confectioner's sugar
1/4 c. orange juice
1/2 c. finely chopped walnuts

Mix crumbs, bits, sugar & walnuts. Add syrup & juice. Mix well. Form into 1" balls. Roll in confectioner's sugar, cocoa, or finely chopped nuts. (Store in tight container & allow to ripen.) These are nice enough to be given as gifts.

Chocolate Raisin Clusters (makes 30)

1-1/4 c. chocolate bits
1 c. seedless raisins

1/2 c. coarsely chopped nuts

Melt chocolate bits in top half of double boiler. Stir until syrupy. Add raisins & nuts. Stir until they are coated. Drop by teaspoonfuls onto wax paper lined cookie sheet. Chill 10 hours.

Mr. Nelson's Peanut Brittle (makes 18 1" x 1")

2 c. white sugar
1 c. white corn syrup

1 t. baking soda
1 T. butter
1-2 c. peanuts

Put sugar & syrup in large cast-iron skillet. Stir to mix. Bring to hard boil. Boil 5 minutes. Add butter; stir in & wait until mixture darkens. Add peanuts. Wait until it boils again. Add soda. Stir in & immediately pour onto oiled cookie sheet. Cool for 15-20 min. Crack with hammer.

Plain White Pull Candy

1/4 c. water
1-1/4 c. granulated sugar
2 T. mild vinegar

1-1/2 t. butter
1/4 t. baking soda
1 t. vanilla
candy thermometer

Oil platter. Place water, sugar, vinegar, butter in pan. Stir over low heat until sugar is dissolved. Increase heat until thermometer reads 268°. Remove from heat. Add vanilla & soda. Stir just enough to blend. Pour onto platter; let cool until a dent can be made in top with finger. Gather into a lump & pull with oiled fingers until candy is light & porous. Dip fingers in cold water often. Roll candy in long strips & cut into 1" pieces. (Place candy in tightly covered tin if creamy quality is desired.)

VARIATION: Molasses Pull Candy

Follow the same procedure, using these ingredients:

1 c. molasses	1/2 c. granulated sugar
1 T. butter	1/4 t. baking soda
2 t. vinegar	1 t. vanilla

The history of cookies & cakes is the history of bread—& bread is as old as Man. The early nomadic peoples had to carry nourishment with them as they traveled. They made a meal by grinding grain & seeds & added water as a cementing agent. The resulting rock-like loaves were the earliest forms of bread—man's first manufactured food.

Gateau a la Brochette

3/8 c. evaporated milk mixed with 3/8 c. water (or a bit less)	
3/8 c. salad oil	1/2 t. baking soda plus
3/8 c. CRUSHED walnuts	1 t. cream of tartar
5 egg yolks	1 c. honey plus 1/2 t. soda
2 c. plus 4 T. sifted cake flour	3/4 t. salt

Mix oil, yolks & nuts together. Sift together: salt, flour, soda, & cream of tartar. Add to nut mixture. Now stir in honey combined with soda. Add half of milk, a bit at a time. Once flour mixture is moist, beat batter 250 times. Add remaining milk & beat 120 times.

Put a lump of dough on an oiled brochette (skewer); turn brochette until dough clings to it. Hold brochette in front of an open fire & keep brochette constantly rotating. From time to time, add more dough to that on skewer until (after 2-3 hours) a cake, eight inches in diameter, has been produced.

When cake is thoroughly cooked, carefully slide it off brochette. (This recipe is included only as a curiosity & is adapted from one found in THE ARTISTS' AND WRITERS' COOKBOOK, by Beryl Barr & Barbara Turner Sachs, eds. (Sausalito, California: Angel Island Pub., 1961), p. 273.

Cookie Recipes:

That old favorite, "Marshmallow Treats"

1/4 c. margarine	5 c. Rice Krispies brand cereal
4 c. tiny marshmallows (or 40 big marshmallows cut up into pieces)	1/2 t. vanilla

Melt margarine in a pan. Add marshmallows & cook over LOW heat, *stirring constantly*, until marshmallows are melted. Add vanilla. Add cereal & stir until it is well coated. Press warm mixture into an oiled pan. Press down firmly. When mixture is *cool*, cut into squares.

And now, The Quickies (makes 30)

1 can sweetened condensed milk (1 1/3 cups)
1/2 c. peanut butter
1 c. chopped nuts, 3 c. shredded coconut, or 2 c. raisins

Blend all ingredients well. Drop by spoonfuls onto a buttered cookie sheet. Bake at 375° for 15 min. or until golden brown. Remove from sheet at once.

Quickie-Cookies (for little children)

1 graham cracker for each child
1 marshmallow for each child
1 red cinnamon drop for each child
   (or 1 chocolate kiss)

Assemble as shown & place under the broiler for a minute, until marshmallow melts.

Turtles* (makes 24 little turtles)

2 squares baking chocolate	1 c. flour
1/3 c. margarine	1 t. vanilla
2 eggs, beaten	2 t. cream
3/4 c. sugar	chocolate icing

Melt chocolate & margarine. Mix together eggs, sugar, flour, vanilla, cream. Add chocolate mixture. Lightly oil waffle iron; heat iron until quite hot (steaming). Drop 4 individual T. of batter onto iron & bake 2-4 min. (thus making 4 turtles at 1 time). Chocolate icing (mix) may be prepared while turtles are being baked. Cooled turtles are frosted & 2 silver shot eyes may be added to each if you like.

---

*Name refers to crosshatch markings of cookie.

No-Bake Brownies (makes 36)

2 c. chocolate bits
1 c. evaporated milk
3 c. finely crushed vanilla wafers
2 c. miniature marshmallows

1 c. chopped nuts (pecans)
1 c. sifted confectioner's
   sugar
1/2 t. salt
2 t. evaporated milk

Stir chocolate bits & milk (1 c.) over low heat until melted. Remove from heat. In a large bowl mix vanilla wafer crumbs, marshmallows, nuts, sugar, salt. Save 1/2 c. of chocolate mixture for icing; stir remainder into crumb mixture. Mix well. Press firmly into a buttered 9 x 9 pan. Stir 2 t. evaporated milk into the reserved 1/2 c. chocolate mixture. Mix until smooth. Spread evenly over mixture in pan. Chill until icing is set. Cut into squares.

Coconut Bars (makes 36 bars)

1/2 c. butter
1 egg slightly beaten
1/2 lb. flaked coconut
1 c. chopped nuts
1/3 c. brown sugar

2 c. crushed graham crackers
1/2 c. milk
1 t. vanilla
1 c. pink butter icing

Cook egg, butter, sugar over low heat for 1 minute. Stir in crackers, nuts, vanilla. Press into 9 x 9 pan. Mix coconut & milk thoroughly. Press on top of crumb mixture. Refrigerate until firm. Frost with pink butter icing. Cut into small squares.

Pink Butter Icing: Beat 1-1/2 T. butter. Gradually add 1 c. sifted confectioner's sugar. Blend until creamy. Add 1/8 t. salt, 1 t. vanilla, & a few drops red food coloring. Additional confectioner's sugar may be added if consistency of icing is too thin.

Miscellaneous Recipes:

Popcorn was introduced to the English colonists at the first Thanksgiving dinner on February 22, 1630, by Quadequina, brother of Massasoit. As his contribution to that dinner he brought a deerskin bag filled with several bushels of popped corn.

Popcorn Crackle

1 foil-wrapped pan of
   ready-to-pop corn
1/2 c. light molasses
3/4 c. light corn syrup

2 T. margarine
1-1/4 c. granulated sugar
candy thermometer

Pop corn according to directions on package. Pour into a bowl. Mix remaining ingredients in a large saucepan. Boil until 285° is registered on candy thermometer (stage at which liquid forms hard ball when dropped into cold water). Stir liquid into the corn. With oiled hands, spread over a 14" square cookie sheet. Cool. Break up. (Store in an air-tight container.) A.F.S.C.

Nut Log (makes 24)

1/2 gallon plastic-coated milk carton	2 c. Spanish peanuts
	2 c. chopped pecans
1/4 lb. margarine	1 c. raisins
1 c. semi-sweet chocolate morsels	3 c. popped popcorn
1 10-oz. pkg. miniature marshmallows	
1 8-oz. pkg. crisp rice cereal	

Open out the top of the milk carton. Wash & dry. Melt margarine, chocolate morsels & marshmallows together in the top of a double boiler. Mix remaining ingredients in a very large bowl. Pour melted chocolate sauce over dry ingredients in bowl. Mix *well.* * Spoon the mixture into the milk carton. Pack *tightly.* Refrigerate until hard, (1 hour). Peel back the carton & slice Nut Log. (I've made this often & its robust flavor always seems to please "the cooks.")

No-Bake Fruitcake (makes 3 lbs.)

2 c. miniature marshmallows	3/4 c. chopped raisins
2/3 c. evaporated milk	1/4 c. candied cherries
6 T. *undiluted* frozen orange juice	(chopped)
1 c. chopped pecans	1 t. cinnamon
1 c. mixed candied fruits (chopped)	4 c. graham cracker crumbs
	1 t. nutmeg
3/4 c. chopped dates	½ t. cloves

Put marshmallows, milk, orange juice in large pan. Stir over medium heat until marshmallows melt. Remove from heat. Stir in pecans & all fruit. Mix crumbs & spices & add to marshmallow mixture. Press firmly into a loaf pan lined with wax paper. Cover tightly. Chill 2 days.

Ice cream was first recorded in the first century A.D. when Nero Claudius Caesar, then Emperor of Rome, ordered snow to be

---

*"A wooden spoon is useless without an untiring arm to wield it": from *A Treasure House of Useful Knowledge.* a 19th c. "Ladies Home-Companion."

brought by fast runners from nearby mountains. Fruit juices & flavoring were added to the snow. It is believed that Marco Polo found recipes for water & milk ices in China & Japan in the thirteenth century, & he is thought to have brought them with him when he returned to Europe.

Homemade Ice Cream: crank style (makes 1 quart or more)

3" vanilla bean pod	3/4 c. sugar
(or 1 T. vanilla)	1/8 t. salt
1-1/2 c. milk	3-4 egg yolks
(1 T. cornstarch)	2 c. whipping cream

(Whenever possible, the mixture should be made the day before & refrigerated. This helps to increase the volume.) Split pod & scrape seed into milk; drop in pod, also. Scald milk. Dissolve sugar in milk over heat. Combine cornstarch, salt & slightly beaten eggs; mix well. Beat in a little of the scalded milk. Combine the two mixtures & cook over low heat, stirring constantly until mixture is thick & smooth. Chill. Stir in stiffly whipped cream & pour into freezer can (2/3-3/4 full). *Chill thoroughly.*

VARIATION:*No-Cook Recipe for Ice Cream (Chocolate):* Beat 5 eggs in large bowl of electric beater at medium speed. Mix in 2 (13 oz.) cans of evaporated milk, 2 c. sugar, 2 c. whole milk & 2 c. chocolate syrup. Stir until sugar dissolves. Pour into freezer can. Freeze according to following directions. (Makes 1 gal.)

VARIATION: *Vanilla Ice Cream:* Substitute 3 c. whole milk in place of 2 c. called for above, & 1 T. vanilla in place of chocolate syrup. Prepare as directed above.

CRANK PROCEDURE. Crush ice fine (in a burlap sack). Insert dasher into freezer can. Cover mouth of freezer can with wax paper. Put on freezer can lid securely. Fit can into freezer. Adjust frame & crank & tighten screws. Measure ice & salt: use 1/2 c. rock salt for each qt. of crushed ice. (To speed up freezing process, in which case ice cream must be used at once, allow 1 part of salt to 3 parts ice.) Tamp down the first quart of ice evenly in the freezer. Alternate salt & ice until freezer is full. (A two-qt. freezer takes 4 qts. of crushed ice & 2 cups [1 lb.] rock salt). Crank continuously until dasher becomes very difficult to turn: average time is 15 minutes. Drain off excess water. Unfasten the screws. Remove crank & frame. Remove top layer of ice. Carefully wipe top & side of freezer with a clean cloth; this is done to prevent salt from getting into the ice cream. Remove top of freezer can; slowly remove dasher. Ice cream may be eaten at

once, although the flavor is *greatly* improved if the ice cream is
allowed to mellow for 1-2 hours. This is done by covering mouth
of freezer can with wax paper & replacing lid, plugging dasher
hole with a cork. Ice & a double portion of salt are added until
freezer is filled & can is covered. A blanket of burlap sacks &
newspapers is placed over the freezer & it is allowed to stand for
1-2 hours.

Fresh Strawberry Ice Cream (an easier alternative)

1 pt. fresh strawberries, washed & hulled.
Place berries in a large bowl. Crush them
  with a toy potato masher.
Add 1c. sugar; let stand 10 minutes. Then
  add & stir with a spoon:

> 1 T. lemon juice
> 1/2 c. COLD coffee cream
> 1/2 c. milk

Pour mixture into a refrigerator tray; let mixture freeze.
Remove tray & put mixture in a large bowl. Whip with electric
beater until mixture is stiff. Refreeze.

Recipes for Art Supplies

Carving Materials.

Girostone: 2 parts sand, 2 parts cement, 4 parts coarse
Zonolite (available at building supply stores). Mix dry ingredients.
Add water to make heavy paste mixture. Stir thoroughly. Pour
into shoe boxes. Dry for several days. VARIATIONS: 2 parts
cement, 3 parts coarse Zonolite; OR 4 parts fine Zonolite to 1 part
cement; OR 4 parts fine Zonolite to 1 part cement & 1 part sand;
OR 4 parts fine Zonolite, 2 parts plaster of Paris & 1 part sand.

Soapscraps. Collect soapscraps until there are 4 lbs. or more.
Chop up fine. Add 5 gallons water. When soap is melted, add 3 lbs.
wallpaper paste & enough finely sifted sawdust (NOT redwood
sawdust) to achieve correct consistency. Pour into wax-lined milk
cartons (or shoe boxes). Let stand overnight. Turn out of mold the
next morning. This material is durable & easy to carve.

Pearlite Stone: In a plastic dishpan, mix 1 part casting plaster
& 1 part to 2 parts Pearlite Insulation Material (both this & casting
plaster are sold at building supply companies). Resulting mixture
should be similar to wet commercial cement, but not soupy. Pour
mixture immediately into 1-1/2 gallon milk cartons. Material
hardens in 1 hour. When dry, remove from cartons & carve with

beer can openers or butter knives. Carve figures out of material, rather than digging into it; i.e., don't dig out the features of the face.

Plaster of Paris: Mix plaster of Paris with silicate to desired consistency, OR mix 3 parts plaster of Paris, 5 parts Vermiculite, 1 part sand & 1/2 part wheat paste. Pour into molds. Let dry. Turn out of molds & carve.

Vermiculite: Mix 5 parts Vermiculite to 2 parts Portland White Cement. Add tempera or brewed coffee to color material. Pour into salt, oatmeal or milk cartons. Tap sides of cartons to settle material. This hardens in 24 hours, unless it is refrigerated, in which case it will harden in 36 hours. Carve while block is damp. Wrap in damp cloths if unfinished block is to be left out overnight. VARIATIONS: 4 parts Vermiculite & 1 part Portland White Cement. Add coloring. This produces a softer material than the former proportions. OR 1 part Portland White Cement, 2 parts plaster of Paris, 3 parts Vermiculite. Add sand for texture. Let stand for 25 minutes. Carve while still damp.

Used (broken) sand molds can often be obtained from foundries.

Modeling Materials.

Asbestos: Slowly add a small amount of water to dry asbestos. Knead until mixture holds its shape. Wheat paste may be added to mixture. (Quickly makes good finger-puppet heads.)

Baker's Clay (inedible dough): Combine 4 c. unsifted all-purpose flour, 1 c. salt, 1-1/2 c. water in a bowl. Mix thoroughly with hands; if too stiff, add a bit more water. Remove dough from bowl. *Knead dough for a full 5-10 minutes.** Shape into desired forms. Bake on cookie sheets in preheated 350° oven until dough has a golden brown color. You can check on your shapes from time to time to know when to remove them from oven. Baking takes from 15-45 minutes as a rule & depends on the thickness of the shapes. Remove shapes from pans. Allow to cool. Once cooled, shapes may be painted with acrylics which give a nice shine to dough, or with poster or water color paints & then lightly sprayed with Varathane.

VARIATIONS: *Vertical pieces* are possible by using chicken wire as armature. Remember that the finished piece must fit into

---

*This is imperative as kneading "lightens" dough's consistency, causing dough to rise while it is being baked.

the oven! *Large Vignettes* are modeled atop a board (23" x 20")
that is covered with blue foil paper & then with chicken wire.
When modeling the scene, many areas (for sky) are left open. Press
dough firmly into chicken wire beneath. Make use of stamped-in
textures. When dough is baked & cool, use sharp wire cutters to
remove chicken wire above sky areas. (This is not essential—but if
done, must be done carefully.) *Wooden Mold* is dusted with
cornstarch & dough is pressed firmly into it to reproduce design in
mold. *Slabs of dough* are cut into animal shapes. When dough is
baked & cooled, features are applied with vari-colored icings.
Stained glass effect is achieved by using thin ropes of dough,
twisted, for the "leading." Fill each space created by "leading"
with a crushed sourball or bright hard candy. As the dough bakes,
the candies melt, forming thin, transparent "stained glass." A bent
wire may be used as support by making it form the contour of
the dough (see illustration). *Colored dough* is obtained by kneading drops of food coloring into unbaked dough. *Detailed pieces:*
tiny details, i.e., curls, flower petals, eyes, feathers, can be rolled
out of small bits of dough & laid in place on basic shape with a
needle or toothpick. Blanched & unblanched almonds (for rays of
the sun or feathers of a bird) or decorative silver shot can be pressed into dough before baking. Lacy paper doilies or metallic paper
may be glued to under edge of baked dough as trim or for contrsat.
may be glued to under edge of baked dough as trim or for contrast. In Ecuador animals are sculpted of Baker's Clay & baked in
beehive ovens for All-Saints' Day.

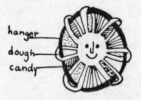

Cooked Salt: Mix 2 parts of salt to 1 part of cornstarch & 1
part of water. Cook over low heat, *stirring* vigorously, until
material is stiff. Ready to mold when cool. Dries in 36 hours if
small in size. 8 boxes of salt & proportionate amounts of
cornstarch & water make enough material for 32 small objects.

Crepe Clay: Cut 1 package of crepe paper into tiny squares;

place in bowl. Add water to cover & allow to soak until paper is soft. Drain off excess water. Mix 1 T. salt with 1 c. flour. Add flour enough to make a stiff dough. Knead mixture until flour is all blended into paper.

Magic Modeling Goop: Mix 2 c. salt with 2/3 c. water. Place in pan over low heat for 3-4 minutes (until mixture is well-heated), stirring constantly. Remove from heat & add 1 c. loose cornstarch that has been mixed with 1/2 cold water. Stir quickly. Mixture should be consistency of stiff dough. If mixture doesn't thicken, return to low heat & stir for 1 minute until a smooth, pliable mass is formed. (Food coloring may be added to portions of the dough.) Makes 1-3/4 lbs. Keeps indefinitely if wrapped in foil. Refrigeration unnecessary. Hardens in 36 hours if object is small. Large objects should be pierced with a pencil when moist in order to allow to dry out. May be painted when dry.

Papier Mâché Pulp: Soak toilet tissue overnight in water sufficient to cover generously; 3 rolls of tissue will provide an average class with pulp for 1 small item each. (To prevent mildewing, 1 t. of boric acid may be added for each pint of water.) Squeeze out excess water. To store, shape into loaves & dry. Then simply moisten & add 1 part flour to 2 parts pulp until dough is not sticky. (If boric acid was not added previously, now add salt or oil of cloves or wintergreen as a preservative.) Knead dough until it is of the desired smoothness. VARIATIONS: In water, soak torn pieces of newspaper until they are disintegrated. Drain. Squeeze pulp as dry as possible. Prepare a very thick & smooth wallpaper paste & mix 2 parts of pulp to 1 part of paste. Add 2 T. salt to prevent fermentation. Add whiting for whiteness. Mix thoroughly. Apply by handfuls directly on the model. OR soak torn-up newspaper in hot water. Beat soaked paper until soft. Make a thin paste of powdered wallpaper paste & water. Drain paper by squeezing in an old nylon stocking. Stir paste thoroughly into pulp. Remove excess moisture again. Shape into objects. OR add shredded asbestos & substitute casein glue in place of the wallpaper paste. This pulp is of superior tensile strength.

Play Clay: Mix 1 c. cornstarch & 2 c. baking soda. Add 1-1/4 c. cold water. Stir until smooth. Cook to boiling point over medium heat, stirring constantly. Boil 1 minute, until mixture reaches consistency of mashed potatoes. Turn out onto plate & cover with damp cloth until clay is cool. Knead. Roll out, & using cookie-cutters stamp out shapes, or model into desired shapes. Thin pieces dry overnight. When dry, paint & then coat with shellac or spray on clear plastic.

Play Dough: Mix 8 c. flour, 2 c. salt, 3 T. vegetable oil with water to make a soft dough. Add food coloring for color. Store in airtight container.

Sawdust & Paste: Use 2 measures of sawdust** to one measure of wallpaper paste. Add cold water—enough to obtain a pliable consistency. An eggbeater is helpful. Finished models are rough textured & can be sanded & painted when dry. VARIATIONS: Mix together 1-1/2 to 2 c. fine pine sawdust, 1 c. water & 1/4 to 1/2 c. wheat paste which is of thick custard consistency. Add 1 t. viscote adhesium OR 1/2 t. powdered casein glue. Makes 1 puppet head. OR mix 2 c. sawdust, 1 c. plaster of Paris, 1/2 c. wheat paste & 1-1/2 to 2 c. water. OR 4 parts sawdust to 1 part wheat paste. OR cook over low heat until clear, 1 c. cornstarch & 1 c. water. Add a few drops of oil of cloves as a preservative. Add sawdust until mixture reaches correct consistency.

Finger Paint: Prepare cornstarch according to directions on package. To each pint of starch add 1 T. glycerine (to obtain a good texture) & 1/2 t. oil of cloves (to prevent paint from souring). Food coloring may be added while mixture is still warm: good idea if paint is to be used by very young children. Or dry powder-type paint can be sprinkled on starch after it has been applied to surface of paper. VARIATIONS: Sift 1/2 c. flour into a cup of water. Make a smooth paste. Cook mixture until it bubbles. Stir continually to avoid lumps. Cool. Add 1 T. glycerine for smoothness. Add 1 t. sodium benzoate if paint is to be stored for more than 2-3 days. OR mix 1/2 box of cornstarch in cold water to make a paste. Add 3 qts. boiling water & cook until glossy. Stir while cooking to prevent sticking, lumping. Add 1/4 c. talc. Cool. Add 1-1/4 c. soap flakes; stir until flakes are evenly distributed. Put in jars. Add color if desired. Talc adds to smoothness but can be omitted. This is enough to supply 20 children.

Fixative: At least 3 weeks before needed, mix 1/2 pt. white shellac & 2 qts. denatured alcohol. Keep tightly covered. Shake well before using. Use as a spray to fix chalk or charcoal drawings. VARIATIONS: Substitute gum arabic (thinned in water to

---

*Found in the *Noe Valley Coop Nursery School Cookbook* & quoted in *The San Francisco Chronicle*, 3/72.

**WARNING: *Do not use plywood or redwood sawdust!*

the consistency of thin mucilage) in place of denatured alcohol OR mix 2 parts denatured alcohol & 1 part white shellac.

Glue (casein or "milk"): Pour a pint of skim milk into an enamel sauce pan & add 1 c. vinegar. Heat & stir until lumps are formed. Pour coagulated milk into a bowl. Cool. Discard excess water that forms, add 1/4 c. water & 1 t. baking soda. This type of glue was used by the Egyptians thousands of years ago. Objects on which this glue was used have been found in tombs today, & the glue is still holding. Furniture makers of the Middle Ages also used it.

Paste: Add 1 T. white alum & 1 c. sifted flour to water, making a thick paste. Keep adding the water until the mixture is like milk: approximately 1 c. water required. Cook over low heat, stirring constantly, until mixture becomes a translucent paste. Add 1/2 t. oil of cloves. Keeps indefinitely.

Art Aids

- For more vibrant colors, mix liquid starch with your tempera paints.
- Cut down plastic starch bottles & wedge them into the paintholder on each easel. Plastic paint containers are, you will find, preferable to all others, as they do not weaken with time.
- Using a funnel, pour mixed poster paints into large plastic bleach bottles. This will greatly simplify storage & will reduce time spent in weekly preparation of paints.
- Tie a pencil by heavy yarn to each easel so that the children will be reminded to sign their paintings.
- Keep a stack of magazines on hand for collage materials, lettering samples & reference work.
- Fill doll-size plastic baby bottles with diluted milk glue so that the children may have individual squeeze bottles to use at their desks.
- Try to keep a bottle of ink eradicator & a tube of "K-2r" in your desk for classroom emergencies.
- Baby oil helps when you're removing gum from a child's hair.
- An ice-cube applied to the fabric will aid in the removal of gum from clothing.

Hannah Adams (1775) 1st American woman to become a professional writer. A contemporary said of Hannah: "No woman can expect to be regarded as a lady after she's written a book."

And with that

An Afterword

I would be very happy to hear from you, to learn your impressions of "Teacher's Almanack," to hear your comments, suggestions, ideas.

I compiled this book, but not without help.

Thank you Gene, for going over the manuscript with me & for going through it all with me too.

A special thanks to my sister Dixie Anter, who has shared her teaching ideas with me for years. She is an unfailing source of those seldom-paired talents: creativity AND practicality.

My thanks to Dorothy Taugher for the hours of loving care & labor she gave typing the majority of the manuscript.

Thank you to David Kronen for the very helpful snake & reptile information, to Viola Bellemans for the instructions for the

erupting volcano, to Beaulah Carswell for the
magnet mimeo idea, Imogene Speiser & her original
'Alexander' puppet & to Robert Skiles who
showed me how to make Giant Pilgrims &
much more, the 1st year I taught.

I do hope to hear from you. You
may write me in care of the publisher.
Warmest regards,
Dana Newmann

Index of Activities